Jean-Luc Nancy and the Thinking of Otherness

Bloomsbury Studies in Continental Philosophy

Bloomsbury Studies in Continental Philosophy is a major monograph series from Bloomsbury. The series features first-class scholarly research monographs across the field of Continental philosophy. Each work makes a major contribution to the field of philosophical research.

Jean-Luc Nancy and the Thinking of Otherness

Philosophy and Powers of Existence

Daniele Rugo

B L O O M S B U R Y
LONDON · NEW DELHI · NEW YORK · SYDNEY

Bloomsbury Academic
An imprint of Bloomsbury Publishing Plc

50 Bedford Square
London
WC1B 3DP
UK

1385 Broadway
New York
NY 10018
USA

www.bloomsbury.com

Bloomsbury is a registered trade mark of Bloomsbury Publishing Plc

First published 2013
This paperback edition first published 2014

British Library Cataloguing-in-Publication Data
A catalogue record for this book is available from the British Library.

ISBN: HB: 978-1-7809-3610-9
PB: 978-1-4725-9130-2
ePUB: 978-1-7809-3703-8
ePDF: 978-1-7809-3798-4

Library of Congress Cataloging-in-Publication Data
A catalog record for this book is available from the Library of Congress.

Typeset by Fakenham Prepress Solutions, Fakenham, Norfolk NR21 8NN

To GG, CR and AW

Contents

Acknowledgements

I would like to express my gratitude to Alexander García Dütmann for his teaching and friendship, to Roberto Cavallini, Sam McAuliffe and David Smith at InC for their generosity, to Adrian Randolph at the Leslie Centre for the Humanities, to Elizabeth Presa at the Centre for Ideas, and to James Tupper at Bloomsbury.

Introduction

The aim of the present volume is neither that of tracing Jean-Luc Nancy's career nor of introducing his philosophical work. Instead the analysis endeavours to follow Nancy's reading of Heidegger in order to investigate to what extent the Heideggerian project motivates Nancy's writing. The conditions for describing the originality of Nancy's thought will emerge from the creative frictions between the two thinkers.

This plan will unfold through a detailed analysis of the notion of Being-with, which is identified here as the moment where Nancy's appropriation of Heidegger becomes at once most distant and most productive.

This framework motivates the presence of the third interlocutor: Emmanuel Levinas. Levinas has been one of the most attentive readers of Heidegger, engaging specifically with questions of otherness and sociality. Finally dismissing the Heideggerian solution – because it is rooted in a philosophy of the world, where the Other is confronted simply as a moment in an otherwise individual and solitary trajectory – Levinas formulates the original command of otherness as epiphany of the face of the other human being. Whilst Jean-Luc Nancy never explicitly engages with the work of Levinas, one has the impression that his 'return' to Heidegger with regard to the themes of sociality and otherness works as a response and critique to Levinas' radically anti-Heideggerian position.

Nancy's 'interpretation' of Heidegger allows one to envisage a possible reopening of the Levinasian question from within Heidegger himself. Whilst Levinas shifts the interest from Being to the Other, Nancy's reading of Heidegger establishes a co-essentiality of the two terms, situating them on the same level. Instead of posing an absolute otherness, Nancy's conception of the co-essentiality of Being and Being-with opens the question of otherness within Being and at the heart of existence. One could suggest therefore that Nancy starts at the point where Levinas seems to envisage the culmination of his philosophy.

Overall the present work attempts to read Nancy's effort as directed to a disarticulation of Heidegger's thinking of sociality (normally considered to be the weakest part of his thinking – Sartre, Levinas, Arendt all agree on this).

Nancy's approach though rarely relies on a historical or literal reading; it is rather a reading that aims at appropriating the underlying ground of existential analysis. Nancy explicitly states his engagement with Heidegger's notion of finite being in his reworking of the idea of finite thinking, by trying to deliver finitude to its own openness, liberating it from a certain Heideggerian rhetoric. In a footnote to *A finite thinking* Nancy writes 'We don't know finitude "in itself" [...] It is with this that we need to concern ourselves, and not the rhetoric of the modesty of thinking within which Heidegger remains trapped' (Nancy 2003: 321).

Nancy starts precisely from a question that Heidegger has left unanswered, that of the body, in order to articulate finite existence at the crossing of materiality and thought. The question 'What a body can do?', posed by Spinoza in his *Ethics*, allows Nancy to force Heideggerian thought to a territory of incommensurable measures. Nancy finds in Spinoza a model where the body is consigned neither to pure materiality nor to the simple extension of the mind. This model frees a space that remains incommensurable to one or the other, opening both from within and making a clear distinction problematic. It is from this consideration of the body that ensues the questioning of finite worldhood, which Nancy approaches in many works, but which is dealt with in a decisive manner in his volume on film. For Nancy cinema offers the possibility of reopening within the finitude of sense the infinity of its destination, namely the impossibility of grasping the *sense of sense* once and for all. By addressing the evidence of sense, cinema insists on the blind spot that the inscription of sense itself is. The world of finite sense opens in itself an infinite measure of sense.

This touch of infinity on which finite sense rests allows one to read the encounter between Nancy and Levinas at the moment where the latter invokes the notion of justice. Levinas' idea of justice springs from the breaking apart imposed by God on the face to face. In so doing Levinas seems to introduce a leap of faith, an impasse where the face to face is outclassed by the encounter with God. A number of commentators have argued that this moment impinges Levinas' argument as to the epiphany of ethics, inasmuch as the distinction between the neutrality of the *il y a* and the intervention of the divine to guarantee justice remains uncertain. Nancy overcomes this difficulty by obliterating, in particular in the two volumes of the *Deconstruction of Christianity*, the clear distinction between secular and religious as well as that between finite and infinite. It is from this argument that a reconsideration of Heidegger becomes possible. Within the Heideggerian framework – existence considered as the disclosure of possibilities through the referentiality of sense in the world – the question of otherness becomes the question of the infinite reopening of the possibilities of finite existence. Finite existence considered in its three moments – *body, world, with* – is caught in the infinite as the continuous exposure of its significations to incommensurable appropriations.

The point therefore will be to see from which concepts Nancy starts and how – namely thanks to what kind of 'writing' – he manages to articulate Heideggerian questions *otherwise than Heidegger*. This move opens also the space to identify the specificity of Nancy's conceptual gestures. The argument will then attempt to name Nancy's original contribution to philosophy, that which allows his writings – whose format is mainly that of the short essay – to move from a complication of Heidegger to a more affirmative and singular position.

Any decision as to the unique character of Nancy's thinking cannot simply be summoned at the end of the argument. It is rather contained in the traces that punctuate the scattered development of his writing. Therefore one has to retrace this decision in the space devoted to each single concept.

However, whilst one can identify a continuity of concerns and strategies, Nancy's fragmentary style makes it difficult to systematize his thinking as well as to isolate one single concept. Each conceptual formulation works on an incessant movement of presentation and withdrawal. What becomes apparent through these negotiations is the struggle through which argumentation seems always to lead thinking to moments of incommensurability which revitalize discourse without being resolved. Each concept therefore is articulated as intensification or an adjustment of the others.

One should thus pay attention to the fact that Nancy's writing responds to the same structure of plural sense and incommensurability that his work attempts to advance as the very core of its conceptual agenda.

For Nancy the problem of writing, the strategy of inscription, becomes co-essential with the demand of the creation of concepts. In the context of Nancy's work the distinction between philosophy as literature and philosophy as the naked re-appropriation of the question of Being is highly problematic. One always has to do with the essential indecision between the two. As Maurice Blanchot writes, then every philosopher is the 'man of duplicitous word: there is what he says and what is important, interesting, original and able to prolong the interminability of discourse, but behind this, there is something that revokes his words' (Blanchot 2003: 49).

For Levinas on the other hand the overcoming of philosophy moves in a different direction. Philosophy should be constantly put under scrutiny since it represents the temptation of temptation, the promise of an unjust life. Whilst Levinas finds in Heidegger's work an exemplary case of this distortion, it is the very name *philosophy* that bears a mark of guilt. Philosophy then should be surpassed because it fails to address its own responsibility; that is it demands to extinguish it before having confronted it. The conditions that Western thought has produced inevitably return philosophy to a position of usurpation. Since philosophy, understood as the specific Western approach to the knowledge of existence, has followed a mastering instinct and formalized this instinct into a logic, thinking has already transformed into hidebound and prejudiced life. This life that wants to know before it acts confounds experience with its knowledge, but demands nonetheless to identify everything and bypass nothing, to include evil and the ambiguous. This life that joins together Ulysses' misfortunes with Don Juan's erotic prodigies and Figaro's crafty remedies finds its values and inspiration in philosophy. Levinas tries to elaborate an antithesis precisely to this philosophy that promotes the 'temptation of temptation'. Therefore he constructs his thinking in opposition to the tempters of postdiluvian civilization, to the dramatic life of Christianity, to the glory of history, the overconfidence of knowledge's total lucidity. When Levinas writes 'the temptation of temptation is the temptation of knowledge' (Levinas 1994: 34) what he is describing is the negative movement that initiates his own philosophical trajectory. Levinas' understanding of philosophy then comes from an ego that is truly separate and not from one that wants to remain pure in the midst of total compromise. To this effect he writes 'what tempts the one tempted by temptation is not pleasure but the ambiguity of a situation in which pleasure is still possible but in respect to which the Ego keeps its liberty, has not yet given up its security' (ibid.).

Contrary to this movement, according to Levinas philosophy should impose to life a continuous act of generosity. In other words, philosophy should constitute itself – against theoretical exploration – as a praxis that overcomes the dialectic engagement–disengagement and produce therefore an alternative to the relation between being and knowing. Being and acting do not proceed from knowing, consent does not follow exploration, responsibility preexists both choice and freedom. Philosophy is overcome not in absolute knowledge or faithfulness to evidence but in the impossibility to resist one's own responsibility: acceptance before inspection and practice before adherence. Levinas does not seek the limit of Reason, freedom of thought, but looks for Reason's predecessor, a pre-history, and finds it in responsibility. Commenting on the giving of the Torah, Levinas writes 'Being receives a challenge from the Torah, which jeopardizes its pretension of keeping itself above or beyond good and evil' (ibid.: 39).

It should be clarified here that it is ontology that Levinas has in mind when he writes of the *guilt of philosophy*. It is in order to counterbalance the priority of Being that he restructures the conditions for philosophy. Levinas finds a coincidence between 'the anteriority of acceptance in relation to freedom' (ibid.: 40) and 'the essence of the real' (ibid.). Being is at this point wrested of its neutrality, of its indifference and obtuseness to the good and becomes immediately meaningful. The work of ontology is reduced to nothing if ontology does not reinforce the affirmation of responsibility. Ontology is justified only because it introduces the ethical order, acceptance of guilt prior to any understanding of Being. The subordination of philosophy to the ethical order is given by Levinas at the very moment of creation and produces a complete reversal of the terms. As Levinas puts it, 'the true which offers itself in such a fashion is the good, not allowing the one who receives it time to look around and explore' (ibid.: 46). The philosophical priority that wants an investigation of the conditions of existence to found the possibility of ethics is here inversed. The world does not provide a neutral ground for the possibilities of ethics, at the opposite Levinas writes that 'the world is here so that the ethical order has the possibility of being fulfilled' (ibid.: 41). Levinas' strategy though does not aim simply at shocking logic in order to affirm faith. The inversion of the philosophical rule does not seek to substitute one mode of understanding with another, but to shift thinking and theory after the fundamental response to the call of responsibility. Levinas substitutes the idea of philosophy as original mediation with the lack of mediation between doing and hearing. Philosophy thus starts not with the clarification of the call, but following the response to the movement of the call. Philosophy must now abandon its moral suspension and act towards the good. Levinas shapes then a philosophy beyond philosophy, where *doing* substitutes *understanding*. As to the sense of this doing Levinas writes: 'the doing at stake here is not simply praxis as opposed to theory but a way of *actualizing without beginning with the possible*' (ibid.: 43). Levinas aims to do philosophy with the Other and for the Other as an obligation towards his face and towards his neighbour (the Third), even if and in particular when the risk one runs is to lose philosophy completely. What Levinas calls 'ethics as first philosophy' is perhaps nothing other than this ruin from which one can start philosophy all over again.

For the sake of the analysis and of coherent presentation this work will be structured around three motives. However, as it should have become clear from these preliminary remarks, it is not only what the concepts do, but also how the concepts are orchestrated that helps characterizing both Nancy's and Levinas' gesture. Whilst the fragment is one of the preferred forms of Nancy's writing, this does not simply dissect an original identity. The shattering precedes the unity: each fragment collaborates with the other, but not in order to reconstitute a lost coherence.

Nancy is willing to risk turning philosophy into literature where such a gesture grants the possibility to save the argument from presenting concepts as absolute. Fragments therefore do not only mark an insufficiency or establish a derivation of philosophy from literature; instead they respond to 'the movement of meaning in the suspension of signification, which withdraws meaning in giving it, in order to give it as its gift' (Nancy 1993b: 151).

The following concepts will be analysed:

- the *body* as the exposure of Dasein's existence and what of Dasein's existence is exposed;
- the *world* as the opening of the question of sense understood in terms of 'what happens between us';
- the *with* as the opening of the problem of otherness as incommensurable distance in the circulation of sense.

Following Nancy one could move then from the characterization of the body to the definition of an ethical world. However one could also describe this constellation starting from the opposite movement: a world whose ethical stance lies in the impossibility of reducing the contact of bodies in separation (*with*) to a category.

If the body is that which consistently keeps moving 'towards the world', the world being the very place where this transcendence becomes factical, the *with* is the hyphen that separates and maintains this transcendence. Such a manner of thinking permits to see the place of ethics in a perpetual form of displacement where the world is both what it is and also what constantly separates itself from mere presence and givenness. The *with* is not then a simple device, but this very logic of unsettlement, a logic that prevents the becoming absolute of the ethical in a principle beyond the sense of the world.

The work is organised in three chapters, each devoted to one concept. The first chapter focuses on the question of the body in Nancy's work *Corpus*. The text does not present a systematic treatment of the question of the body. Instead Nancy's attempt to expose the intertwining of materiality and thought is elaborated according to a strategy of displacements achieved through a series of resolutions. Concepts such as body, flesh, incarnation, are adopted momentarily and only strategically. The fragments are often organised or culminate with long lists, which at times lead to what Derrida has called *aposiopesis* (Derrida 2005: 71).

Nancy's discussion of the body is framed as an attempt to open Heidegger's silence on the question of the body, taking this silence to be a *praeteritio*: the body receives emphasis through its own absence. Nancy's work will be read in the light of Spinoza's *Ethics*, in particular there where the latter seems to offer a model to liberate the body.

The work of Emmanuel Levinas is introduced towards the end of the chapter, since the notion of *position* developed in his early writings provides a point of contact with Nancy's attempt to link the question of the body with that of existence.

Nancy elaborates his notion of the body in order to develop his deconstruction of Christianity and rework at the same time Heidegger's existential analysis by completing both the insufficient development of Being-with and the silence on corporeality.

Levinas on the other hand uses his early analysis on the body to attack Heidegger's empty notion of Being, which Levinas names the 'there is' and to start developing the notion of separation which will then make possible his phenomenology of desire and the movement of Infinity.

Nancy and Levinas move then from two opposite points of view: for Nancy the body is always entrusted to otherness, whilst Levinas introduces the concept of position to discover inner regions, ipseity and separation. However, given these differences, both philosophers read the body as an event opening the singular moment of existence. The body signals the arising of singularity and opens simultaneously the horizon of sharing and otherness.

If the problem of contemporary thought, of thinking after Heidegger, is to affirm the disenchantment of the world, the loss of a cosmic order and of organising principles, then Nancy adds that this project cannot avoid a deconstruction of Christian onto-theology. To put it with Nancy's words, 'the effacing of God is the sense of the world' (Nancy 2010: 46). For this reason Nancy's reading of Heidegger always moves in parallel with those of Descartes, Spinoza and Leibniz. It is within this rationalist tradition that Nancy detects the initial steps of a deconstruction of divine principles and it is from here that Nancy turns again to examine the Christian message of incarnation.

The second chapter attempts a reading of the question of the world, mainly from Nancy's volume *The Creation of the World or Globalization*. Here Nancy embarks in a deconstruction of the onto-theological tradition that has presented the world as dependant from an external principle. Since throughout the Western tradition the principle is primarily a divine one this deconstructive gesture cannot be completely separated from a deconstruction of Christianity. Following a reading of Heidegger's notion of Being-in-the-world, Nancy's analysis understands the world as the site for the opening of sense as that which responds to the question 'what happens between us'. 'Us' can be pronounced only insofar as it is pronounced within the limits of this world 'here'. The sense of the world is always given, but only insofar as it given to 'us'. Given to be given again.

Heidegger's attempt to extricate the question of the world from the subject–object relation and his own project of *destruction* are subject in Nancy's text to a creative re-appropriation. This becomes more apparent when the question of a world without principle is read in the light of Heidegger's examination of Leibniz' *Principle of Reason*.

In order to expose the logic of a world without principle, the chapter will investigate the relation between the cinematographic image and the real, as explored in Nancy's *The Evidence of Film*. In particular the work of American director John Cassavetes will be presented as an attempt to figure out a strategy of sociality based on distance.

The third chapter will take its cue from Levinas' notion of metaphysical desire and intends to question the notion of originary otherness. Levinas' refusal of Heidegger's Being-in-the-world constitutes the point of departure to develop the dialogue between Levinas, Heidegger and Nancy. The phenomenology of desire that occupies the central part of *Totality and Infinity* will be re-opened in a debate with Heidegger. The question of originary otherness and Levinas' relationship to the work of Martin Buber will be confronted with Nancy's work on the incommensurable.

Heidegger's notion of Being-with, refused by Levinas because organised around an indifferent crowd and because grounded in individualism, provides Nancy with the possibility of understanding a co-essential plurality at the heart of singular existence.

In this light therefore the *with* remains inappropriable, its logic is that of separation. Without being a thing, the *with* is that which commands a logic of relation based on the distinction of the terms that engage in the relation. The separation of the terms imposed by the *with* is that which allows the two terms to keep relating to each other.

With therefore designates relation in terms of that which happens and withdraws between us. *With* is nothing, meaning that it is not some thing, but that which happens between things. As Nancy puts it the law of the *with* is that of 'the distinct that distinguishes itself in entering the relation [...] coming to the other and separating itself from it' (Nancy 2001b: 22).

The fact that the *with* remains incommensurable guarantees the opening towards the other that Levinas was seeking to address.

The problem of otherness will therefore be understood in terms of decision over singular existence. Existence is the work of otherness inasmuch as it has always to decide itself. This decision is always co-appearing along the *with*.

The work of otherness at the heart of existence will be explored finally in the conclusive remarks where the attempt will be to understand Nancy's incommensurabilities as the work of *powers of existence*. Those name both the primacy for Nancy of philosophy as demand towards the open and the necessity of plunging philosophy into limit-thoughts and incommensurable distances.

On the one hand philosophy responds for Nancy to the demand of keeping open the exercise of questioning; the stress is therefore always on the possibility of retaining in philosophy the primacy of the question. The work of philosophy is that of questioning acquired significations in the name of a reopening of sense, whose consequences cannot be completely calculated. Finite thinking must retain a completion in incompletion.

On the other hand the incommensurable is introduced by Nancy in order to avoid binary structures and the reification of philosophical concepts. Nancy acknowledges that the work of philosophy is always an attempt to recover the *advance of existence*. In this act of retrieval philosophy does not represent or explicate existence, rather it maintains the openings and interruptions that are there constantly produced. Philosophy opens a space where the evidence of the real is exposed as that which philosophy has to decide upon, without extinguishing neither the real nor its own (in)decision. The opening of any question to the incommensurable is what prompts the most decisive transgression and allows philosophical discourse to proceed.

The return to Heidegger in the conclusive section then explores another silence, this time on the question of love. In 'Shattered Love' Nancy reopens the possibility for a discourse on and of love from within the Heideggerian ontological constitution of Dasein. The proposal is that a logic of the broken heart would allow one to envisage a new opening of the notion of otherness in Heidegger's thinking. The movement of love, which disrupts and at the same time widens the discourse, rather than determining the closure of the argument, should explode the enquiry towards a reconsideration of what still remains unthought.

Nancy's absolute realism matures through this constellation without a privileged point of entry. Nancy intertwines existential analysis with the disassembling of onto-theological substances to announce a world whose *telos* is submitted to the sparkle of singularities and to the density and intensity of bodies, which constitute the structure of sense, bare and transimmanent. Such a configuration does not provide a privileged access; it rather produces a sequence of movements through which its form constantly exceeds itself. As Nancy writes in *Adoration*, 'these are the opportunity and the joy of thinking: that it is essentially a relationship to its own excess, to the absolute excess which we can name "being", but also "world" or "sense"' (Nancy 2010: 23).

Rather than gathering fragments towards a solid form, the figure of thought peculiar to Nancy's work then is constantly entangled in the thinking of how such figures contribute to the texture and presentation of concepts.

Exposures

Heidegger: A review

Heidegger does not speak about the body. Famously *Being and Time* contains almost no reference to corporeality. To be more specific, the only reference one finds is a rather dismissive statement: '"Bodily nature" hides a whole problematic of its own, though we shall not treat it here' (Heidegger 1962: 124). Heidegger explicitly declares his intention to forego a discussion of Dasein's bodily nature. However one could have reasons to be suspicious given that this passage appears in Section 23, at the point where Heidegger takes up the question of de-severance (*Ent-fernung*) and directionality (*Ausrichtung*). It is in Section 23 that Heidegger discusses Dasein's way of orienting itself in the world. Perhaps this hasty dismissal should then be read as a *praeteritio*, a figure that allows one to achieve emphasis by passing something by. The passage from Section 23 seems to produce an interruption, whilst leaving at the same time an empty space there where the ek-statical opening of the world promises a phenomenological and existential investigation of the body.

The only mention of the body therefore appears when Heidegger sets off to explain what it means for Dasein to spatialize. De-severance is 'a kind of Being which Dasein has with regard to its Being-in-the-world' (ibid.: 139). It is a constitutive state of Dasein's Being, a state whose factical modes go from 'extremely close' to 'absolute remoteness'. Dasein opens space, makes space for itself. Dasein's spatiality is linked with its Being-in-the-world; it is one of the ways through which Heidegger specifies the nature of 'in' and the concept of world. Dasein's spatiality is not that of an object inside the world, Dasein is not in the world as present-at-hand; rather its happening in a space has an ontological connection to the world. In *Being and Time* Heidegger writes that

Dasein's spatiality 'cannot signify anything like occurrence at a position in a "world-space", nor it can signify Being-ready-to-hand at some place' (ibid.: 138). Dasein's way of being in space is of a different nature: Dasein relates to things present at hand by becoming familiar with them, by concerning itself with them. It is through this concernful dealing that Dasein situates things in space, making them available and accessible. Dasein brings what it encounters within-the-world into its sphere of concern, namely it brings things at a distance.

Heidegger insists on assigning this kind of spatiality to Dasein's existential characteristics. The expression 'bringing close' indicates not only objects drawn near for immediate use, but denotes also that which is cognitively discovered. However one should not deduce from this that Heidegger is implying here a subjectivist stance. Dasein does not change the nature of the entities it encounters; it rather reveals them as that which always already matters. This 'primordial spatiality' precedes every measuring (whether rigourous or casual, scientific or everyday) because it is intended as a way of relating, rather than serving as a device for quantitative calculations. This is what Heidegger means with the example of the street, whose touch one feels at every step – 'it slides itself as it were along certain portions of one's body' (ibid.: 142) – whilst at the same time it remains more remote than what one can encounter at a distance on that same street. Dis-stancing as bringing close does not mean drawing something nearer to my body, encumbered by my body as it were; it means bringing something at a distance existentially, becoming concerned with it. The corporeal involvement of Dasein appears here as existential: it discloses a world without necessarily bringing this world here.

In order to understand the existential character of one's body, one should pay attention to the body's involvement with the world. This involvement implies the activity of reaching as that of disclosing a region without performing any particular action. Furthermore it entails the almost passive situation of being always stretched between here and there. One could say that in these passages Heidegger is pointing to a structure that understands the body as never fixed, never belonging to one place, but always at each time opening the conditions for a 'somewhere'. This is the starting point where Jean-Luc Nancy takes up the Heideggerian silence over the body and develops it into the relation between the body and existence. This relation – that one could call 'exposure' – is struc-tured around the fact that Dasein moves between a 'here' in which it finds itself (without ever simply being or resting there) and a 'there', which it 'makes' each time. The fact that Dasein ex-ists and that its nature is ek-statical – always already played out in the outside where it has transcended all beings, including itself – constitutes the central question of the body. As François Raffoul puts it: 'transcendence is the taking place of any place' (Raffoul 1999: 152). Therefore, despite the fact that in *Being and Time* Heidegger does not articulate any explicit argument with regard to the body, it seems possible to reopen the aforementioned question from a Heideggerian perspective, regardless or even because of Heidegger's silence.

As mentioned the existential character of the body is disclosed moving from Section 23 of *Being and Time*. It is at this point that Heidegger attempts to liberate the body from its metaphysical 'history': the body is not a substance, but a particular way of existing in the world. The body is a fundamental way of being of Dasein, exposing Dasein's throwness, its involvement with the world (Being-in) and with others (Being-with). This suggestion and its links with Dasein's there is precisely what Nancy attempts to retrieve from Heidegger's silence. As Heidegger puts it: 'Dasein is proximally never here but yonder; from this "yonder" it comes back to its "here"; and it comes back to its "here" only in the way in which it interprets its concernful Being-towards' (Heidegger 1962: 142).

In Heidegger's work the question of the body becomes then the question of Dasein's leaping over and of its concernful Being-in-the-world as dealing with and working. Because Dasein is neither *vorhanden* nor *zuhanden*, neither present-at-hand nor ready-at-hand,[1] one could say that it is not only factically that the body occupies a crucial juncture in Heidegger's thinking. The body is not only what is present-at-hand for other Daseine. Existentially it is the ek- that displaces any place. The taking place of any place happens existentially with the body. It is as a body that Dasein assumes a distance and inhabits the world as the outside towards which it has transcended. The body is in charge of possibilities as the horizon of ek-sistence. This could also be put in the following way: something about the body is already explained by its bare being-there, but this something comes to be articulated only once the body exists as dis-stance from the world.

Despite the fact that the question of the body is again not addressed frontally, the *Metaphysical Foundations of Logic* takes up the question of Dasein's neutrality. Heidegger makes clear that his choice of 'Dasein' over 'man' is made in the name of neutrality. Dasein's neutrality allows Heidegger to investigate the being for which its own proper mode of being in a definite sense is not indifferent prior to factual determinations: existence prior to its concretions. This peculiar neutrality, however, should not be taken as indifference. It is a way of addressing

Dasein's potency. Neutrality here stands for openness to possibilities disclosed by Dasein in view of the realization of factual humanity. As Heidegger puts it, 'neutral Dasein is indeed the primal source of intrinsic possibility that springs up in every existence and makes it possible' (Heidegger 1984: 137).

This line of reasoning allows Heidegger to separate his existential analysis from worldviews and philosophies of life. As neutral Dasein gets immediately dispersed. Its dispersion is what *exists*. Dasein exists as its own dispersion. Seen in this light neutrality translates an original situation: Dasein is originally neutral, its neutrality stands for 'the not yet of factical dispersion' (ibid.). It is at this point that Heidegger inscribes bodiliness: 'as factical Dasein is in each case dispersed in a body' (ibid.). One should immediately caution that Heidegger does not introduce dispersion as a negative term, and that the lexicon deployed at this stage – splitting, dissociation, disaccord, division – cannot be heard only in its negative resonances. As for other concepts belonging to Dasein's facticity – falling, throwness, They and destruction, among others – the register suggested by the terminology should not be taken literally. Dispersion – further defined as *bestrewal* [*Streuung*] and *dissemination* [*Zertstreuung*] – is first of all a descriptive term. It describes Dasein's relation with the 'multiplication' of possibilities, its standing against and disclosing of this proliferation. This multiplication is already present in Dasein's neutrality and is realised in its essence: existence. Heidegger writes that embodiment is an organising factor of this dispersion. Dispersed in a body, Dasein then assumes its proper multiplication, it occurs in the world as extension [*Erstreckung*]. As Derrida writes commenting on these passages: 'Erstreckung names a spacing that, "prior to" the determination of space as *extensio*, comes to extend or stretch out being-there, the *there* of being, *between* birth and death' (Derrida 2008: 20). The extension that Dasein assumes as factically dispersed in a body belongs to its ontological character, to its existential structure, and decides of both Dasein's temporality and of its spatiality. As dispersed Dasein is *in between*: both in a temporal sense (extended between birth and death) and in a spatial one ('here', 'there' and all other spatial connotations belong to this dispersion). The body is at this point the organising factor of this original dispersion. Heidegger again stops here. Nothing more is mentioned with regard to how embodiment organises the aforementioned dispersion. Nevertheless what one could retain from these passages of *The Metaphysical Foundations* is the 'lexical swarm', invoked by Derrida, the scattering of *dis-*, 'the series of "dissociation", "distraction", "dissemination", "division", "dispersion"' (ibid.: 17).

In the Zollikon Seminars hosted between 1959 and 1969 in Zurich by the psychiatrist Medard Boss, Heidegger takes up the question of the body in more explicit terms. The first emergence of the term is to be found within a discussion of the phenomenon of making-present. Heidegger tries to clarify to an audience of non-philosophers the philosophical presuppositions that natural and physical sciences take for granted when explaining physiological and psychological processes.

The phenomenon of making-present, Heidegger says, cannot be considered as self-evident and immediately understood. Heidegger criticizes science for its assumptions and blind attitude: 'Science becomes blind to what it must presuppose and to what it wants to explain' (Heidegger 2001: 75). According to Heidegger there is then something unsatisfactory in the way sciences approach perception. Heidegger shows the impossibility of distinguishing between body and mind, saying that a simple principle cannot be found; instead, one moves in a circle. Contrary to what Nietzsche thought, the phenomenon of the body is not the more distinct and comprehensible and this is why, Heidegger says, its treatment has been passed by in *Being and Time*. Given these premises one can explain why Heidegger always appears sceptical with regard to the possibility of providing a solution to the question of the body. His intention is rather to open a field of questions.

Phenomenologically the body is the most resistant of concepts.[2] In a tone not different from the one deployed in *Being and Time*, Heidegger says that 'Dasein is not spatial because it is embodied. But its bodiliness is possible only because Dasein is spatial in the sense of making room' (ibid.: 81). As a consequence of this, the body is not identical to any 'being-here' of Dasein's being in a particular place. The body is the most distant to us in space. These passages serve Heidegger to develop the argument according to which whilst the body is a relation with my 'here', this relation is not that of presence-at-hand or readiness-to-hand; Dasein's mode of presence is other. One cannot properly say that the body is here in some place, 'in each case the *here* is this one' (ibid.: 94). Rather the body always leaps forward and in so doing takes up space. The fact that the body takes up space, rather than occupying a point in it, means that the 'here' of the body is never specified, because it is simply a 'somewhere': the body discloses a somewhere, without ever identifying with a specific site. At each time the body discloses a somewhere, this somewhere is opened, made by the body at each time and resists being reduced to specific coordinates.

From these remarks one could conclude that Heidegger intends the human body differently from a simply corporeal entity. *The body has to be linked more intimately with the question of Dasein, with existence.*

The limits of the body are not the limits of the body as a corporeal thing. They extend beyond, and in this beyond one should understand existence. Thus the question of the mineness of my body has nothing to do with the limit of my skin. My body is not limited by or within my skin. Heidegger says that 'the bodying forth of the body is determined by the way of my being [...] The limit of bodying forth (the body is only as it is bodying forth: 'body') is the horizon of being within which I sojourn' (ibid.: 84).

Further on, Heidegger attempts to explain the body as organising factor in the following terms: 'within philosophy [...] we must characterise all comportment of the human being as being-in-the-world, determined by bodying forth of the body' (ibid.: 90). The body is an organising factor in that it *expresses* Being-in-the-world. This expression, which manifests itself as gesture – 'one's gathered bearing and comportment' (ibid.) – should not be taken as an expression of something interior – the body pushing to the outside that which exerts a pressure from the inside. The body is an *interpretation* of Being-in-the-world in the way of an existential disclosure. As Levin says, this gesture could be heard perhaps in terms of 'a deep sense of inherence, belonging, rootedness, and grounding that normally and for the most part remains deeply, darkly implicit, pre-reflective, unthematized, unquestioned' (Levin 1999: 132).

These few passages – from the almost total silence of *Being and Time* to the explicit argumentation as a response to natural and medical sciences in the *Zollikon Seminars* – do not exhaust the list. What emerges though is the possibility of reading the body in relation to Dasein's existential disclosure of the world. The path, however, remains in Heidegger's work nothing more than a prospect, whose articulation is always precarious. Nevertheless those references provide a possibility to understand how Jean-Luc Nancy's work tries to address the question of the body within a Heideggerian perspective, whilst remaining silent with regard to Heidegger's silence.

Nancy endeavours to re-open the question of the body from within Heidegger, which in a few words means to *link the body most explicitly with the question of an existence without essence.*

However it should not be surprising that one finds no explicit reference to Heidegger in Nancy's *Corpus*. The volume in fact tries to make its own space. Thus it often takes on trajectories that, whilst respectful of the procedure of philosophical praxis, do not follow a specific model of philosophical presentation. The risk of this discourse betraying the canon of philosophical writing is always open, in particular when one stumbles upon propositions that can neither be derived nor refuted and that therefore prompt and never abandon the 'syncopation' of philosophical discourse. *Corpus* inhabits this syncope by relying constantly on those undecidable series that Nancy evokes in discussing Kant's work (Nancy 2008c: 10).

As it is frequently the case with Nancy, the way Heidegger is read allows for an indirect appropriation where the proper name *Martin Heidegger* seldom appears, whilst at the same time one can feel the German philosopher watching over the curve of the argument. This kind of appropriation does not repeat Heidegger's discourse; rather, it attempts to open Heidegger to his own possibilities.

If it is true that *Being and Time* 'strives to understand meaning as a question that precedes itself hermeneutically' (Nancy 1990: 225), then the work of Nancy on the body recalls that of the subject in the hermeneutic circle: the sense of the body cannot be separated from the body of sense.

Nancy will not treat Heidegger. He will not openly address the criticism that Heidegger never talks about the body, but nevertheless his question, which finds references elsewhere, namely in Spinoza, springs from a recess of Heideggerian silence. Nancy takes up Heidegger's *praeteritio* to re-mark what has been said only by being passed by.

Situating the body

Nancy takes up much of Heidegger's argument in refuting to consider the body as mere extension. His discourse attempts to preserve the idea of extension whilst highlighting the complexity of the relationships that the body harbours with sense. The latter is then defined as that which, dis-identical to itself, is irreducible to the assignment of significations. As Nancy writes: 'sense isn't a matter of something having or making sense. It is rather the fact that sense grasps itself as sense' (Nancy 1994: 92).

The angle at play within Nancy's work on the body is then an existential one, which means that questions regarding the body emerge from a reworking of existential analysis in view of what Nancy calls an *ontology of bodies*.

The first movement Nancy's work points to acknowledges that existence is disclosed at the threshold of the relationship between sense and the body.

The body is that which makes sense, but at the same time, residing in the passage sense-matter, it is resistant to signification, resistant to the play of signifiers/signified.

As Nancy writes 'the body is neither a "signifier" nor a "signified". It is exposing/exposed, ausgedehnt, an extension of the breakthrough that existence is' (Nancy 2008a: 25).

The argument that Nancy elaborates stresses the body's relation to existence, sense and creation in order to present the body as excess resisting the system of references. In this light the body constantly weaves and disrupts the ground in which this system finds its ultimate position.

It is not then a matter of translating the materiality of the body into a discursive gesture or of saying that materiality is itself a process.[3] The problem is to situate bodies beyond pure materiality. Bodies inhabit the passage or fracture that distances materiality and sense, the movement that exceeds both in circulating from one to the other. Although this program – a body that refuses the dualism sense-matter in order to take position beyond the two and that plays a pivotal role in the disclosure of existence and the world – might resonate with that of phenomenology, there are nevertheless important and crucial differences between the two. In a different way from Merleau-Ponty or Michel Henry and the approaches associated with their work, Nancy does not employ the term *flesh*. Whilst Henry carefully lays down the difference between flesh – '(that) which experiences itself and at the same time senses what surrounds it' – and body – 'senseless to the universe' (Henry 2009: 8) – in Nancy's discourse the word flesh is deliberately overlooked. In fact Henry writes not just that 'flesh and body are as opposed as to feel and not to feel', but that 'just our flesh allows us to know [...] something as «body»' (ibid.). In an interview with Roberto Esposito, which opens the Italian translation of *Being Singular Plural*, Nancy explains that his avoidance of the word flesh is due to its inscription within the Christian and phenomenological register. On the contrary, the word body retains some kind of lightness. In addition Nancy says: '(flesh) is a word of the in-itself and not of the outside of itself' (Nancy 2001: xxviii). Whilst Merleau-Ponty uses a register of intertwining that develops in his later writings into the notion of chiasm (Merleau-Ponty 1968), here the register on which to insist is one of discontinuity: not an inscription, but a writing out, a relation as limit that exceeds what it inscribes. It is precisely by stressing the outside of itself rather than the in-itself that Nancy marks the distance with the body of phenomenology. Nancy's refusal of phenomenology can be summarised as follows: every analysis of self-touching – including those remarkable passages in Husserl and Merleau-Ponty – returns the thinking of the body to interiority, consciousness and properness. At the opposite what thinking encounters when thinking the body is the whole extension of the outside. Nancy expresses the paradoxical structure of phenomenological discourse as follows: 'the phenomenological analyses of "self-touching" always return to a primary interiority. Which is impossible. To begin with, I have to be in exteriority in order to touch myself. And what I touch remains on the outside' (Nancy 2008a: 128). This is also the reason why Nancy refuses every reading of the body proper, of corporeality's two sides, 'inaccessible to others, open in principle only to itself' (Merleau-Ponty 1988: 197). For Nancy the body proper evokes on the one hand the already mentioned embodiment of Being-to-itself and on the other 'a vast tangle of images stretching from Christ musing over his unleavened bread to Christ tearing open his throbbing, blood-soaked Sacred Heart' (Nancy 2008a: 5). Behind the body proper lies the body of God, the desire to be and eat the body of God, to sacrifice the body in the name of God.

Whilst it is true that one finds in Nancy's work a constant reflection on the lexicon of incarnation, which traces the question back to a broader questioning of the hearth of Christianity, this project largely differs from that of Merleau-Ponty and also from that of Henry and is crucial to an understanding of Nancy's work on corporeality and his reference to Spinoza. What still survives in Henry's argument on the essential and productive difference between flesh and body is the presence of the *body of God*, that is to say an external, eminent Cause or Discourse, a *beyond*, which is called to confer sense on the body. On the contrary Nancy's project of *deconstruction of Christianity* (of which *Corpus* could be considered as the first – condensed – volume) attempts precisely to understand the body in the absence of Gods or as the place that the withdrawal of Gods has left open. As Nancy writes: 'we can in no way think the body in terms of incarnation [...] where that which is without place, without exteriority, without form, without matter (God) comes into flesh' (ibid.: 132). It is therefore a matter of replacing the emptiness of the body before the moment of incarnation, with the density of bodies that are not incarnated, but constantly tend towards existence. The question of incarnation must be dislodged from the Christian ground that informs everything we know and think about it. It must be substituted with the register of Being-there, but it is then a matter of articulating this 'there' and of doing so generously and rigourously. To express the 'there' means to articulate it as a body (and therefore at once within and away from Heidegger). The body is that which triggers the relation to the outside: it establishes the fact that every relation can only be a relation to an outside. Existence itself can only sense itself as existence, removal of essence, putting at stake of essences, in-decision. With the body one always has to do with a 'there' that constantly extends itself, 'following a perhaps impenetrable formula in Heidegger with "being the there" [...] the "there" itself is made only of opening and exposition' (ibid.: 133). The concept of incarnation bears for Nancy even broader connotations. In the second volume of the deconstruction of Christianity – *Adoration* – Nancy suggests that incarnation inaugurates an 'ontological degradation [...] "Being" as fall, that is to say a movement triggered by the lack of ground' (Nancy 2010: 105).

It is from this initial gesture that Nancy revives the rationalist traditions and turns in particular to the work of Spinoza. It is the withdrawal of God, announced precisely by Spinoza's *Deus sive Natura*, that liberates the question of the body and sets in motion the discourse of the body's relation with the open character of existence and the transimmanent movement of sense in the world. The body as an open space, the space opened by bodies and the movements of sense in the world form in Nancy's philosophy the core of a conceptual constellation that occupies the place left free by the withdrawal of Gods. If there is no beyond, no body of God, then the question of the body can be put alongside the obsession, peculiar to Western thought, for *what is*.

   Questions will then be structured around the fact that the body is that which exposes existence. These questions can be posited as demands concerning the very fact that the body *is* and that it is always what is *there* (in thinking as in the actuality of experience). What is left is the body as an obsession with the real.

Approaching the body in the light of an obsession with the real, without falling into defining it as either discourse or matter, amounts to questioning the body's relation with an existence that cuts across its own essence. Nancy's program addresses the body as body, at once away from and within the apparent tautology, in excess of signification, as that which constantly exposes and is exposed to existence. Nancy suggests thinking the body not as referring to clear and distinct signifiers or fixed moments of meaning, but to existence's coming to presence. To put it differently, Nancy advocates a thinking of the body in terms of existence as the sharing that creates the world as *world*. The body writes out this absence of teleology: the world is its own existence, the 'happening' of existence.

Nancy's reopening of Heidegger's *praeteritio* is played out through Spinoza's liberation of the body: the body as extension participating in God; the mind as idea of the body. It is Spinoza's understanding of God as one substance (or Nature) to open the space for the liberation of the body from the body of God. As Nancy writes:

'God is the unique substance. There is nothing else. The unique substance for Spinoza is not a mass, it is in itself double: it is thought and extension [...] Which is why, from this moment on, we can forget God' (Nancy 2008a: 129). Moving from the definition of the 'body as a mode which expresses [...] God [...] as the thing extended' (Spinoza 1949: 79) and the mind as idea of the body, one can draw a trajectory that culminates in Nancy's thinking of the body as the place of existence.

Spinoza's claim that 'no-one has hitherto determined what a body can do' (ibid.) echoes the idea of the body as resilient to signification, of the body as excess, as that which resides in the passage sense-matter. Given the nature of the Spinozian God, Nancy considers him to be the first thinker of the world. The famous formulation '*Deus sive natura*' bears a relation with Nancy's reading of existence and the question of the world.

Banality of bodies

To speak of the banality of the body would mean here that the word 'body' itself does not touch the ground anymore. It means to touch on a *generalogy* (a logos of the general, posited as generally as possible).

As Nancy puts it:

> Capital, no doubt, also produces a banalizing generalization of the body and of the neighbour. Photographic obsessions with crowds attest to this fact, with their misery, their panics, with number as such, or with erotic obsessions filtering in throughout ... (this, too, is why the body has also become the most insipid, the flattest, finally the most disconnected of themes and terms – in an irreversible coma).
>
> (ibid.: 91)

Nancy goes on to indicate two versions of this banality, two shades of the same phenomenon: 'that of the model (the magazine register, a canon of streamlined, velvety bodies) and that of the *indiscriminate* (no matter what body, ruined, wrecked, deformed)' (ibid.: 91).

This distinction outlines the circumstances into which the question of the body has fallen. On the one side, the body matters when it can be subjected to a process of beautification (*cosmesis*), what Stendhal calls *la promesse du bonheur*.[4] On the other, a body is always called upon to signify or stand in for something else. Any other body, which does not belong or subscribe to a body of signs, which does not inscribe itself within a system of signification, falls into the category of the *whatever* (*n'importe que corps*).

Along this same path the theme of proximity, the space of the one next to me, loses its depth. One's relation with the fellow man becomes a question of a simple juxtaposition of bodies. Exposing the theme to its banality requires reopening again the Heideggerian horizon, in particular at the juncture where a crossing is produced between the questions of Being-with and the question of the world.

What happens once, as Nancy writes, 'the body is simply there, given, abandoned, without presupposition, simply posited, weighted, weighty' (Nancy 1993: 197) and what if bodies were 'first masses, masses offered without anything to articulate, without anything to discourse about, without anything to add to them' (ibid.)? To the lightness and inconsistency that the concept of the body has come to assume, it will be here opposed a thinking that tries to give weight to this notion in an attempt to acknowledge the nature of our bodies as local extensions exposing existence and exposed to existence.

The aim is that of understanding existence's coming to presence and what of existence is present. In relation to the body this means questioning the *pure contingency of my place*.

The urgency for an enquiry into what bodies are can be located on two limits, which themselves form the edges of a polarized structure. This polarization is determined on the one side by 'starving bodies' and on the other by bodies excessively sated or nourished. It is here between these two poles that one should situate the sense of the body, there where the sense of the word 'body' has become too light and too cruel, incommensurable. The former is the place where sense disappears from the body, the sign is in withdrawal, no longer present; it has left space for a mere thinness, which presents itself like a shortage of existence. The latter establishes a pole on to which too much signification is concentrated. Sense disappears in the wake of a body that dazzles.

It is in this cleft that the two banalities arise, in their spacing out which sees this cruelty inflicted upon them: a cadaverous and gaunt body and a pleonastic one, each incommensurable to the other in the lightness they have become.

What they have grown to be recalls precisely the Socrates of Aristophanes' *Clouds*, the philosopher caught in pointless speculations, walking upon air and descrying the sun: Socrates has become Σωκρατίδιον (sweet little Socrates).

One should then ask, as with Strepsiades, for a *katabasi*, for this body to come down. It must be repeated here that the body is a matter of weight and thickness.

Impenetrable outline

On the 30th of October 1921 Franz Kafka wrote in his diary: 'the impenetrable outline of human bodies is horrible' (Kafka 1974: 396). This sentence provides a useful starting point to separate the body from the two regimes of banality just mentioned. The passage outlines the effort to give the body its dimension, a dimension that does not rest upon a system of significations, but rather one into which signification has not yet entered.

The Kafkian outline sets the limit, that limit one has to question in order to let the body expose sense and disclose the world. Rather than occupying a place, the body occupies a limit. This is precisely what is horrible about it: the body, its outline, is always the limit that discloses sense; it is always as limit that it makes sense. As Nancy writes: 'a thought of limit is always a thought of excess' (Nancy 1997: 40). The outline then is horrible because as limit it is always in excess. In excess of itself, always open and about to reject itself – the limit where existence comes to presence. Secondly it is also in excess of signification and the symbolic order, since the outline of the body is the limit where sense is articulated, and articulated as the border of signification, irreducible to it.

Nancy writes that the general logic of the limit is such that 'the limit unlimits the passage to the limit' (ibid.: 40). According to the excesses just mentioned, the body unlimits itself, existence and sense. It unlimits itself as open; it unlimits existence's coming to presence; it unlimits sense as the denial of identity, as a resistance to signification.

The sense the body exposes is 'beyond the appropriation of signifieds and the presentation of signifiers, in the very opening of the abandonment of sense, as the opening of the world' (ibid.). The body, a situation of excess and a passage of excess (sense), goes beyond the play of the symbolic–cultural order, it resists this reduction. It resists it as matter (the thickness of its outline, almost a crust) and it resists it as the opening of sense (as the horrifying power of its outline, the silhouette of excess). There is something about the body that signification never grasps since it is the element without which signification could not be opened. Meaning confronts the body always as its most uncontrolled *nescio quid*, horrible outline.

It is from this movement, the body as excess of signification and disclosure of sense that Nancy's work crosses the first two books of Spinoza's *Ethics*. It is from an attempt to give voice to Heidegger's silence about Dasein's body and the bodies of others and to do so in the place left vacant by the withdrawal of Gods, without simply producing a return to the divine, that Nancy encounters Spinoza. The geometrical mode of the *Ethics* works as a key to inaugurate a deconstruction of the body of God and to expose Heidegger to his own silence. Whilst Nancy never explicitly undertakes such program, he nonetheless announces Heidegger's limits in Spinozian terms. Nancy concludes a text on the coincidence in Heidegger of fundamental ontology and originary ethics with the following proposition:

> Heidegger cannot but have kept deliberately quiet about the only major work of philosophy entitled *Ethics* that is itself an 'ontology' [...] To say that *ethos* is the ek-sisting of existence itself might be another way of saying that 'blessedness is not the reward of virtue, but virtue itself.
>
> (Nancy 2003: 195)

Whilst Heidegger deliberately avoids any reference to Spinoza, Nancy's introduction of the concept of *adoration* strikes as an attempt to explore an unthought residue of Spinozism at the heart of Heidegger's analysis. Within Nancy's second volume of the deconstruction of Christianity one can hear the echoes of the fifth volume of the *Ethics* reopening the Heideggerian analysis of existence. Spinoza's knowledge of the third kind, through which blessedness reveals itself not as the reward of virtue, but as attitude towards existence, moves from the attentiveness to singular beings. This specific kind of devotion to singularities opens the path to the love of God (or Nature). Nancy's linguistic turn brings adoration outside of its religious dimension, replicating the shift Spinoza performs on the concept of blessedness. Adoration becomes therefore a special kind of attentiveness, directed not towards the divine principle, but towards the opening of existence, according to a principle of non-equivalence. If Spinozian blessedness is not just the outcome of a privileged register of knowledge, but contemplation of *nature*, Nancy's adoration is a relation to existence in the excess that existence itself produces with regard to an ultimate reason, a final destination and an original sense. Adoration is a leap beyond philosophy itself and becomes 'attention to the movements of sense' (Nancy 2010: 31).[5]

Spinoza: The liberator of the body

At the very beginning of his remarkable *Spinoza: Practical Philosophy*, Gilles Deleuze comments on the groundbreaking consequences of Spinoza's thought insofar as it has provided philosophy with a new model: the body. Commenting on the *Ethics*, Deleuze writes: 'one seeks to acquire a knowledge of the powers of the body in order to discover, in a parallel fashion, the powers of the mind' (Deleuze 1988: 17).

What Deleuze is referring to can be found in EIII, P2, where Spinoza writes: 'the body cannot determine the mind to thought neither can the mind determine the body to motion nor rest, nor to anything else, if there be anything else' (Spinoza 1949: 130). The mind is determined by the attribute of thought whilst only another body, that is to say, God understood as an extended thing, can affect the body to motion and rest. Whatever then arises in the body cannot come from the mind, but from God in the mode of extension.

A first stop followed by a diversion is needed here in order to clarify the context of the expression 'to come from'. Whilst it is true that Spinoza adopts the terms *sequire* and *effluere*, this should not induce one to understand Spinoza as a Neo-Platonist. As Deleuze emphasises, the differences between an emanatist Neo-Platonic understanding and the essentially immanentist theory of Spinoza are incommensurable. In particular the line has to be drawn between the conceptual core of the *Ethics* and Plotinus' theory of the emanation *ex-deo*. Spinoza situates himself on precisely the opposite side, since his *cause* is an immanent one. As Deleuze argues, if it is true that both an immanent and emanative cause can be said to produce without leaving themselves, the emanative cause does not retain its effect. It is precisely from this latter element that Plotinus developed the theory of degradation. To this Spinoza replies with a cause that, instead of being remote, is everywhere equally close. Spinoza's God 'produces things as he formally exists, or as he objectively understands himself' (Deleuze 1992: 180). It is important to note that in Spinoza expression is 'freed from all traces of emanation [...] Far from emanating from an eminent Unity, the really distinct attributes constitute the essence of absolutely single substance' (ibid.: 182). Nancy's remark that Spinoza is the first thinker of the world takes its cue precisely from this understanding of expression.

According to the theory of parallelism then body and mind have to be considered as one and the same thing precisely for this reason: neither of the two can limit the other. The theoretical thesis known as parallelism assumes no primacy of the mind over the body and vice versa. It is clear how this explicitly undermines the Cartesian idea, which wants the mind to act upon the body and the latter to act upon the mind. However whilst the work of mind and body is one, at the same time, body and mind have to be understood as autonomous since they depend on two different attributes. Their relation – and this is what it is addressed as parallelism – is established by the fact that the order of ideas corresponds to the order of things. As in Spinoza there is no primacy of any attribute over any other, mind and body share the same (im)perfection.

In EII, P13 then one reads: 'the mind is the idea of the body' (Spinoza 1949: 89). The mind is the idea of a singular extension, of an outside relating to itself, of a *being-outside*. The irreconcilable difference between inside and outside comes to an end with Spinoza. Interiority and exteriority coexist. This also amounts to saying that the singular mind (my mind) constantly understands itself as being outside, articulating itself towards other minds and other bodies. There are not two bodies, the aerial body of the soul and the material, extended body. As Nancy puts it with Spinoza for the first time, 'the soul signifies that the body is what knows or senses it is necessary in its contingency' (Nancy 2008a: 130). The mind is the body's relation to itself, its own difference, which defers every ownness and properness, but which also makes a body into a singularity, this body opened to itself and offered to others.

The suggestion is here to read this statement next to a posthumous fragment by Freud on which Jean-Luc Nancy has extensively commented: 'The psyche's extended: knows nothing about it' (ibid.: 21). The proposal can be justified looking at how both Spinoza's proposition and Freud's fragment draw a trajectory of incommensurability. Both passages point to a thinking of the mind as extended. In both cases one is facing an incommensurability. Commenting on this union Nancy writes 'there is no measure one can attend to here. It is the incommensurable that makes possible the *quasi permixtio* of the union and that makes of this an incommensurable thought' (Nancy 1979: 161). How to think then this incommensurable community in extension of thought and body?

Nancy understands this incommensurability in terms of holes. He employs a metonymy: 'the incommensuable extension of thought, is the opening of the mouth. The mouth that opens itself and forms "ego", this mouth is the locus of the union as far as the union opens itself up and stretches itself' (ibid.). Nancy thinks the mouth for everything else, as accounting for the whole body. He suggests that what is to be thought, in order to make sense of Psyche's extension, is the mouth, 'psyche's body, the being-extended and outside-itself of presence-to-the world' (Nancy 2008a: 21). One should then think the mouth, but starting from it one must also pay attention to other entrances, ways in and ways out. In order to think this extension of Psyche, it is necessary to think a mouth before orality, doing things other than speaking, spacing out thought, thus reconciling the incommensurability. The mouth assumes this importance because it is the place where the 'I' is thrown. The mouth creates space, making available the conditions of extension, including that of thought. Spinoza writes that the mind is not an Other to the body, it is not that which is in opposition to our corporeal nature (receptacle in the tradition of all degradation and incapable of resisting temptations) for the very reason that mind and body are united (EII, P13, Note). Whilst thinking the body one then should not take for granted that there is a soul on the other side, which is overdetermined or which overdetermines. What 'Psyche ist ausgedehnt ...' and EII, P13 point to is the outside of the body, the idea of the mind as the body outside itself, in relation with itself.

Nancy suggests that once one elaborates a discourse on the body one is in fact already implicated in a discourse about the mind. One should then reason keeping in mind the parallelism introduced at the beginning of this discussion. On the one hand this discourse demands not to think body and mind as exactly the same thing, whilst on the other it also asks to resist giving in to a dualistic vision. What is at stake is to think with Spinoza, at the very heart of his P13, at the very heart of parallelism: the mind as the idea of the body or Psyche being stretched out. In other terms, one is here asked to conceive the mind as the difference of the body to itself; that which accompanies the journey of the body from itself to itself. This idea has at different times agitated Western thinking and has performed with Descartes' second meditation (certainty as the verbalization of the '*Ego Sum*' – '*Ego sum, ego existo; quoties a me profertur, vel mente concipitur – necessario esse verum*') a deconstructive interruption. As Nancy says: 'the setting up and inauguration of the Subject have provoked the collapse of its substance [...] the collapse of the substance belongs to the setting up of the Subject' (Nancy 1979: 33).

Nancy suggests thinking the *unity of the articulation*, which means to understand the extension of the mind and its relation to the body in terms of movement, of a common *e-motion*.

What Spinoza writes in the propositions following P13 is fundamentally that the mind is the experience of the body. In addressing the question of experience, it should be made clear that the word – from the latin *experiri* – always holds to an idea of movement towards the outside.

As long as sense is all that is available to us, then bodies *make* sense – in the double and ambivalent sense of the expression. This is why to talk about bodies is a matter of touching on that which is not discourse at all. If one argues – with Nancy – that the world is the exposed of the human and that the human being is that which exposes the world, then sense requires a body in order to gain such a name. As Nancy points out, if we are to rebuild ontology the only one available would be one concerning the body. Bodies do photography, they write the light in making space for sense, but sense needs to stop on the edge of this writing, it has to squeeze itself into this writing the body is.

Sense finds in the body a second skin, whilst at the same time the body invests itself in sense. It is not the skin of an incarnation, but the skin as the surface that makes space, that exposes sense, that takes the place of sense.

In EII, P13 one reads that the mind does not know anything else but the body, 'the object of the idea constituting the human mind is a body [...] and nothing else' (Spinoza 1949: 89). If the body is the extended thing informing the very and only idea of the human mind, then the mind makes sense of itself by ways of the affections of the body. Body is the extension of the mind on which the mind bases its knowledge of itself. What a mind is capable of is what a body is capable of. This last discussion inscribes the present argument once more there where the body escapes the dialectic signifier/signified. The body does not stand for anything else. Instead the body is sense in itself, as such, as extension, as dense, solid and open. The body is there where sense comes to presence, sense in se and per se.

In the Note to the second proposition of EIII, Spinoza argues: 'for what the body can do, none has hitherto determined' (Spinoza 1949: 131). The body surpasses the knowledge that one has of it. Bodies are somehow free from the understanding we have of them. Spinoza liberates the body not just from the legacy of scholastic and medieval philosophy, where following a Platonic framework the body was detached from the elevation of the mind and could not achieve any perfection whatsoever[6] – but also from Cartesian dualism. Deleuze will return to this point few years after his work on Spinoza in *Cinema 2*, referring to this position as a philosophical reversal. In the section of the volume devoted to the cinema of bodies, a cinema that through the body would build its alliance with thought, Deleuze still seems to be thinking with Spinoza when he writes that:

> the body is no longer the obstacle that separates thought from itself, that which it has to overcome to reach thinking. It is on the contrary that which it plunges into or must plunge into, in order to reach the unthought, that is life [...] The categories of life are precisely the attitudes of the body, its postures [...] To think is to learn what a non-thinking body is capable of.
>
> (Deleuze 2005: 182)

The mind cannot and should not act in order to dominate the body, for passions arise in both and, most importantly, *for what a body can do, none has hitherto determined*. One should thus not consider the mind to be the master of the body, insofar as a significant number of bodily states – drunkenness and insomnia for instance, but also effort and resistance – are unavailable to the mind.

It could be argued here that one should be reminded of the fifth book of the *Ethics*, the volume devoted to 'the method or way which leads to liberty' (Spinoza 1949: 252). This volume certainly poses additional problems to the theory parallelism. Here Spinoza argues that 'we possess the power of arranging and connecting the modifications of the body according to the order of the intellect' (ibid.: 260). A number of commentators have taken this proposition as undermining parallelism and in fact, when read in isolation, it does indeed seem to confirm this position. However upon reading further one finds clues that seem to convey the opposite: persistence in determining the body as parallel to the mind; the body as an irreplaceable intermediary on the way towards knowledge. If EV, P10, the proposition just quoted, could be read as saying that the mind acts upon the body in order to subdue the body's passions, one should nevertheless not forget that the liberation from passions springs from a clear and distinct knowledge of oneself. This particular kind of awareness must necessarily include knowledge of the body that allows the latter to act. Furthermore, in propositions 30 and 39, it is possible to find further confirmation of such a reading. In EV, P30, Spinoza writes that 'our mind in so far as it knows itself and the body under the form of eternity, necessarily has a knowledge of God' (ibid.: 272). One can see here how the body is not excluded from the knowledge of God and of one's being in God (the subject matter of the third kind of knowledge, the one we must acquire in order to set ourselves free from passions). In EV, 39 then Spinoza pursues an old philosophical question, first debated by Aristotle and then by Maimonides among others: whether or not the body can bring anything to the perfection of the mind. Spinoza's reply is affirmative. The body helps our mind to experience during lifetime the liberation from passions, for 'He who possesses a body fit for many things possesses a mind of which the greater part is eternal' (ibid.: 277).

Spinoza conceives of the body, as Deleuze puts it, as 'composed of an infinite numbers of particles; it is the relation of motion and rest, of speed and slowness between the particles that define a body [...] a body affects other bodies' (Deleuze 1988: 123). The body is here described as a set of relations: no longer in terms of form and function, no longer simply as a substance.

As Deleuze writes: 'one never commences; one never has a *tabula rasa*, one slips in, enters in the middle; one takes up or lays down rhythms. Also Spinoza provides the body with a great deal of power, for its affective power is core to its definition' (ibid.). There is an additional idea here: 'one never commences, one never has a tabula rasa, one slips in, enters in the middle'. It is important to underline this point: *one never starts with the body, nor with it one ever ends; one always finds oneself caught in its coming.*

There is then a last element according to which Spinoza removes the body from its traditional position: the body is a mode of God; God is also body, extended thing.

In EII, D1, Spinoza says: 'by body I understand a mode which expresses in a certain and determinate manner the essence of God in so far as He is considered as the thing extended' (Spinoza 1949: 79). To the definition of God as thought Spinoza adds God as extension. From this it follows that the body shares the same ontological status as the mind. It takes part in God, it is in God.

From these preliminary lines it is already apparent the degree of novelty Spinoza brings to the understanding of the body. To this effect Deleuze writes: 'Every reader of Spinoza knows that for him the bodies [...] are not substances or subjects, but modes' (Deleuze 1988: 124). Spinoza allows for a definition of the human body that already opens a path beyond subjectivity: 'you will define a human being not as a subject, but by the affects of which it is capable' (ibid.).

With Spinoza therefore one comes across a body that shares in the essence of God. The body is an expression of God as extended thing; its powers are not fully graspable by the mind and its definition relies on relational properties: motion, rest and its capacity to affect other bodies and to be in turn affected by them.

Following a Spinozian path Dr Nahum Fischelson in Isaac Singer's storey finds redemption through his body whilst in the last stages of his life. His body comes to liberate him from a state of abandonment; an abandonment that he pays, at an intellectual level, in finding shut each and every door that would open onto a true understanding of the *Ethics*. This private revolution is triggered by the encounter with a woman 'tall and lean and as black as a baker's shovel' (Singer 1973: 14). Dr Fichelson, old, sick, and almost entirely deprived of physical strength, is quite unexpectedly led back before his physicality. He retrieves it when Miss Dobbe, the woman he has just married (a wedding that, involving such a feeble and tired man, is without joy), enters his room 'wearing a silk nightgown, slippers with pompoms, and with her hair hanging down over her shoulders' (ibid.). Dr Fischelson starts trembling, whilst Spinoza's masterpiece falls from his hands. When she kisses him, murmuring 'Mazel Tov', something miraculous happens. Suddenly all the pain, the pressures, the ailments and aches stopped, 'he was again a man in his youth' (ibid.). After this awakening of the body he seems for a single second to be able to grasp the Spinozian system, finally accepting the truth with which he is confronted. Whilst Dr Fichelson watches the night sky in which a shower of meteors is shedding light, the narrating voice comments:

Yes, the divine substance was extended and had neither beginning, nor end; it was absolute, indivisible, eternal, without duration, infinite in its attributes. Its waves and bubbles danced in the universal cauldron, seething with chance, following the unbroken chain of causes and effects, and he … with his unavoidable faith was part of this.

(ibid.: 24)

No one knows what a body can do.

Touching the word

To claim that one does not know what a body can do also means that it will not be possible to find its 'truth' in the realm of signification, in the symbolic order. The path traced by a Spinozian understanding of the body frames the question of corporeality in terms of extension and relational qualities. In conceiving of the body in terms of its relation to the One Substance and in terms of the mutual affection it performs on and receives from other bodies, the aim is to bring forward a discourse that explores the truth of the body elsewhere than in the dialectic signifier/signified. Following Spinoza, one can say that a body is in the world as relational extension, well before it is in the world as *subject of*. The attempt to resist subscribing to the idea of the body as signifier leads to the body as untranslatable. The primary concern resides in the following situation: *a word for the body is missing* or *the word 'body' fails to touch upon that to which it refers*. A word, in order to account for the body, should designate a physical extension or structure, whose power relies on the ability to enter a complex set of relations; it should, as it were, *exist the body*.

What is questioned here is the 'properness' of the words used to invoke and define the body. Nancy's *Corpus* evokes this idea by referring to the catalogue and the body of work the word corpus entails. The question of polysemia underlines his discourse. It is this same question that Jacques Derrida investigates in his reading of Aristotle. The question could be formulated in this way: when is a noun proper? Is the noun *body* proper? Derrida argues that a noun is proper first of all when 'it has but a single sense. Better it is only in this case that it is properly a noun. Univocity is the essence' (Derrida 1982: 247).

Derrida suggests posing the question of properness along with the ones relating to polysemia:

language is what it is, language, only insofar as it can then master and analyse polysemia […] A nonmasterable dissemination is not even a polysemia, it belongs to what is outside language [...] Each time that polysemia is irreducible, when no unity of meaning is even promised to it, one is outside language.

(ibid.: 248)

In the context developed here one could ask: is it possible that the word *body* resides exactly there, at the limit or even beyond the limit of language? The question would be then that of a polysemia only partially reducible to meaning, a polysemia that resists being reduced completely, but that nevertheless makes itself understood. Polysemia would have here entered one single word, the word *body*, obliging it to always engage a dynamic game of in and out, within and beyond univocity, always approaching the limits of meaning.

The Ancient Greek dictionary expresses the idea of a body with more than ten words; it is a *polisomatic* dictionary. What the Greek dictionary does not do is designate the body with a single term; it does not provide a word for an organic unity, which would support the individual in the multiplicity of his vital and mental functions. Univocity is excluded, though one is not exactly outside meaning, never too far from it.

For the Greeks what exists is instead a corpus, a list, a catalogue without an index, without a unity, precisely orphan of its object. A catalogue without an object is that which creates its object through a continuous process of naming. It is a catalogue without a table of contents, a catalogue comprised not of the totality of its terms taken together, but of the declination of each one of them. It is a catalogue one would find difficult to use as a reference, as one would make use of a dictionary.

The word that has survived in the philosophical tradition to designate one's body is σῶμα. Modern languages still employ it in reference to a whole range of expressions such as somatic, to somaticize, somatology, psychosomatic. In the Greek dictionary the word σῶμα originally indicates a corpse. It seems to designate the very opposite of a body, an antibody as it were. Σῶμα is what remains of an individual after his incarnated life and physical vitality has left him. It is the body of bereavement and waiting. Σῶμα is an inert figure, it is immobility, stillness, absence of life, lack of movement, lack of bodily functions; a symbol, an effigy, an imitation, an image (μιμέομαι means to imitate, but also shadow, ghost). It is what remains of me, or better still what remains of me after *me* has departed. It is then an exposition, an object on display. The object of display and lamentation, cries, tears and screams. It is the shadow of the beloved for the ones who are left celebrating him/her. It is the minute before dust, before all disappears in the burial, ashes. Σῶμα, rather than indicating or standing for the word 'body', invokes the instant before invisibility, and as such it thus accomplishes this invisibility's initiation. It reminds us of Socrates' statement in the *Cratylus*: 'there is a lot to say, it seems to me – and if one distorted the name a little, there would be even more. Thus some say that the body is the grave of the soul' (Plato 1998: 30). In Σῶμα resonates the word σῆμα (grave).

The term δέμας indicates an individual's stature, the whole individual as various pieces in assemblage. It is employed in combination with εἶδος. The two together account for the image of someone standing in front of us, the idea that one gives when offering his body to another. Similarly χρώσ (from which derive the English *crust*, the French *croûte* and the Italian *crosta*) stands for the outside of the individual, the hard outer layer, what is most likely to touch and be touched, the place of contact, the place that links one's body to the surface of another. These four terms all indicate bodily properties or parts; they do so, however, without entailing any idea of life. A body that lives, moves, escapes stillness, is immersed in the stream of life is expressed with still different terms. γυῖα and μελέα both communicate an idea of movement, of a being possessing the quality of life, activity, strength and ability to hold tools and make use of them. Suppleness, agility, flexibility, elasticity, plasticity, even smoothness, grace, style. γυῖα and μελέα articulate a wholeness, a physical entity that holds itself, that is self-contained, that can bring itself from one place to another as a whole.

Σῶμα; δέμας; εἶδος; χρώσ; γυῖα; μελέα; κάρα; πρόσωπον; καρδία; πραπίδες; μένος; νόος

What keeps presenting and withdrawing its features under these many curtains is a human body. The positive aspect of this dissemination resides in the fact that the Greeks were reaching a productive compromise with regard to the idea of the body as in constant change, immersed in a set of relations that it is not possible to simplify.

All the words the Greek dictionary employs account for a part of the body, or for the body's being in a particular state (thus somehow confirming the Deleuzian account that by thinking the body with Spinoza one is driven to think it as a complex set of relations). The whole is never taken into consideration, purely *partes extra partes*. The Latin word *corpus*, which then gives birth to the French *corps*, the Italian *corpo* and the Spanish *cuerpo*, means simply 'that which has a form', leaving the question of the body in an indisputable indeterminacy, for that which has a form does not tell us anything about the changes this form may undergo and the relations in which this form can engage. The English word body (from the German root *bodig*) is itself a metonymy, originally standing for chest. Whilst the Greek dictionary proceeds through dissemination, always drawn into detours, and thus setting aside the possibility of having one word which would without remainder account for the body, the strategy of modern languages on the contrary seems to privilege a single component (the idea of form or a part of this form), which then comes to account for the physical structure as a whole. There is a sort of exuberance when one attempts to trace bodies in language, a sort of enthusiasm of and for language. Language persists pronouncing a single word, keeps unravelling its own imperfection in addressing the question of the body (or maybe here one is asking of language too much, because this is exactly what language does, it continually expresses and unravels a lack). The part goes beyond itself and names the whole. In this case language, rather than allowing for an intervention to be made on to the body, instead of opening up a series of paths, lifts up a curtain on the in-trans-latability of the body, maybe even the impossibility of talking about it. This is the reason why a discussion concerned with the body should avoid starting from the body in the midst of signification or from the body overwhelmed with signification. In doing so, it seems one will eventually find oneself within that other body of signification, translation, meaning, therapy, interpretation, giving up any attempt to understand the body as that thick rim which makes sense *in se*, that which constitutes the solution of sense by articulating it. If one wants to put it into a synthetic formulation: *the body is the solution of sense*. If absolution indicates the state of being free from … depending on nothing, solution would then be its opposite: that which opens up the opportunity for a bondage, for *to solve* is always – even in its chemical meaning – to call for a fastening. This is the nature of the relation between body and sense. In order for sense to make sense, a body must expose it, must solve it by coming together with it.

An absolute sense (or sense absolutely, that is, a sense *free from* …) does not properly exist, for it is not exposed to anything, it keeps coming back to itself; absolute sense would be the identity of sense. When it comes to the body one has to do with a 'certain interruption of sense' (Nancy 2008a: 125). If one looks at this relation from the opposite side one could also add that the truth of bodies resides somewhere other than in absolute sense (that which would make of the body a pure signifier). To treat the body in this manner would mean touching merely upon the words we use for it and not on its thickness and volume. The word 'body' is the word without word and without body, unable to speak for itself, that which cannot be uttered. As Nancy writes: 'perhaps body is the word without employment par excellence. Perhaps, in any language, it's the word in excess. At the same time however this "in excess" is nothing' (ibid.: 21).

At first glance the program outlined above may appear to simply register the fact that sense, as the incorporeal, needs flesh and requires an incarnation. However it is something different that is at stake here: not that sense requires embodiment, but the very fact that a body is sense's *end* (in both senses of the word, as ending and as aim). As Nancy writes:

> in no way is the body of sense the incarnation of the ideality of 'sense': on the contrary, it is the end of such an ideality – and thus the end of sense as well, since it no longer returns to itself or refers to itself (to an ideality making sense of it) – suspending itself at a limit that makes its own most proper 'sense' and exposes it as such.
>
> (ibid.: 23)

The body is the end of sense in two ways: as *ending*, because sense ceases to direct itself towards the purely incorporeal, and *aim* because the body is that by and through which sense begins. One must reach that point where signification comes to a stop, where the body resists; one must always bear in mind the solid outline Kafka was so terrified by, and bear in mind that sense comes with it, that sense is exposed as this limit.

A further misreading is possible here and it concerns temporality. That sense begins with the body should not be taken as an attempt to establish any kind of anteriority of bodies with regard to the order of signification. The point that needs to be stressed is the need to addresses their co-appearance. This is not at all to say that a body may come at any time, that it comes already loaded with signification, but rather that sense cannot come if not at the limit of the body, on its border, with its border.

In principium erat verbum; but then *verbo caro factum est*, otherwise *verbum* would not be able to express itself. It would remain caught up in the *principium*. Despite the reference to the Christian logos it is not a matter of incarnation, but of conceiving a body as both *verbo* and *principio*, 'not a body produced by the production and reproduction of the spirit, but a body given, always already given, abandoned, and withdrawn from all the plays of signs' (Nancy 1993: 197). If one repeats the gesture previously mentioned and turns the relation upside down, one could then say: not a sense made available by its incarnation in a body, but a sense given over, delivered over just to bodies; sense as a bodily event, a passage that cannot be thought in abstraction from the body. Sense becomes then the very possibility of bodies. There is no supposition here; the body does not presuppose sense and vice-versa, the nature of this relation cuts short all presupposition in favour of a co-appearance. As Nancy puts it:

this doesn't mean that the body comes before sense, as its obscure prehistory or preontological attestation. No, it gives it its place, absolutely. Neither before nor after, the body's place is the taking-place of sense, absolutely. The ab-solute is the detached, the set-apart, the extended, the imparted. (We can say the finite sense …).

(Nancy 2008a: 119)

If sense therefore needs a body it is in order not to be the sense of itself, in order to escape a return to itself. Speaking of the joy of the body Nancy suggests: 'this joy is its birth, its coming into presence, outside of sense, in the place of sense, taking the place of sense, and making a place for sense' (Nancy 1993: 197). Thus, instead of incarnation, one should speak here of a making-place.

Instead of a fragile version of a body floating in significations and language, one must be able to set out a different program, one that will enable us to touch upon that fear the body seems to provoke, the undetermined of the *none has hitherto determined*. It is this solidity, this delimitation and this fear that one should address, for these terms constitute the triad of a body extended, dense and open. This will in turn require a program. Further on in *Corpus* Nancy adds:

A discourse of the body or on the body is both touched by and touches upon something that is not discourse at all. Which means quite simply that the body's discourse cannot produce a sense of the body, can't give sense to the body.

(Nancy 2008a: 124)

What is required thus is to pursue the body through nails and hairs rather than by questions of genders and identities, not because these are lacking in relevance, but because bodies indicate their limit, that is their starting point. A limit is the place where several opportunities remain open, and what is of interest here is the condition of emergence of these possibilities. To say it better: that which allows for their coming, that which makes consistent and dense their availability.

First of all one should go straight to the body. One should go there where bodies make place for sense, contemplating at the same time what the body expels (its outwards, or the body itself as outward and onset). To touch on the density, solidity, terrible outline and open traits of the body.

For Nancy sense is a movement that never returns to itself, that never goes back to ideality and never presents a pure identity. The body writes sense in this way, in disclosing sense as this openness, as a dis-identity, which cuts off and exceeds ideality and signification. What the body expresses is a writing of this limit, this *closure into openness*. As Nancy puts it: 'sense, as that which the world is, is only insofar as it never constitutes a ground [...] rather exists as passage, as movement to or as creation or birth' (Nancy 2003: 8).

The body writes the light by rendering sense as the limit – by weeding out any possible ground where sense could be reduced to its identity – whilst at the same time disclosing it as the 'stuff' of existence. In this constellation where sense is always the sense of a limit – a passage, a being-to – bodies write light. Prior to being *subjective* or to being inscribed into language and signification, the body opens up the world as the writing of the limit from which sense can't come back to ideality, but is delivered over to infinity and maintains infinity 'open, inexhaustible, in excess of' (Nancy 2010: 23).

According to what has just been said, the body would be the only photographer who never printed an image, who never developed the film, for this writing of the light is the writing of a movement, a movement of disclosure, which never rests upon itself. There is no withdrawal here. There is not even mimesis, for there is no ground or identity on which mimesis can be achieved. The outcome of this photographic act is never an image, but the dispersal of writing itself.

Body's origin

Once one has departed from the body's inscription in the realm of signification, the body's relation to the creation and sharing of sense – to sense *as* creation and sharing – provides a new entrance into the argument relating to the body's existential status. Any questioning as to the nature and the origin of the body calls into question simultaneously the structure of sense. It has already been underlined that in no way one can interpret Spinoza as being a Neo-Platonist. In EI, P16 one reads: 'From the necessity of the divine nature, infinite numbers of things in infinite ways must follow' (Spinoza 1949: 51). The relation between things and God is derivative in kind, and the modality of this relation is one of necessity. Further on, in EI, P17, Note, Spinoza says that the singularities one finds in the world 'flow' from God: 'From the supreme power of God, or from His infinite nature, infinite things in infinite ways, that is to say, all things, have necessarily flowed, or continually follow by the same necessity' (ibid.: 52). This relation of necessity – in which things follow on (*ex natura* [...] *attributi Dei sequuntur*) from God in a constant flowing – contains an idea of movement as well as one of dislocation. The latter is implied within the notion of divine extension: for EII, P2, individual things, this and that thing, are modes that express the nature of God in a certain and determinate manner. God therefore possesses an attribute, in this case extension, the conception of which is involved in all individual things.[7] God then would have many places and would be equally close to all of them. Is this not confirmed at the very beginning of the *Ethics*, when Spinoza lays down the foundational principles of his system, and also in his most evocative formula, which has somehow come to define Spinozism itself, *Deus sive Natura*?

In EI, P15 one reads that 'whatever is, is in God, and nothing can either be or be conceived without God' (ibid.) (*quidquid est, in Deo est*), a proposition that develops out of D3 and D5, so that modes can only be in the divine nature and only through it they can be conceived. God would thus be the movement of dislocation, although this dislocation, the outcome of the movement according to which things flow from God, would not be separated from God himself. Again one here has an echo of Nancy's statement: 'in saying this [Deus sive Natura] Spinoza becomes the first thinker of the world' (Nancy 1997b: 54). The One Substance is the always-existing movement that – by flowing towards its own outside – results in extension. This flowing does not make its way towards an Other, as if the world would already be there, a tabula rasa upon which God forces his powers, as if singularities would be a degradation of the One (this would be essentially the doctrine of Plotinus). The outside towards which the One Substance moves is an outside-to-itself; an outside that is comprised within. Acknowledging that in Spinoza there is no separation between God and the world means articulating the fact that the world expresses God whilst God expresses itself in the world.

God is immanent in the world, the creation is *ex-nihilo*, in the sense that *the nothing grows out of itself*. According to Nancy, the expression *ex-nihilo*, the world as coming from nothing, 'does not mean fabricated with nothing by a particularly ingenious producer. It means instead that [...] the nothing itself or rather nothing growing as something' (Nancy 2007b: 51).

The creation *ex-nihilo* here is understood differently from the way in which the Christian onto-theology would have it. *Ex-nihilo* for Nancy means 'that it is the nihil that opens and that disposes itself as the space of all presence (or even as one will see, of all the presences)' (ibid.: 62). This is why Nancy defines Spinoza as the first thinker of the world: '*Deus sive natura* does not simply say two names for one thing, rather that this very thing has its outside on the inside' (Nancy 1997b: 54). Nancy writes that with Spinoza one moves from 'creation as the result of an accomplished divine action, to creation as activity and incessant actuality of this world in its singularity' (Nancy 2007b: 64).

In the world God feels himself eternal, that is to say, necessary. It is in this relation of God with the world that the concept of expression can be developed to its most productive consequences. The term *expression* is in Spinoza a technical one. It is a term that he inherits from a philosophical tradition that stretches across several centuries. As Deleuze writes in *Expressionism in Philosophy*:

> Expression is on the one hand an explication, an unfolding of what expresses itself, the One manifesting himself in the Many (substance manifesting himself in its attributes, and these attributes manifesting themselves in their modes). Its multiple expression, on the other hand, involves Unity. The One remains involved in what expresses it, imprinted in what unfolds it, immanent in whatever manifests it.
>
> (Deleuze 1992: 16)

The notion of expression relies traditionally upon four concepts. These concepts respond to different stages of expression and are organised in a binomial structure: involution and evolution; implication and explication. The idea of expression would then be the synthesis of these four conceptual moments. This synthesis takes the name of *complicatio*. In the context of Spinoza's system (and taking into account his geometrical mode) *complicatio* indicates that the attributes are points of view on the Substance – not external but contained within the Substance itself, the latter then would comprise the infinity of its points of view within itself. The transformation of the notion of expression in Spinoza is fittingly explained by Deleuze: 'it is no longer a matter of finite understanding, deducing properties separately […] it is now the object that expresses itself, the thing itself that explicates itself' (ibid.: 22). A very important point has been anticipated in view of the fact that the idea of expression serves as the point from which one can begin to draw a line connecting the philosophy of Jean-Luc Nancy to that of Spinoza. The idea of the Substance having in itself all that is external to it comes back in Nancy's idea of the coming to presence of existence and of existence's *sharing out*. In *Corpus* Nancy articulates a precise reference to Spinoza's atheism (Nancy 2008a: 129) and in various works the Dutch philosopher is brought into play as the paradigmatic figure exposing creation *ex-nihilo*.

Nancy's volume *The Creation of the World* is devoted precisely to this idea: the thinking of the world on the basis of a transcendental principle (a principle from which it would attain its sense) has come to an end. This 'exhaustion' starts manifesting itself in particular with Spinoza's Substance.

The argument there presented is that according to a tension present in our tradition, the world shows itself as that which is 'without a model, without reference, without a first step, without origin, without even the possibility to say «without»' (Nancy 2001a: 187). The world has come to coincide with itself; this is what lies in the word *mondialization*. What the term coincidence expresses is precisely the 'becoming-world of the whole that was formerly articulated and divided and expressed as the nature – world – God triad' (Nancy 2007b: 20). This is what allows Nancy to claim that 'the world resolutely and absolutely distances itself from any status as object in order to tend towards being itself the subject of its own 'worldhood – or "world-forming"' (ibid.: 20). The world has stopped to be represented, to be the object of a representation, and has become itself the subject of sense. The possibility for a vision of the world has been exhausted; the world has escaped a world of representations: in its wholeness and with all its weight it has now entered this vision, it has become this vision, it has swollen it. It is with Spinoza and from him that we can start tracing that auto-deconstructive development of external principles and divine places that Nancy identifies in our thinking tradition. The sense of the world, Nancy warns, is not anywhere else than in the world itself, there is no outside to which we can refer to in order to find the sense of the world. This sense resides precisely in the possibility of this world, in the actuality of its taking place, the inescapable thinking that *there is* this world. What is left is the experience of the world, its internal revolution and the domestic movement from one end to another.

In Spinoza the passing away of a transcendental entity providing the sense of the world (in terms of ground or organising principle) is announced in the idea of God itself. In EI, P28 one reads:

> An individual thing, or a thing which is finite and which has a determinate existence, cannot exist nor be determined to action unless it be determined to existence and action by another cause which is also finite and has a determinate existence; and again, this cause cannot exist nor be determined to action unless by another cause which is also finite and determined to existence and action, and so on ad infinitum.
>
> (Spinoza 1949: 64)

As one can see, the Spinozian God unambiguously negates the religious God. Since the early stages of his philosophy, Spinoza, following the method of the Collegiants, challenged the idea of God as persona, a God able to lavish miracles, an object of an unreasonable cult.

In fact God in Spinoza is equated to nature; in the demonstration of P15 for instance one can read:

there are those who imagine God to be like a man, composed of body and soul
and subject to passions; but it is clear enough from what has already been demon-
strated how far off men who believe this are from the true knowledge of God.

(ibid.: 105)

As previously mentioned, unlike the God of religions, the Spinozian divinity is
not a God that responds to a principle of creation, for – in order to assume a
principle of creation – one should also imply a principle of exhaustion, since any
creation has an end in exhaustion. The God of the *Ethics* keeps auto-producing
itself; it shares itself out. This is how the world comes to presence: in sharing out
its essence and therefore crossing this over before the latter can be posited as a
ground. Thus it derives that the Substance is never alien to the world since the
world is its expression, it is its outside without being unrelated to its inside. The
truth of this God is that it shares itself out. With the theory of modes Spinoza
seems to claim that the world is the ways of being of God, the attitudes and the
postures of God, if one can dare to use such terms. The world does not refer to
a unity, a single wholeness; rather world stands for a multiplicity of singularities
(*natura naturante*), since the attributes of God are infinite. Similarly in Nancy's
text: 'a world is a multiplicity of worlds and its unity is the mutual sharing and
exposition of all its worlds – within this world' (Nancy 1993: 185).

The fact that Spinoza employs two verbs such as *sequire* and *effluire* and
the idea of movement that they imply allows us to read Spinoza's Substance
alongside Nancy's idea of coming to presence. The One Substance, according
to the characteristics mentioned before and the principle of expression, recalls
the idea of existence as that which is always engaged in coming, which informs
much of Nancy's ontology. The kind of auto-production Spinoza talks about and
the fact that everything follows and flows from the One Substance allows one to
read the Spinozian creation in terms of an auto-production *ex-nihilo*. It has been
mentioned that the term *ex-nihilo* should not be intended here as referring to a
Creator or Idea delivering the world starting from nothing. In Nancy's reading
the question of the creation *ex-nihilo* assumes different connotations from
the ones established according to a Judeo-Christian philosophical tradition.
Ex-nihilo is taken to mean that there is not a *nothing* to start with, neither is
there some kind of rough material, uneven matter that the Architect will work
on, crafting the ordered world. The *nihilo* is God himself and the *ex* is what is
left in the sharing out of God.

if creation is ex-nihilo, this does not signify that a creator operates «starting
from nothing» […] this instead signifies two things: on the one hand, it signifies

that the 'creator' itself is the nihil; on the other hand, it signifies that this nihil is not [...] «something from which» what is created would come, but the very origin...of some thing in general and of everything.

(ibid.: 16)

As in Spinoza, here one has existence as at the same time some thing in general and every thing (where *every* stands for *each* singularity). The nature of this coming to presence contained in the *ex-nihilo* is such that with it, Being shares out; that which exists is precisely the outcome of this sharing out, or better said, the sharing out itself. Nancy writes:

Creation takes place everywhere and always – but it is this unique event, or advent, only on the condition of being each time what it is, or being what it is only «at each time», each time appearing singularly ... If 'creation' is indeed this singular exposition of being, then its real name is *existence*.

(ibid.)

God then is all in the *ex*, in this movement, in this dislocation. The One Substance – *causa sui* and *per se concipi* – ex-produces itself, and in this continuous production it constitutes the immanent cause of the world.

What has been just mentioned can be put in another way: if God is the immanent cause of the world, which follows from him as its own dislocation, then God never withdraws from the world, because this would mean that God can also withdraw from Himself. For Spinoza God is eternal (EI, P19), which means that God is the *there*, which has *always* and *already* been there (without these terms assuming temporal connotations). Creation, if one can still call it by this name, is always occurring: 'it is the being-already-there of the already there that is of concern' (ibid.). Origin is thus an each time. One could then think Origin as the lack of a thing called by this name, or better said as the multiplication, the unextinguishing echo of this name. *Origin is ongoing*, it is contained in that 'effluxisse', it is a movement. In Nancy's words: 'Origin does not signify that from which the world come, but rather the coming of each presence of the world, each time singular' (ibid.: 26).

Having worked out this parallel, one can now move back to the question of the origin of the body and observe what room the notion of God as an extended thing has made for it. In EII, D1 one reads: 'by body I understand a mode which expresses in a certain and determinate manner the existence of God in so far as He is considered as the thing extended' (Spinoza 1949: 79). The problem of origin and creation of the body asks to be thought in terms of extension, that is to say in terms of that which makes room for existence. In the second place it then demands a thought on the matter of access to the origin. Making room for existence here means that the body is that which exposes the coming to presence of existence. It is that which manifests the singular being as shared out, for my body makes me here and you there. The expression indicates the impossibility for me to speak at the same time and from the same place you are speaking from.[8]

To make room for existence means that the body as extension or place – the body thought here both with Nancy and Spinoza and with their lexicon – exposes the very fact that existence is always in a coming of some sort and must be decided in the open. Body is the dislocation of this coming, dislocation of existence's coming. In order for the coming to presence to persist in its name and to preserve the meaningfulness of this name (without this name becoming just an echo, caught in a meaningless bouncing back), it cannot be identical to itself, it has to be – always – encumbered in coming, for its very essence is in this movement. To exist means exposing existence precisely to its *to*.

The mode of the coming to presence thus cannot be identity; quite the opposite, it has to be a movement against identity. If coming to presence has to keep coming – otherwise it would be just presence, but presence of itself to itself, saturation – it needs in each coming to move from itself, it needs to come at a distance from itself.

When Nancy makes use of the expression 'world of bodies' it is this constant refusal of existence to come to itself that he has in mind. Existence performs in its appearance a rejection of its own face, the refusal of its identity, a room with no mirrors.

Dislocation is the dis-identity of the coming, the lack of evenness and saturation. Coming comes always elsewhere; it is in this way that one can make sense of the multiplicity of singularities. The world does not happen in one moment, it does not suddenly burst out, but it is present every time this refusal comes to presence, thus every time existence appears as dislocated. This is what bodies expose; the body exposes this dis-identity. The body is the extension of this not-having identity (or the necessary and eternal refusal of identity) of the coming. But nowhere is the body simply a figure, an illustration of existence's dis-location – it is instead its very limit.

If existence is that which 'pre-vents supposition itself, or that which overcomes it by surprise […] the same thing completely different' (Nancy 1997b: 69), then it is in this light that one can read Nancy's words: 'the body is the being of existence […] registering the fact that existence has no essence, but only ex-ists' (Nancy 2008a: 15).

This last thought connects the present discourse to the one that has been previously anticipated: bodies are the limit where sense quits referring to that ideal it is and starts *making* sense. Bodies do photography, but this has something of the skills proper to medieval amanuenses, who copy a manuscript, crafting one letter after the other, whilst already engaging in the exegetical effort.

The body makes room for existence: along with each body, the whole is exposed, but never recuperated as a system or determined as a closed totality. The body then makes room for existence by exposing the logic of exposition: not identical and not appropriable. One could attempt to summarise all this in three points:

- the body is that which makes room for existence; the body is existence in action; not created, not produced, without supposition, simply placing itself continuously outside, in the 'other'.

- The body is the presencing of existence. There is no anteriority of the body to existence here because the coming of existence is also the coming into existence.[9] It has been mentioned earlier on that bodies could also be conceived in terms of access. This claim is grounded in the analysis worked out in the previous paragraph: it has to be conceived in relation to the ongoing characteristic of origin. Given that the extension of the body, or better the body as extended, is that which exposes existence – constant coming to presence and dis-identity – bodies allow us to touch on the origin and to have access to it. The body is that by which I can gain access to the *at each time*, to the singular origin and to the plurality of origins. Body is my plastic *locality* exposed to other *localities*; hence the access to the origin is realised in the fact that I can conceive of myself as exposed to the multiplicity of existence and its ongoing origin just through my body. My body is what spaces me from other beings, thus allowing me to touch on that plurality constituting the continuous arising of origins. Body is access in these terms: it is the extension of God – the *there* of existence – and the existing presence of the ongoing origin.

- The presence of existence and existence presencing: one can think the body as the *ex*, the presence of that outside which follows from existing.

'Bear in mind, Dear Friend ...'

At the very end of EP4 – a letter addressed to Henry Oldenburg – Spinoza writes the following: 'bear in mind, Dear Friend, that men are not created, but born

and that their bodies already exist before birth, though under different forms'
(Spinoza 1969: 17).

In this passage Spinoza tries to reply to his friend's objection to EI, P1 and
EI, P3. What is anticipated here is something that Spinoza will develop more
extensively in EII, Lemma VII, Note,[10] namely the continuity, indivisibility
and indestructibility of God as extended thing. Such a statement leads one to
notice that, as to the mind we can attribute a 'certain eternity', so one must do
with the body. Bodies exist independently from the individual subject; they
are born and not created, with the singular body one is in the midst of the *ex*,
which constitutes the difference of God to himself. In its constant sharing out,
the Substance dislocates itself. This dislocation differentiates the Substance
from itself. What Spinoza seems to address is that the body is always already
there in the substance and that birth is the appearance of this dislocation. The
argument of the eternity of the body, this 'certain eternity' satisfied through
body's eternal presence in the One, follows logically from two points: the
expressive implication of modes and substance; according to EI, P19: 'God is
eternal or in other words, all His attributes are eternal [...] eternity pertains
to the nature of the substance. Therefore, each of the attributes must involve
eternity' (Spinoza 1949: 59); the idea of bodies and minds as having the same
ontological status.

In addition if the body were to be thought as dying and being created anew
each time, this would mean that God as an extended thing would perish or be
divided, which is not possible. The body is then eternal, although it exists within
God in forms that may well be different from the human body. As Nancy adds
though, the eternity of the body does not indicate that this lasts forever, that the
body is caught up in an indefinite waiting for time. The eternity of the body does
not coincide with being sempiternal, at the opposite this eternity, as already
mentioned, is of the order of necessity. As Nancy writes: 'as my body itself,
along the extension and exposition of my body, God (or substance) feels itself
necessary [...] God feels and knows itself to be necessary in his contingency'
(Nancy 2008a: 130).

Oddly enough, if one turns to Christian logic, it is possible to trace a
similar proposal; that is to say, there is nothing before the body. Although
this might appear in sharp contrast with the Εν αρχή ην ὁ λόγος, it is
exactly this incipit that allows for such a statement. What is before the body?
The answer should be something of this kind: it is the angelic revelation
that stands before the body, the angelic logic of Christian creation, that
which has and is no-body. The coming to presence of the Angel happens,

however, under the features of a body, because any presence is the presence of a body, even this presence of God. Body makes space for the verbum. '*In principium erat verbum*', Εν αρχή ην ὁ λόγος: what takes place before the body actually claims the body's eternity as necessity. In this *principium* is already contained the idea that *verbum caro factum est et habitavit in nobis*, the two co-appear, their coming is simultaneous. The word has to *caro se facere*. This body that the verbum becomes is nothing else than the sharing out of logos itself, what makes the logos come to presence. Everything that comes without a body is just principium, not even verbum, for verbum needs a body to become that which it is. *In principium erat verbum, verbum caro facto est* = the verbum, in order to become what it is, to make sense, has to come on the edge of a body, otherwise it remains principium, that is to say the beginning of sense and its ideal principle (Goethe's Faust, struggling with the logocentric diktat and the mediation of signs to which he saw himself subordinated, retranslated the question as 'in the beginning was the deed' [Goethe 1949: 59]).

What this biblical detour attempts to express is that once one poses the verbum one is at the same time posing the body, and necessarily so. *Principium* – as Nancy points out – indicates that which has always already been there (it is the religious equivalent of the metaphysical *nihilo*) the incipit that already also implies an excipit. Verbum = corpus = incipit. They all come together, at the same time in the same place, or they do not come at all, or there is no way out of the inertia of the principium. Either there is just an incipit without the body of the text or there is an incipit with an excipit. It is not by chance that Christianity starts with a body. It starts with it and from it twice and in two ways:

a) there is no Christianity, there is no verbum of Christianity, without the body of Christ, without God becoming flesh; this body of Christ makes room for the existence of the Christian God;

b) moreover there is no Christianity without this body of Christ being extended until the end of every possible extension; until he starts rising and engages in an *anabasi*, becoming untouchable, becoming again the body of logos, the body of God, God as extended; *quo tangere non vis*.

Body and the wound

Always open, always already wounded, a fracture of existence: this is the condition of the body.[11] Following the path traced by Jean-Luc Nancy, the question of the open nature of the body can be thought of in three ways. When Nancy writes that the body is 'what is neither shit nor soul' (Nancy 2008b: 127), he is advancing a consistent argument. One could summarise it as follows: soul and faeces constitute the difference of the body to itself, 'in and of itself a body is also its consumption, its degradation' (ibid.: 105). In this way the body is always open, always ready to think its form and its manner in terms of its own rejection and expulsion. As Nancy remarks, the open body or the body-as-open is never a void, a blank page; it is an open calling for a double action or double movement: relation to itself that is already relation to the outside.

The openness of the body, its breach, revolves around this double movement. In order to configure itself as appropriation – as itself or as self full stop – the first movement demands the second. The body, as the dis-identity of the coming to presence, cannot withdraw from its openness. 'A world of bodies in which bodies, identically, decompose the world. Identically: dis-location, dis-localization' (ibid.). The body keeps extending and dislocating itself towards itself. The dislocation, which is its creation, its mode, its art, keeps opening the body and keeps the body wide open. The body cannot contain its origins, its ends and its beginnings, as it cannot contain its immersion and emotion towards other bodies.

The body is open in at least two other ways. It has been mentioned already that for Nancy bodies are not a full space, they are rather open space, the opening of space. One can take this to mean that bodies are what make room for existence, thus they constitute the taking place, the taking the place of existence. The body creates the conditions for space and then, maintaining itself as this dislocation, persists (without its persistence ever perduring in the same) in making room for existence. Open would thus mean the presence of the always and forever there, terms that in turn indicate permanent access to the origin, for this origin is ongoing, always possible, always arising, incipient.

A body is the continuous being outside of existence, it is that which never stops coming to presence and always makes space for an outside. What Nancy names the ontology of bodies would be nothing else than this fracture or spacing. One would then say: *the opening of existence* and *existence as the open*.

There is then also a third way: my body is local; it is the local extension that makes me-here and you-there. It is here that one approaches the singularity of the body, but it is also here that one touches on the question of singularity in general as always already exposed to the resistance of bodies, exposed through bodies and from one body to the other. It is worth recalling that Spinoza focuses his attention on the relational value of the body. In Spinoza's *Ethics* the body is not defined as a subject but on the basis of kinetic and dynamic properties. When Spinoza writes 'we do not know what a body can do' and 'the human mind does not know the human body itself [...] except through ideas of modifications by which the body is affected' (Spinoza 1949: 99), he shows the presence of the body to other bodies. For Nancy mentioning one body leads not only to its *partes*, but also to a great number of other bodies. One comes to place oneself in the midst of the system of relations and exposures the body is made of, relations which extend across and through the world. Nancy's ontology of bodies opens up and unfolds through the singular contact – like the Aleph that in its three centimetres contains the 'populous sea, dawn and dusk, the multitudes of the Americas and London as a broken labyrinth' (Borges 1998: 283). The world of bodies is a corpus constantly pierced and crossed by sense, where the singular event explodes and brings up the very structure of sense. It is not possible to employ the word body without necessarily letting the space free for this burst, since everything the body is exposed to comes about as an eruption. Nancy uses the list to describe the infinite resonances of the body:

> a body is an image offered to other bodies, a whole corpus of images stretched from body to body, local colours and shadows, fragments, grains, areolas, lunules, nails, hairs, tendons, skulls, ribs, pelvises, stomachs, meatuses, foams, tears, teeth, droolings, slits, blocks, tongues, sweat, liquors, veins, pains, and joys, and me, and you.
>
> (Nancy 2008a: 121)

The body is always exposed to and always exposes *alium/aliud*. The definition Nancy proposes of our world as the *world of bodies* seems to indicate this: that our body is always offered to otherness. By otherness one should read here not only other human beings, rather the very movement towards that which does not come from the body and does not return to it, a movement that does not recuperate an identity, nor establish a propriety. The body is delivered to other bodies and to sense as always other from itself. However this other is not more foreign than my 'own' body. 'There is not, on one side, an original singularity and on the other, a simple being there of things, more or less given for our use' (Nancy 2000: 17). My body is always my outside, an outside I offer to the other.

I will never perceive my body as such, as mine; what I will perceive are others as bodies. Body is open to other bodies, and this word *other* should include both *alium* and *aliud*, both other human bodies and all the other bodies of whatever nature. A body suspends even this separation.

If my body is an opening, it is then all a question of access, of acknowledging that my local density is always handed over to the other, for, every time a body rises up, this inception immediately brings forth all the other inceptions. My relation to these others is not such that I can stop sharing with them; on the contrary, it is such that having access to them also assures me access to myself.

One can then summarise the three modes of the body-open:

- open as rejecting itself; as incontinence of its own density, of itself as origin;
- open as the taking place of existence; constantly moving with the coming to presence of existence; constantly placing itself in existing;
- open as other; open in the sharing of an ongoing origin, open for its being local extends to all the other localities.

An interesting position

Nancy's body occupies the place left vacant by the withdrawal of the Gods: it is open as the existing of existence and delivered over to otherness, sharing and exposition of sense. Nancy thus releases the Heideggerian project through a deconstruction of the body of God. Starting with a glorious body (*hoc est enim corpus meum*) Nancy attempts to extract the substance from the ground of corporeality. The operation that Heidegger set aside – to liberate the body from the metaphysics of substance – is performed in a radically different tone by Nancy.

However, Heidegger's silence over the body provides the ground for a different kind of interpretation. Whilst Nancy reads Heidegger's *praeteritio* as an unfulfilled promise and sets therefore to continue Heidegger's work, for Emmanuel Levinas that same silence exposes Heidegger's philosophy to its own responsibility and demands a radical interruption. Following Heidegger's omission of the body from *Being and Time* Levinas operates with great conceptual vigour an inversion of philosophical priorities. The attempt is to move into the territory charted by Heidegger, whilst performing a reversal of the very terms deployed in *Being and Time*. This effort is already visible in *Existence and Existents*, written in 1945 whilst Levinas was a prisoner of war (which also means that it does not take into account almost any volume published between 1940 and 1945). In this preliminary volume the task is to describe the relation between the *there is*, the impersonal Being, and existents, what Levinas calls 'the distinction between that which exists and its existence itself' (Levinas 2003a: 1). Levinas is looking for the way in which 'a being, a subject, an existent, arises in impersonal Being' (ibid.: 3). The notion Levinas develops to introduce the aforementioned question is that of *position*. This idea contains *in nuce* most of Levinas' mature philosophical concerns and will retain its place up to *Totality and Infinity*.

On the one hand then Jean-Luc Nancy writes that 'Being takes place, but its place spaces it out [...] being is an area, and its reality gives itself in *areality*. It is thus that being is a body' (Nancy 1997b: 35) in order to open a lexicon of *exscription* and *exposition* that can be employed to announce the question of the body in terms of 'absolute realism'. Nancy's argument is that 'a world is the common place of a totality of places: of presences and dispositions for possible events' (Nancy 2007b: 42).

Levinas introduces the notion of position on the other hand to express how a subject can arise from impersonal Being, from the rumbling of the *there is*. His argument moves then from an analysis of limit states such as fatigue, insomnia, sleeping to describe the detachment these bodily phenomena produce from the *there is*. The position in which the subject arises is a position before any understanding, even before any world; it is the very essence of any existent to have a position, to hold himself. To this effect Levinas writes: 'the here we are starting with [...] is the very fact that consciousness is an origin, that it starts from itself' (Levinas 2003a: 68). The event of position is the very opportunity a body possesses to become a subject, to realise its position and the opportunity of opening spaces.

Position then cannot be conceived simply as a location, a point in space, because before the body no spatial possibility is given.

Levinas insists on this point:

> body is nowise a thing [...] because its being belongs to the order of the events [...] it is not posited; it is a position. It is not situated in a space given beforehand; it is the irruption in anonymous being of localization itself.
>
> (ibid.: 69)

To reinforce once more the idea that the taking position is the foundational concept of an analysis of the body Levinas adds:

> a subject does not exist before the event of its position. The act of taking position does not unfold in some dimension from which it could take its origin;

it arises at the very point at which it acts. Its action does not consist in willing, but in being.

(ibid.: 81)

Position is then an awakening. It indicates both the sheer location on earth and the possibility of vision. The beginning, as beginning of a subject that will turn to the structure of the for-the-other, is intrinsically linked with this act of positioning, where corporeality grounds me to my place and at the same time discloses the horizon of singular existence within anonymous Being. Through Levinas' shift of emphasis, Heidegger idea of one's own place becomes radical rootedness, the seduction of a new paganism. Levinas' intention to move away from the Heideggerian rhetoric of the land, of the specific geography, but also from the most abstract formulations of *Being and Time* to return philosophy to a concern for the place of human beings is even more apparent in passages like the following: 'to posit oneself corporeally is to touch an earth, but to do so in such a way that the touching finds itself already conditioned by the position, the foot settles into a real which this very action outlines or constitutes' (Levinas 2003a: 128).

The notion of position therefore introduces the body as constantly caught in a major equivocation. On the one hand the body produces the detachment from anonymous Being whilst on the other it marks the initial betrayal of the ethical order. Through the body my singular existence begins, but this inaugurates at the same time my usurpation of the other. In a deliberately polemical text on Christianity and Judaism, Levinas asks: 'What is an individual if not a usurper?' (Levinas 1997a: 100). At the same time though it is precisely the awakening of the body as position that can lead the individual to attention for the others. It is through position that one's own place becomes the acknowledgement of respon-sibility. In this connotation position becomes the refusal of empty utopias, one chooses to 'remain here below [...] choosing ethical action' (ibid.).

As mentioned earlier on, Nancy highlights three ways in which a body is open. Nancy claims that body is always *bodies*, because I will always perceive it as present with and to others, as sharing their same origin. It is the question of this sharing out that is decisive, because this sharing out between bodies constitutes the very condition of a shared space; it sets down the coordinates for a world of bodies. What Levinas wants to affirm in introducing the question of position is that it is possible to begin thinking of sense and consciousness only if one acknowledges the crucial role played by the taking position of a body in the coming of Being, in the rumbling of the *there is*. In *Totality and Infinity* he further develops the question of Being and beings, assuming a radical perspective, unknown to *Existence and Existents*. One encounters here the question of the body framed by the broader aim Levinas has set for his philosophy: the possibility for existents to overcome Totality, the same, the ontological enclosure. The core question of *Totality and Infinity* is already announced in *Is Ontology fundamental?* an essay Levinas published well before he started his first major work. In this text Levinas asks: 'how is this simultaneity of a position in totality and a reserve or separation with regard to it achieved?' (Levinas 2006a: 13). The concept of separation is introduced to elicit a disruption at the heart of Western ontological traditions. Levinas aims to revise a recurrent mistake in our philosophical practice by opposing to ontological completeness the idea of Infinity. In the context of Levinas' philosophy infinity is realised in the possibility for *ipseity* to contain in itself what is not of itself, the welcoming of the Other, gentleness and the face. In *Totality and Infinity* Levinas writes 'to think the infinite, the transcendent, the stranger is not to think an object' (Levinas 2005: 50) it is to do more and better than that.

For Levinas it is crucial to resolve the question of infinity in terms of resistance to totality, the very possibility of thinking a way out of the same. Infinity then comes to be defined as 'that which arouses desire, that which is approachable by a thought that at each instant thinks more than it thinks [...] the measure through the very impossibility of measure' (ibid.: 63). The chances of Infinity are opened precisely through the break away of separation, which recalls in its movement that of position. Similarly to what happens with position then the fracture produced by separation affirms singular existence and Levinas proceeds from this to a more explicit treatment of personal responsibility. It is in the creation *ex-nihilo* that the occasion for separation arises for the first time. This notion has been discussed already with regard to Nancy and Spinoza, but Levinas' interest in this idea lies elsewhere. On the one hand Nancy stresses the fact that the body is the created par excellence and created always refer to a creation *ex-nihilo*; on the other, Levinas sees in this movement where the *nihil* comes to presence the possibility for the first detachment from totality. The *ex-nihilo* is the moment where Levinas introduces for the first time the *equivocation*, which the body constantly exposes:

> the creation ex-nihilo expresses a multiplicity not united into a totality; [...]
> Creation ex nihilo breaks with system, posits a being outside of every system [...]
> Creation leaves to the creature a trace of dependence, but it is an unparalleled

dependence: the dependent being draws from this exceptional dependence, from this relationship, its very independence, its exteriority to the system.

(ibid.: 104)

In the *ex-nihilo* Levinas envisages the sparkle where the novelty of the 'I' is introduced, the nascent development of separation. The foregoing passage also sets the ground for the dependence – independence equivocation that constitutes for Levinas the plurality of existence. It is in fact through the prospect of separation, of every existent disposing of its own time, that Levinas makes sense of plurality.

Separation, Levinas warns, cannot and should not be regarded just in negative terms. It has to be the outcome of a positive movement, a movement where the 'I' and the 'I can' grow. The movement Levinas has in mind is a movement towards the inside, for separation can only happen as *ipseity*. Separation is a movement that has in view inner life, for 'inner life is the unique way for the real to exist as a plurality' (ibid.: 50). Separation however cannot rest merely on a dialectical opposition. If the intention is to breach into the *there is*, then separation has to come not from an opposition, but from a positive movement. Resistance to totality cannot simply be resolved in opposing to the totality of the same another kind of totality, that of the 'I' completely shut, isolated, withdrawn into its inner life, a desert island. Separation is instead the way in which the 'I' comes to be freed from the site in which it finds itself. Separation, then, is produced when the 'I' starts loving life, inaugurating that process through which it begins to love what it lives from, to become preoccupied with itself. Levinas warns that this existent preoccupied with itself is not the same as Dasein, and its enjoyment is not care for Being. The existent is confronted with something more dear than its own being: 'thinking, eating […] distinct from my substance but constituting it, these contents make up the worth of my life' (ibid.: 112). Whilst Dasein always cares for its existence, for it is always there to comprehend Being, for Levinas the 'love of life does not love Being but loves the happiness of being' (ibid.: 145).

Separation thus constitutes itself first in creation *ex-nihilo*, as pure trace of the intertwining dependence – independence; secondly in the closure of *egoism* and finally in the *living from*.

Living from…

The notion of *living from…* articulates another step towards separation, psychism and the inner life. Through living from… 'each existent comes to have its own time' (ibid.: 57), separation appears to be resolved. When an existent has come to recognise itself in ipseity, it then turns towards life, towards its dependence on the other. Living from... is the ground of enjoyment: there the individual recognises that her dependence on the other, on the world, characterises also the contents of her life. In Vittorio De Sica's movie *Miracolo a Milano* the paupers leaving in the shanty town at the border of the big city happily praise their poverty by singing '*Ci basta una capanna per vivere e dormir, ci basta un po' di terra per vivere e dormir*' ['*All we need is a shack to live and sleep in, all we need is a bit of ground to live and sleep in*'].

For Levinas *living from...* is marked by a double meaning: it is poverty and dependence, πενία, but also the very exercise of existence, the fact that there is a life to be lived, ἐνθουσιασμός, dwelling with God. To this effect Levinas writes: 'what I do and what I am is at the same time that from which I live' (ibid.: 113). Need is the need *of* enjoyment, it is that which makes enjoyment possible.

In this construction the body plays a central role, for it is the body that bears more than any other the weight of this ambiguity, it is the body that concentrates in itself πενία and ἐνθουσιασμός. The body is the very articulation of this equivocation, of this game between dependence and independence life is made of. The chance for the human being to leave the realm of absolute autonomy (nature) is all in the body as that mode making possible the movement from need to enjoyment, from life as self-sufficiency and nutrition to life as happiness, love, responsibility. To this effect Levinas writes: 'my body is not only a way for the subject to be reduced to slavery, to depend on what is not of itself, but is also a way [...] of overcoming the alterity of what I have to live from' (ibid.: 116). Without the body I would not be able to realise this distance from the world, which assures my movement from need to enjoyment. The 'here' of the body, my place, both usurpation and initiation to ethics, exercises itself in this double movement between dependence and independence, need and happiness. The body realises separation towards what Levinas finally comes to call *desire*: I allow myself to exercise life, I gain time. As Levinas writes 'to be a body is to have time in the midst of the facts' (ibid.: 117). Looking back at *Existence and Existents* it becomes clearer what Levinas attempted to formulate there: the position of one's body is an event and not a substantive. Position is not a site in being – not already posited in a pre-existent space – but the arising of human beings as subjects in the nameless rumbling of the *there is*. In *Totality and Infinity* the approach becomes even more radical, for the body becomes almost irreducible to thought; it even appears as the very contestation of consciousness. Similarly to Nancy, where sense starts making sense by coming at the edge of the body, in Levinas' text the body is 'a permanent contestation of the prerogative attributed to consciousness of "giving meaning" to each thing' (ibid.: 129). The very question of the body – its truth as it were – must be traced in the taking position and in the equivocation that this taking position implies.

Taking position means thus situating oneself on earth in a way that is conditioned by this very being. The body is this taking position that makes available the future, a future that nevertheless has already been announced. 'To be a body is to be master of oneself and on the other hand to be encumbered by one's body' (ibid.: 164). The body is this participation of health and sickness, of openness to the other and belonging to one's place, abandoned to need and elation, it is the process of separation, the 'somewhere' of the separated being as separate.

In between bodies

At the beginning of the argument it was said that Nancy reopens the question of the body from within Heidegger's *praeteritio*. Starting from Heidegger's silence Nancy develops the idea that the body is what *existence exposes* and the *exposure of existence*. One could say that the *existence of the body* is the *body of existence*. The crossing of the praxis of existing happens through the materiality of our world. In the reading Nancy offers of it, materiality is not a property of matter, but the resistance of sense to Ideality, to a non-actual referent. The praxis of existing is already the distance and circulation of materiality. Existence transcends this materiality not towards pure spirit or pure soul. This means that materiality itself is always already sensible, predisposed to and predisposing sense, and that sense is cut across by its own actuality.

At the same time the existence of the body is nothing but a force of appearance between a here and a there, a 'here' and a 'there' of sense, a 'here' constituted by body's evidence and a 'there' formed by the stretching of this evidence, which is nothing if not filtered through, suspended, abandoned. The evidence of a body is nothing if not the movement of sense towards something other than itself. This evidence should be understood not only as that which, by being under my eyes, conflates the obvious and the obscure, but that according to which 'my eyes and the world are opened together, the first included in the second, which, at the same time, penetrates them' (Nancy 2010: 70). It is therefore a force of sense inasmuch as it is a force of spacing. The body spaces itself out and spaces sense out. Sense circulates through bodies and on bodies: this is Nancy's 'absolute realism' (Derrida 2005: 46). One could say that as body existence is already decided, already in action, cutting across the substratum of its essences. In a very Spinozian fashion, Nancy writes:

> The existence of a body is a free force which does not disappear even when the body is destroyed and which does not disappear as such except when the relation of this existence to an other and destructive existence is itself destroyed as a relation of existences, becoming a relation of essences.
>
> (Nancy 1993: 102)

The existence of the body indicates also that the body itself is not a whole, it is not self-same but always already crossed by existence, and unable to recover itself as a property. The property of the body is not to be found in some determination of matter, but in its implication in the praxis of existing. This praxis sends the body to the open, remits it to the open and brings the open into the body. And again the open does not become itself a substance, but keeps signalling to the fact that the body negotiates its existence against substance. The body guarantees that existence comes to have no essence, no interiority into which it can withdraw. This means that at the same time the body itself has no guarantee, it remains completely *delivered over*.

The body is what existence exposes (of itself): existence exposes through the body the logic of a putting at stake of interiority; from this existence receives its name. This does not mean that existence recalls or gathers its interiority and puts it outside, but rather that existence decides only and always in favour of the outside and is only decided when it is left outside. Through the body existence exposes the fact of subsisting only in the restlessness of a 'going to' that, despite its obviousness, cannot be made into a property. That the body is what existence exposes means that existence offers its evidence precisely by remaining outside the field of vision that it creates.

The body is the exposure of existence: existence touches on its sense only in detaching from itself the 'sense' of 'existence'. In spacing sense, therefore, bodies place it at a distance, there where a final completion would have to be negotiated once again, anew. Sense is thus never the ideality of recurring significations or the ultimate destination of meaning, but an entangled circulation, a mass of strands, that bodies expose precisely in excess of conceptual formulations. The exposure of existence means the remaining in circulation of existence, despite the closure brought upon it by discourse. Bodies name the actuality of existence, bringing the fact of existing to its bareness, to an exuberant and mute absence of mediation that conceptual formulations can write out without making less bare and resistant.

What appears from this double signification is that the body pronounces about existence the latter's being nothing: *everything* that is *not a thing*. The body therefore can be articulated only in a multiplicity of figures or as a figure of proliferation, always more foreign than proper. As Emmanuel Levinas writes: to talk about the body means talking about an advent. The notion of *position* – which in a way identifies a body preoccupied with itself – determines still the space for a growth, a space not yet saturated, but constantly in the making, offered to others, opened.

It is by means of this opening that it is possible to proceed in the analysis and make sense of a world of bodies. The attempt is to move the focus from the body as standing alone to a body exposed to any other body. The spaces where bodies keep each other company.

In reading *Corpus*, I summarised that the body could be open, an aperture, as rejecting itself, as that which cannot contain its own density. The apertures as rejection that Nancy evokes – playing on the sounds of the French words *cent*, *sense* and *sang* (Nancy 2008a: 107) – all highlight this necessity for bodies to pull out something of themselves. This same discourse informs the idea of the mind as relation and difference of the body to itself.

The body is then open in a second fashion: as the exposure of existence, constantly open to the coming to presence of existence, thus open as constituting the space for existence. Recalling Nancy once more: 'the world of bodies is the nonimpenetrable world, a world that is not initially subject to the compactness of space; rather, it is a world where bodies initially articulate space' (ibid.: 27). Bodies do not just articulate space, making available the conditions for space, arising in a position which was not posited before; as Levinas makes clear, bodies also articulate a space for contact. Bodies are open to the contact of all other bodies. The point here is to show how the aperture that a body is articulates a space for contact, co-appearance, sharing and otherness; how singular bodies necessarily make available the proximity to other bodies and how this space of company becomes the necessity of their presence. It is essential to see how the body creating an outside of itself, being itself an outside, necessarily opens the conditions for a more general outside. This space of extended existence is not configured as a possibility the body can avoid, a responsibility it can decline; quite the contrary, it is the space without which it would not exist. It is indispensable to acknowledge that the two steps just delineated, the body as making available itself through the conditions for its own space and the body as articulating the space of contact, company, the space of bodies, do not occur as consequential – first a body that constitutes itself as a closed locality and then one that opens up to share this inner place. At the opposite, what is a stake here is the co-presence of these two possibilities at the very point where a body exposes existence. When a body exposes its own existence it is already exposing to the whole of existence. One cannot take the coming to presence of the body as a point of closure, after which existence arrests its coming just to move to another singular creation. Quite the contrary, one must think that the arising of a body as extension of existence is also the way existence articulates itself as space of contact, as a world of bodies. The body contains both its space and the space for contact. Its presence is always a co-presence. It is present to itself inasmuch and as long as it is present to other bodies. It is in this sense that Levinas writes that the body is *separation*, for in the body there are, from the outset, two dimensions of space.

The body is existence extended but also that which extends itself towards the plurality of existence. Separation indicates that the body is that space which contradicts itself by tending towards any other possible space, and in so doing making these spaces possible. There is no choice: a body is always offered to a space of co-presence. As Nancy writes:

> the opening is neither the foundation nor the origin. Nor is the opening any longer a sort of receptacle or an extension prior to things of the world. The opening of the world is what opens along such things and among them, that which separates them in their profuse singularity and which relates them to each other in their coexistence.
>
> (Nancy 2007b: 70)

One must therefore acknowledge that it is from the body that one can question the idea of the space of the other(s). There where Levinas writes of the spacing of bodies, of their *here below* as the possibility for 'ethical action' (Levinas 1998: 100), Nancy intends this spacing of bodies as a matter of justice, at once singular and absolute. This justice should be addressed

> not only to the whole of existence, but to all existences, taken together but distinctly and in a discontinuous way, not as the totality of their differences, and differends – precisely not that – but as these differences together, coexisting or co-appearing, held together as multiple [...] and held by a *co-* that is not a principle, or that is a principle or archi-principle of spacing in the principle itself.
>
> (Nancy 2007b: 61)

From this space of the single body, from its trait of separation – where in the opening of one's locality this body is also thrown towards constituting the space which is not its own, but its outside – derives the possibility of an analysis beyond the single body. A discourse on the space of the other needs to arise from this analysis of the body as a place for existence, a place that makes possible not only its own expression of existence, but existence's expression. A body is never alone with itself, it is never known as a single body.

In Levinas' thinking the first step towards separation is played in the realm of discretion and retreat – the separated being arises in egoism, ignorant of the Other – but this withdrawal reveals a strategic ambiguity. It is in this ambiguity that the separated being, the body that has taken position, living within the dialectic dependence–independence from the world, can produce an encounter with heteronomy. Levinas writes that 'in the separated being the door to the outside must hence be at the same time open and closed' (Levinas 2003a: 148). Closed because the inner life necessary to approach infinity must remain such in order to keep itself out of the dialectic of the same, but simultaneously open, for within this interiority 'there must be produced a heteronomy that incites to another destiny than this animal complacency in oneself' (ibid.: 149).

Thus, once the separated existent has come to love life, it has to open itself in order to rise from the animal condition; it has to let itself be shocked by heteronomy. This shock, Levinas warns, is not the shock of the Other negating me, of the 'non-I' negating the 'I', it is *the Other who comes directly from gentleness.*

On this former structure Levinas will then configure another opening, even more decisive, the possibility of a movement beyond essence. Levinas approaches the questioning of openness again at the end of *Otherwise than Being*:

> How can the openness upon the other than being be conceived without the openness as such forthwith signifying an assembling into a conjuncture, into a unity of essence? Can openness have another sense than that of the accessibility of entities through open doors or windows? Can openness have another signification that that of disclosure?
>
> (Levinas 2006b: 178–9)

How can on shed light then on the question of the body expressing the world of bodies, always having this possibility as its inner nature? What is the place of the other, what kind of space is allocated to the other in the world?

Any possibility for a sharing, must be, to put it in the words of Jean-Luc Nancy:

elaborated as a quite particular space – the word space being understood here both in the literal sense, since the existents are also bodies, extended beings, and in a figurative sense, which would answer the question: 'What takes place between us?'

(Nancy 2008d: 119)

What is the space opened between eight billion bodies?

Between Us

Turn of phrase

The question 'What happens between eight billion bodies?' can be arranged according to a second configuration, so that it would read 'What happens between us?'

The distance between these two expressions is apparently minimal, but by looking at them more closely one finds that the latter insists precisely on what the former omits. It is not the same thing to ask what happens between eight billion bodies – without having defined any attribute with regard to the way in which these bodies share a *between* – and to ask what happens between *us*. It is precisely the 'us' that draws the line here, as it is not established that the 'us' follows naturally, organically as it were, from the mere juxtaposition of a number of bodies. The pronoun 'us' contains something that goes well beyond a space simply filled with bodies. It contains that which lies beyond mere proximity, even the closest and most intimate one. The 'us' is a leap, a movement forward with respect to the simple assemblage of bodies. At the same time it pronounces what is most proper to them: that bodies are 'us', in this odd grammatical fashion, or that we are as bodies. However the two aforementioned propositions do not articulate any valuable statement on 'us'; the latter rests, therefore, on an unresolved inertia. 'Us' is never a given, it is never posed in something; it is never presupposed, unless one situates oneself within a perfectly immanent community, a community by definition destined to constantly restate its natural intimacy.

What asks to be treated here is the way in which bodies find themselves in between one another. 'Us' lays *in between* bodies; not just as the space between one body and another, but most properly as that between, the articulation of one body with regard to all others. The task consists then in looking not solely for the space opened by my locality, but also for the exposition of one locality to the other. The 'between' is intended here precisely as this space bodies articulate, but whose determination goes beyond their pure juxtaposition. It is this indetermination that allows 'us' to speak.

There is one more point that requires clarification. The questions ask: *What happens between eight billion bodies* or *What happens between us*. That which 'happens', rather than addressing the firm and clear visibility of an actuality, holds the quality of a coming to, of an open possibility, of an ongoing movement towards presence. If one pushes the reading to the limit of the word it is not incorrect to list, along with other connotations, those of 'spontaneity', 'fortuity' and 'accident', of an unexpected emergence. To put it in other terms, what happens between us could possibly not happen at all. That which happens always embeds also its very opposite. It is then worth questioning what 'to happen' means, investigating the nature of this *happening* when related to the space between us.

The main argument elaborated here is that the conditions of the space identified 'between bodies' do not just provide a background for the emergence of the question 'what happens between us', but constitute and occupy the very movement of such questioning. In other words, the *where* of this happening is also its *how* and indicates furthermore the order of the exposition. The space of the 'us' is intended here as bearing also a physical dimension. This space is identified as the *world*. The study of this concept, through Jean-Luc Nancy's work and its references to the Heideggerian idea of 'Being-in-the-world' and the closure of the onto-theological horizon, draws the coordinates for most of the following argument. Nancy's conclusion that the world rests on a lack of principle, essence, creator or organising factor – the world of bodies – constitutes the point of departure on which to situate the happening of 'us'.

With regard to the impossibility for the world to represent its own premise, Nancy speaks at times of the *end of the world*. However this end

> cannot mean that we are confronted merely with the end of a certain 'conception' of the world, and that we would have to go off in search of another one or to restore another one. It means that there is no longer any assignable signification of world or that the world is subtracting itself from the entire regime of signification available to us.
>
> (Nancy 1997b: 5)

A world without reason, a world that has escaped its own ground, is a world where what remains are bodies, their propagations and exposures to one another. Similarly in Deleuze's cinema of bodies what remains, once characters and plots have been stripped away, are forces supported only by the belief in this world *here*, a world whose sense corresponds to its confines. Among the filmmakers whose gesture can be exposed according to such logic Deleuze pays particular attention to American director John Cassavetes.

Cinema here will work as our model. The method will follow one rule: that the philosophical approach to a filmmaker cannot be taken simply as the possibility to unravel a convergence between concept and image. The task cannot only be that of treating a film as a philosophical example or that of using a concept as a comprehensive approach to a particular cinematographic work. It is a matter of investigating how both philosophy and cinema creatively confront a problem, in this case the problem of our being-together in its relation with the question of the sense of the world. It is therefore not a matter of providing an entrance into Nancy's philosophy or of describing Cassavetes' cinema but of how cinema reopens the sense of what happens between us. Moving between philosophy and cinema one is always asked to look for their internal alliance and their creative frictions. It will be thus a matter of following and exposing the cinematographic idea as it happens in the image and not of imposing ideas from the vantage point of a conceptual constellation.

Along with Deleuze's argument, one can read modern cinema as reestablishing our belief in this actual world, the articulation of the world's *here* with regard to all its *there*. Understood in this fashion, cinema establishes the very modern fact that we do not believe in another world anymore. As Deleuze puts it: 'what is certain is that believing is no longer believing in another world, or in a transformed world' (Deleuze 2005: 167). In the account provided by Revault D'Allones – who elaborates on Deleuze's work – 'starting with World War II [...] a number of directors have decided to turn their cameras to the world itself, "as it is", "raw"' (Revault D'Allones 1994: 9).

As the world happens and happens between us, so cinema essentially contributes to free a motion, accompanying the presencing of presence. One can see at work here the same relation the 'us' entertains with the world, since cinema, Nancy writes, 'shares the intensity of a look upon a world of which it is itself part and parcel' (Nancy 2001c: 16). Cinema does not represent the world; it does not mirror it; reality is not simply registered in its immediacy. In cinema experience is not reduced and incorporated. Instead the impossibility of capturing it under the regime of truth liberates once more the sharing of experience's evidence as undecidability. Cinema allows Nancy to express the intrinsic differential structure of the world: relation to itself as relation to an outside. This structure does not apply to the world as a category – it is neither the world's disposition nor its organising principle – it is the world itself. It is the constant creation of finite sense, infinitely relating to an outside of itself, which composes (and at once, in the same gesture, decomposes) the evidence of the world.

The 'real' at stake in cinema, what Nancy calls the 'evidence of film', exposes this logic: sense is not the set of significations sent and received, infinitely sealed on themselves, but sending and receiving as they infringe acquired significations and release a tension that opens up the immanence of the world. It is following this gesture that Jean-Luc Nancy's engagement with the writing of film responds also to a wider reconsideration of the question of the image. It is from within the image (and from within the curvature of imagination) that Nancy reverses the order of absence and presence and their priority. For Nancy what comes to presence is the force liberated by an absence. The evidence of presence is nothing other than the effect produced by the drawing out of absence. It is absence that constantly occupies that which finally comes to presence. Within Nancy's philosophy the writing of film mirrors the writing out of the structure of sense in the world. The writing on film therefore responds to a double demand: on the one hand it aims to illuminate the status of the cinematrographic image – what cinema is, cinema's ontology, the body and the gestures of this particular Muse – and on the other hand it interrogates how cinema exposes finite worldhood by making the world evident. Cinema allows an entrance into the ontological moment where the world – delivered over to us – is separated from its character of mere given and its sense is made remarkable, our attention being called to it. Cinema always runs this risk: to open within the world a space where everything becomes possible, but nothing is possible yet. Through cinema the world opens up to its own sense and to its own images, whose final meaning cannot be calculated. Cinema's relevance for Nancy's ontology resides then in the possibility of presenting the unseen, not as the extraordinary, rather as defeat of ultimate significations, sense's constant withdrawing from its own horizon, deferral of its arrival. The notion of evidence should thus be understood within this ontology of finite sense, where the world is always presented as the absolute novelty of sense, in absence of ultimate disclosures, salvations, providence or last judgements. Cinema does not mimic the world, it gives presence to it, but this giving presence again should be understood under the mode of absence: 'the image gives a presence that it lacks—since it has no other presence than the unreal one of its thin, filmlike surface—and it gives it to something that, being absent, cannot receive it' (Nancy 2005: 63). The something that cannot receive this presence is precisely sense, which cannot be situated anywhere else than in the existence of the image, 'sense exists, or rather it is the movement and flight of existing' (ibid.: 68). Cinema presents 'the opening and the communication of sense as possible, indeterminate and unachievable' (Nancy 2010: 20). The reversal here operated – from the world as that which *has* sense to that which *is making* sense – develops in parallel with a general revision of the notion of *subject of sense*. Talking about the possibility for sense to listen (thus to sense) itself, Nancy writes 'sense reaches me long before it leaves me [...] there is only a "subject" that resounds, responding to a momentum, a summons, a convocation of sense' (Nancy 2007a: 30). There is a coincidence between the affirmation of sense and its failure to recuperate itself in a whole. This fault should not be eliminated since it is precisely from this insufficiency that sense proceeds.

The philosophical mirror, as it were, of the world of bodies would then be the cinema of bodies, a cinema that undoes the character and the plot in order to follow and reduce both to bodily attitudes. In the cinema of bodies, as Deleuze conceives of it, the space is also reduced to bodies' articulations, 'in order to get to attitudes as to categories which put time into the body, as well as thought into life' (Deleuze 2005: 185). Deleuze identifies in John Cassavetes the most successful example of this strategy:

> this is what Cassavetes was already saying in *Shadows* and then *Faces*; what constitutes part of the film is interesting oneself in people rather than in the film, in the human problems more than in the problems of the mise en scene; so that people do not pass over to the side of the camera without the camera having passed to the side of the people.
>
> (ibid.: 149)

Although Deleuze's analysis of the work of Cassavetes is detailed and generous, there is a second strategy developed by the American filmmaker, which is overlooked in Deleuze's *Cinema 2*. This relates to Cassavetes' use of close-ups. The question asked here is how, in particular in a film like *Faces*, close-ups take on a contrapuntal structure. It is by way of the contrapuntal use of the close-up that Cassavetes is able to elaborate a model of being-together based on distance.

What happens between us

What is the space opened between eight billion bodies?
What happens between us?

The second question exposes a set of quandaries on the nature of this happening, but in particular on the status of 'us' and on its measure.

If the first chapter has been almost entirely devoted to the analysis of the body and its radical openness, here the gesture extends beyond the local position of the body to reach bodies in relation with one another. It is here a matter of relation, because one is moving from an analysis of the status (*stare* – to lay, to rest) towards a dynamic investigation, the investigation of a passage.

The argument takes its cue from the space opened by eight billion bodies, moving into the density of this opening to investigate *what happens between us,* retaining entirely the previous analysis so that the space of the one next to me will not lose its meaningfulness and become a simple summa of more than one body. The aim here is to be able to pronounce something about 'us', about the space where 'us' takes its place, the space where we are essentially with 'us'.

Following Nancy, the problem of understanding the space of the 'us' reveals itself in all its urgency:

> the with understood in terms of existence, must therefore be elaborated as a quite particular space – the word space being understood here both in the literal sense, since the existents are also bodies, extended beings, and in a figurative sense, which would answer the question: 'What takes place between us?'
>
> (Nancy 2008d: 119)

A discourse on the space of this relation (which amounts to a discourse on the space of otherness) needs to arise from the analysis of the body as a place for existence, in the double connotation already described. A body is never alone with itself, it is never known as a single body, 'bodies are first and always others, just as others are first and always bodies. I'll never know my body, never know myself as a body [...] *An other is a body* because only *a body is an other*' (Nancy 2008a: 31).

Already in the first chapter the question of space as intimately linked to that of the body was of crucial importance. This space, opened to a plastic lexicon, a register of plasticity, was needed in order for the excesses of the body to appear, so that the latter would not fall either into the symbolic, hysteric reduction or into its opposite, the purely material one, where the body forms just an irreducible crust, what Heidegger in the *Zollikon Seminars* refers to as the mere corporeality of a thing.

The kind of space thus described, the space of this language, was announced as one whose suture is unknown, or, better said, as an opening that is not anymore in the realm of knowledge. However this openness should not be dismissed as vagueness. As Nancy says, 'tightly woven and narrowly articulated, it constitutes the structure of sense qua sense of the world' (Nancy 1997b: 3).

One of the main issues the previous reading of the work of Jean-Luc Nancy was concerned with was the fact that bodies are open-space. The open nature of the body was pursued along three lines: the body rejecting itself; the body open as the exposure of existence; the body exposed to other bodies, the world of bodies.

One could even say that the first chapter in its entirety had an implicit centre constituted by the question of space. Even when the discourse turned to the work of Emmanuel Levinas and its notion of position, the focus was on bodies' way to articulate space. There it was said that position is never already within Being; instead it is a rage, a movement, the opening up of a space that was not there beforehand. The lengthy analysis devoted to this concept was in fact pointing to the same direction as the reading of Jean-Luc Nancy: bodies do articulate space by spacing each other out.

On the other hand it was said that through a reworking of the phenomenological body Levinas attempts to refute what he calls the concreteness and usability of Heidegger's world. The notion of position also allows Levinas to distance his thinking from the geographical–political connotation of Heidegger's thought. In later writings Levinas will express his concerns towards Heidegger's reasoning on the place of Germany and on the primacy of certain topography. This will lead Levinas strategically to oppose to Heideggerian 'entrenchment', the courage of Gagarin who 'left the Place. For one hour, man existed beyond any horizon – everything around him was sky or, more exactly, everything was geometrical space. A man existed in the absolute of homogeneous space' (Levinas 1997a: 233).

In *Otherwise than Being* the body becomes a necessary element in the construction of the ethical relation: 'the body is not only an image or figure here; it is the distinctive in oneself of the non-contraction of ipseity and its break-up' (Levinas 2006b: 109). Levinas announces his strategy in clear terms:

> in contradistinction to the philosophers of existence we will not found the relation with the existent respected in its being [...] on being in the world, the care and doing [...] Doing, labour, already implies the relation with the transcendent.
>
> (Levinas 2005: 109)

In other words, Levinas tries to formulate a concept that would precede and exceed the instrumentality of Heidegger's Being-in-the-world. From this search for an 'otherwise than the world' will spring the third part of this work.

Two notions will be retained here from the analysis that has occupied the first stage of the research:

- the body as what spaces me from other beings; thus the problem of access and origins from which the question of relations *between us* also springs;
- the world of bodies – that is to say, 'a world that is not initially subject to the compactness of space [...] rather, it is a world, where bodies initially articulate space' (Nancy 2008a: 27).

The world of bodies

The world of bodies bears no relation to a beyond or an outside of itself, for it is that which has escaped every representation. In order to get to what the world is, to the apparently simple fact that the world is, Nancy draws largely on Heidegger's *Being and Time*. Despite the fact that Heidegger's work is never mentioned, nor referenced explicitly, it constitutes the inevitable background throughout both *The Sense of the World* and *The Creation of the World and Globalization*.

Nancy moves from the same difficulty already envisaged by Heidegger when the German philosopher writes that 'the concept of the world or the phenomenon thus designated, is what has hitherto not yet been recognised in philosophy' (Heidegger 1982: 165). Confronting this lack for Nancy means first of all being attentive to 'the diction of word *world*' (Nancy 2007b: 47, translation modified).[1] Nancy aims to establish the notion of the world as a relational totality, constantly open and where what is at stake (sense) is at stake *in* the very structure of this world here and nowhere else (not beyond). The preliminary gesture required in order to pose the question of the world beyond the traditional external principle is to examine the subject–object model. As long as one places the thinking of the world on such a model, one necessarily understands the world as an ob-jectum, illuminated by the gaze of a (divine) subject.

The world, Nancy writes, is a fact, our fact. Namely, any reference to a principle conferring sense has now left space for the immanent experience of the world. As one can see, what resonates here is the idea of Being-in-the-world as a particular kind of absorption, absorption in a set of references, from which there is no way out.

What one should look into is therefore:

the very movement of the occidental history of *sense* as the movement of an ontoth-eology in principle involved with its own deconstruction, the *end* of which, in all

senses is precisely "this world *here*", this world that is to such an extent "*here*" that
it is definitively beyond all gods and all signifying or signified instances of sense.

(Nancy 2007b: 25)

The very attempt Nancy engages in revolves entirely around the possibility to
reach an open conclusion on what the sense of the world is. That the sense of
the world is to be found in the world itself and absolutely in what is immanent
about it (although for this immanence Nancy uses the expression *transimmi-
nence* to mean that sense belongs to the structure of the world, but precisely as
the ex-position of this structure[2]) could be said to rely on Heidegger's discussion
of significance as 'that on the basis of which the world is disclosed as such'
(Heidegger 1962: 182). According to Dreyfus' commentary this suggests that
'the world and Dasein are ultimately so intertwined that one cannot separate the
world from Daseining' (Dreyfus 1990: 94).

Nancy retains most of the Heideggerian argument, despite the fact that he does
not explore the modes of our everyday dealings with the world. In this way he
avoids entering the discussion of how one encounters things in the world, ultimately
limiting himself to define this relation in terms of exposition. 'Man is the exposing
of the world' – he says – 'and the world is the exposed of man' (Nancy 2000: 28).

Nancy finds in Heidegger's work – in his critique of Descartes' use of the
concept of *substantia* for example, whereby the substantia is not defined and
thus makes it impossible for philosophy to pronounce any statement with
regard to what the world is and to the being of this world – an understanding
of the world as being 'world' only for the ones inhabiting it. Since the structure
of the world, its worldliness and its significance, are thoroughly connected with
Dasein's Being-in-the-world, by way of a twofold transcendental movement of
disclosure and discovery, the world cannot be read in reference to a substratum
that does not participate in it. Heidegger writes that 'the world is therefore
something "wherein" Dasein as an entity already was, and if in any manner
it explicitly comes away from anything, it can never do more than come back
to the world' (Heidegger 1962: 106–7). This passage contains one of the main
points Nancy wants to advance: there is no way out of the world; the only way
out still resides within the world. By saying that one cannot escape from this
world, I am not proposing to give to the world some kind of Pascalian connotation, as if the world were a sort of *cachot*. What is at stake here is the internal
opening of the world, a relation of the world to itself.

The possibility to represent the world's premise is replaced by the facticity
of the world, by the world as 'our fact'. Such a proposition calls for a double

reading. If it is true that the world is *our* fact, it is also true that the world is our fact and nobody else's – this 'negative' connotation should not be overlooked. In *Being and Time* Heidegger argues that due to its structure the world could not be understood by a rational entity, which does not inhabit it. Nancy, following Heidegger, articulates on this point a wider argument, emphasizing the idea of dwelling as the moment where a participatory definition of the world becomes possible. As mentioned earlier on, Nancy conceives of the world as something within which one is absorbed, otherwise the world is not such anymore. If one can give a detailed description of the world, if the latter offers itself as an object of representation, one is already looking at something else. The only way to access the world is to access it as the 'wherein' one inhabits; according to Heidegger's formula 'the world is such just for those who inhabit it'. Nancy then specifies his understanding of *inhabiting* as the taking place of the possibility of a world to exist (the world exists itself, in a transitive fashion). In our inhabiting we hold ourselves to the world, we take place in the world, where 'in' does not address just 'insideness' as 'being contained' or 'resting inside'. 'In' addresses in fact something quite different: the 'in' of 'this taking place in' sustains my very singular happening.

For Nancy the taking place as happening provides the world with a structure, or better with an ex-perience, whilst at the same time what takes place, takes place by way and within this world here. This taking place then not only recalls the double structure according to which Dasein is always already in the world – at the same time as it reveals the world's significance by a double 'attitude' of disclosing and discovering – but seems to elaborate directly on a number of passages that can be found in Heidegger. In *Basic Problems of Phenomenology* for instance Heidegger writes:

> the world as already unveiled in advance is such that we do not in fact specifi-cally occupy ourselves with it, or apprehend it, but instead it is so self-evident, so much a matter of course, that we are completely oblivious to it.
>
> (Heidegger 1982: 165)

Furthermore, Heidegger specifies the nature of the 'in' of the compound expression Being-in-the-world by clarifying that we should not think the in as the insideness of an object into a container. The 'in' is thus not a spatial repre-sentation whose expression renders Dasein as contained into the world; rather, it stands for Dasein's concern towards the world, a concern Dasein is invested with, prior to its disclosure of the world:

> Being-in [...] designates the kind of Being which an entity has when it is 'in'
> another one, as the water is 'in' the glass, or the garment is 'in' the cupboard [...]
> Being-in, on the other hand, is a state of Dasein's Being; it is an existentiale [...]
> So one cannot think of it as the Being-present-at-hand of some corporeal Thing
> (such as a human body) 'in' an entity which is present-at-hand.
>
> (Heidegger 1962: 79)

Heidegger draws his analysis of Being-in from the etymology of 'in', which he reads in the Latin terms *habitare, diligere, colere*: to dwell, chose and cultivate. These terms, rather than specifying a container and a contained, bear a direct relation with being-familiar-with and being-connected-with. Heidegger explicitly links the expression 'having a world' with the connotation of *habitare* that Being-in refers to: 'In its very possibility this "having" is founded upon the existential state of Being-in' (ibid.: 84).

Deploying a similar philological insight Nancy links 'taking place' with the Greek terms *êthos* and *ethos*, echoed by the Latin *habitus* and *habitare*, both related to *habere*, a 'having – Nancy says – with a sense of being: it is a manner of being there and of standing in it' (Nancy 2007b: 42). It is by way of Heidegger then that Nancy seems to reach the conclusion, based on the abovementioned etymological resonances, that the world 'is an ethos, a *habitus* and an inhabiting' (ibid.); our fact. This is what allows Nancy in turn to attribute to the world its own proper mode, its way of standing and occupying a place. 'A world is an ethos, a habitus and an inhabiting: it is what holds to itself and in itself, following to its proper mode. It is a network of the self-reference of this stance. In this way it resembles a subject' (ibid.: 43).

This last sentence offers a problem (a problem that confirms the kinship between Nancy's thought and Heidegger's, for the German philosopher asked himself the very same question).[3] If the world resembles a subject then one would need to make sense of it through the model of subjectivity. As a consequence one would need to presuppose something, to look for something prior to the subject itself and to seek therefore the substance of this subjectivity. Here one runs the risk of falling again into some kind of Cartesianism, at least the one Heidegger moves against, whereby an undefined substance comes to define the world. Against this argument Heidegger writes that 'the world comes not afterwards, but beforehand, in the strict sense of the word' (Heidegger 1982: 165). Moreover one should keep in mind that the analysis Nancy devotes to the world aims at defining it beyond a subject–object relation and beyond any presupposition according to which the sense of the world would have to be found beyond the world itself. If the world can be called subjective, this is not because it can be placed somewhere within the subject/object relation, but because the world presupposes itself outside any premise. The only possibility left open to the world-as-subject is its own revolution, the fact of turning on itself, from one end to the other. To this effect Nancy writes: 'the world does not presuppose itself: it is only coextensive to its extension as world, to the spacing of its places between which its resonances reverberate' (Nancy 2007b: 43). Thus, following a Heideggerian path, Nancy tries to resolve the question of the world in terms of experience, a particular kind of experience taking place as the revolution of the world on itself. The word experience has again to be understood according to the logic just exposed:

> there is no experience of sense if 'experience' is supposed to imply the appropriation of a signification – but that there is nothing other than experience of sense if 'experience' says that sense precedes all appropriation or succeeds on and exceeds it.
>
> (Nancy 1997b: 11)

The sense of the world is triggered through the immanent experience the world makes of itself. As Nancy puts it, experience then consists in the circulation of sense infinitely reopening available significations. Experience here is the given of sense delivering itself back to exposure. Hence the experience of the world would be in this case the apprehending of the world as an inhabiting, a self-standing that never presupposes itself. The world opens onto itself and this opening is its experience. The world is thus this *habitus*, this taking place as dwelling that opens onto its own lack of supports.

The points one needs to retain are mainly two:

- the world is such just for the ones who inhabit it;
- the world does not depend; rather it ex-ists itself.

How does the world appear for the first time beyond the subject–object relationship? How does the world appear as that which is available just to those who inhabit it without depending on any substance?

Nancy is here exposing once more the argument regarding the closure of the onto-theological and onto-teleological horizon. More specifically his gesture attempts a re-reading of the Heideggerian composite expression Being-in-the-world. Nancy shares with Heidegger a point of departure: both philosophers attempt to think the world as that which has never been thought before in its being as such. The philosophical urgency Nancy moves from revolves around the need to think the world not as an object, but as a *habitus*, what holds to itself and in itself. The question one tries to respond to, the very question the philosophical tradition has left open, is formulated as follows:

> What has remained unresolved is the grasping of a concrete world that would be the world of the proper freedom and singularity of each and of all without claim to a world beyond-the-world.
>
> (Nancy 2007b: 38)

The world is without a why: Deconstruction of the world

One needs here to take a step backwards and reread the passage that has led us this far. The present discussion started out from this:

> The with understood in terms of existence, must therefore be elaborated as a quite particular space – the word space being understood here both in the literal sense, since the existents are also bodies, extended beings, and in a figurative sense, which would answer the question "What takes place between us?"
>
> (Nancy 2008d: 119)

Nancy's vocabulary draws here more explicitly on Heidegger's concept of *Being-with*. At times it seems as if the entirety of Nancy's effort were devoted to reopening the problem of Being-with as in sections 26–7 of *Being and Time*. Given the question investigated here, a passage from Heidegger's work resonates with particular relevance: 'the world is always the one that I share with others' (Heidegger 1962: 155). Most of the questions this work sets as its horizon derive from and are triggered by an attempt advanced by a group of philosophers after Heidegger's work. The debate formed around this question has tried to reconsider – according to different trajectories and taking in some cases opposite paths – *Being-with* as the possibility to open the question of subjectivity outside individuality.

What is at stake of course is to understand what Heidegger means when he defines Being-with as an existential, rather than a category (a definition which Heidegger himself leaves somehow unfinished). The attempt is then to articulate the *with* not just as a device for juxtaposition or combination, but as co-essential to the existing of existence. At this stage it is important to analyse the space from which *Being-with* emerges and begins to work.

If the *with* in its existential determination articulates itself as a space – both the physical space of a coming-to-presence and the space as relational set – then such a space, denoted as the world, collaborates to define the *with* itself. This is to say that the *with* and the world are so intimately bound up that the first emergence of the *with* can be read from within the question of the world. If the world is our fact, then it is a fact that has first of all to do with 'us'.

For Jean-Luc Nancy the question of the *with* revolves around the question of a space, a space that sometimes is structured as a thin line running between Heidegger's destination, the destining of a people, and a pure juxtaposition of impersonal bodies.

However the analysis of Being-with cannot for Nancy be completely separated from a deconstructive gesture that delimits the conditions for the appearance of something as a 'world'. In other terms, Nancy seems to take up Heidegger's question 'How does the deity enter into philosophy?'

Whilst it is true that Nancy formulates a similar demand, the articulation of this demand is reversed: how does God abandon the world? What happens to the world once God's presence stops signaling the sense of the world from its rearguard beyond the world itself? The nature of that place that was once divine and grounded in the highest cause assumes different traits: 'if the god no longer offers himself, if he no longer even conceals his presence in his divine being, he leaves only bare places, where no presence withdraws or comes' (Nancy 1991: 111).

Both Nancy and Heidegger elaborate on the development of the Western tradition as the search for a ground. This engagement with the idea of a foundation draws the trajectory for the institution of divine places, of the world itself as a divine place, intending with this expression that the world becomes a place caused by a Supreme Being. The argument cannot be completely separated from a deconstruction of Christianity and of monotheism, at least insofar as a discussion of the God of philosophy makes evident that monotheism is not simply the reduction of the Greek–Roman pantheon to one single divinity, but the positing of the divine as an existent being holding real qualities. The question therefore is not just that of a singularity replacing plurality, but that of the place of the divine in the real. One could say that monotheism accounts for Being itself. According to Nancy the very possibility of atheism is already inscribed in the program of Christianity for two reasons: on the one hand Christianity announces the presence of the divine in this world here; on the other the death of the incarnated divinity opens up the appearance of truth in this world here. To this effect Nancy writes, 'Socrates and Christ are the same: their death is opened in the middle of the world [...] exposing the failure of the indefinite quest for an ultimate sense' (Nancy 2010: 44).

With the question 'How does the deity enter into philosophy' – asked in the context of a conversation with Hegel – Heidegger aims to pierce the nature of the onto-theological constitution of metaphysics, the posing of grounds that within the Western tradition has allowed and dominated the thinking of the Being of beings. Drawing in particular on his *What is Metaphysics?* Heidegger inquires on the nature of the God of philosophy, the metaphysical concept of God as *causa sui*. 'How does the deity enter into philosophy?'

Heidegger intends to generate a rupture into the conditions that produce such question and the consequences that the terms of the question have had in the history of Western thought. What is in question in the onto-theological? What are the terms of the belonging together of ontology and theology?

Heidegger makes clear in this context that ontology and theology cannot be thought of as two distinct disciplines coming together in a second stage. What must be considered is indeed the nature of the unity according to which they belong together, which means elucidating the problem of 'beings as such in the universal and primal at one with beings as such in the highest and ultimate' (Heidegger 2002: 62). It is therefore a matter of interrogating that which is grounded through that which grounds it through its height, whilst constantly performing also a reversal of this very order.

The aforementioned unity has established itself as our way of thinking the difference between Being and beings. Philosophy has represented this difference to itself in onto-theological terms. The difference just mentioned, however, is what one encounters at any time – therefore it cannot be said to be simply a contribution of representational and philosophical thinking. Whilst on the one side Being can only be thought of as the Being of beings, on the other beings can only be reached according to the ways in which they account for Being. Being constitutes itself as that which transits the arrival of beings, the difference becoming as a result 'the perdurance of overwhelming and arrival' (ibid.: 65). It is in this way that Being is posed as ground. In turn, and still by virtue of the difference, beings as such – as a totality, a whole – account for the ground. The difference is then thought in terms of Being as that which grounds because it allows beings' presence and in terms of beings as that which accounts for Being because they present Being's active nature. Being as grounding becomes something that is, something that appears as presence and therefore needs 'accounting for through a being, that is causation, and indeed causation by the highest cause' (ibid.: 72).

This configuration is most clearly expressed by Leibniz in *The 24 Theses of Metaphysics*, a text Heidegger recalls both in *Identity and Difference* and *The End of Philosophy*.

Leibniz concentrates his logic in three succinct expressions: 'ratio est in natura'; 'ratio debet esse in aliquo Ente Reali'; 'Est scilicet Ens illud ultima ratio

Rerum, et uno vocabulo solet appellari DEUS' (Heidegger 2003: 49–50)[4]. The totality of Beings must be thought in terms of a ground that justifies its existence. This ground must be identified in the realm of reality. Furthermore the ground must be conceived as a real cause that grounds the actuality of existing things. This real cause must in turn be necessary, which means not grounded in anything else. This necessary being that grounds the existent goes under the name of God.

These passages from Leibniz highlight the specific movement prompted through the onto-theological approach to the question of existence: once the transformation of Being into real ground has occurred, the ground is then identified with God, a real being providing the first cause. Therefore we think onto-theologically because we always think beings both as belonging to a common ground and as a whole granted by the highest being, whose existence is necessary (it is precisely by redefining and breaking up this necessity that the rationalist thinkers mark their distance with medieval philosophy and announce its inevitable end). Beings belong to a common ground that makes their presence possible, whilst this common ground at the same time belongs to beings according to the existence of a supremely original matter that exists necessarily.

Heidegger therefore concludes that the 'deity enters into philosophy through the perdurance of which we think at first as the approach to the active nature of the difference between Being and beings' (Heidegger 2002: 71).

This is the framework on which Nancy too starts his work. His attempts seem to respond to this urgency opened by Heidegger across a number of texts in terms of 'destruction of ontology', what John Stambaugh in the introduction to *The End of Philosophy* defines as 'the unbuilding (*de-struere*) of the layers covering up the original nature of Being, the layers which metaphysical thinking has con-structed' (Heidegger 2003: ix). Nancy is writing here against the idea that there could be an organising principle, 'an other order, an other agency of all things of life and of existence' (Nancy 2010: 42), that would ground the totality of existents and address their distribution.

Although Nancy's argument does not refer explicitly to the Heideggerian notion of 'appropriation', it nevertheless finds its point of departure in the breach operated by Heidegger at the heart of the Western tradition. It is therefore important to take this 'provenance' into account.

To grasp how the deconstruction announced by Nancy in fact participates in the construction of the world of the onto-theological tradition, one could start by reading the very beginning of a text whose title reads *Urbi et Orbi*:

it is no longer possible to identify either a city that would be 'The City' – as
Rome was for so long – or an orb that would provide the contour of a world
extended around this city […] it is no longer possible to identify either the city
or the orb of the world in general.

(Nancy 2007b: 33)

'Urbi et orbi' is the expression used in papal addresses to Rome and the world,
or to Rome as the world. To name the world 'Rome' meant to imagine the world
as inscribed within a particular topography, in that case that of the city of Rome
and the walls – *Murus Servii Tullii, Murus Aurelianii,* the walls protecting the
Civitas Leonina – that separated the city from the surrounding countryside.

'Urbi et orbi' makes the world the subject–object of a metaphor, of a representation. The world has escaped this possibility, the possibility of a being
represented or subjected. The possibility of this break away from its representations – from the ones held true by the tradition – is already at play within
the tradition itself. This is precisely the juncture Nancy tries to bring about
by attempting a deconstruction of the world. The deconstruction of the onto-
theological tradition – *our* tradition, the tradition of the Western world that
comes to extend itself over the entire globe – can once again not be completely
separated from a deconstruction of Christianity. As Nancy writes:

> The opening of the world in the world is the result of a destitution or a decon-
> struction of Christianity, which goes back or which advances in it all the way to
> the extremity at which nihilism breaks up the presence and the value of God,
> breaks up the sense of salvation as an escape from the world.

(Nancy 2008b: 78)

The more one progresses with the imaging of the world – the more one forges
pictures of it from satellites – the less the world resembles a *topos*. When the Pope
was pronouncing his blessing it was clear to everyone that he was thinking the world
as a particular image of God: the order God had wanted for his creatures. The Pope
could say 'urbi et orbi' just because his audience would have immediately understood the world as the subject of This formula was made available moving from the
consideration that the world was the subject of the making of God and of the making
of God itself, God's praxis. According to Alexander Koyré this cosmo-ontological
upheaval is the result of the destruction of the cosmos and the consequential
geometrization of space. By way of this double movement the idea of the world as
a harmoniously and hierarchically ordered whole is replaced with 'an indefinite or
even infinite universe no longer united by natural subordination, but unified only by
the identity of its ultimate and basic components and laws' (Koyré 1957: 2).

The same use of the word *orbe* suggests that the Pope had in mind a particular shape for the world: not just an image as idea, but also an image as form. The rim surrounding the world and providing it with a sense, theological or historical–teleological, filling the word with the consistency of a world, does not include the world anymore.

How could one therefore address the world nowadays,[5] provided that the metonymy – Rome, the Urbe – has ceased to work? It has ceased to work not just because there is no city around which the world is wrapped, but also because the meaning of the word *world* should be readdressed today in a fashion that excludes any appropriation and also any illustration (as the world as a sphere or orbe, would suggest). One would rather have to address the world as a matter of fact. To say that one is left with the world means that the world 'is such only for those who inhabit it', a world without principle.

The expression 'without principle' should be read as inhabiting two poles of any reasoning on the world. This double meaning articulates the opening and the open end of a possible deconstruction of the world. However, 'the world is without principle' may lend itself to a different connotation, a different perspective: 'the world is without reason'. Once translated in such a way, the expression presents a slightly different constellation: there is no reason to engage in a discussion that holds the world as its centre, for – the world being an *ens creatum*, the very here below, placed at the bottom of the hierarchical vertical structure – its very reason, the point of departure as it were for reasoning, would necessarily (and thus eternally) lie beyond the world itself.

This reason thus rests on the specification provided by an *ens perfectissimum*, which itself requires no specification in order to be what it is. Hence, every time one sets oneself out to speak about the world, one needs to define the subject – or creator – of the world. On the other hand 'the world is without reason' means something that might sound just like the exact opposite. It means that the world is in itself in no need, it is determined as self-standing and it requires neither further specification nor further representation. According to this articulation the world would finally be able to confront its own freedom: revolution. This is the world-subject (although one should, it has been mentioned already, always be careful when it comes to the term subject).

What can be highlighted here is how the world, from being that which needs to be rescued from the abyss, becomes itself that which is without a ground (α-byss).

The abovementioned movement is such that one might find in the end that the figure of the subject of the world has been replaced by the world-subject. As Nancy says, after Heidegger, a long tradition has covered up the question of the world by replacing it with something *better*, a creator or a substance accounting for the world. In this scenario the world cannot account for itself, since its sense is deposited beyond its 'thereness'.

The world, augmented by an ideal world, which lays above (ὑπέρ), or via a 'οὐ κινούμενον κινεῖ' that moves it, has never been enough. Nevertheless one can see how even the most radically transcendent, the most vertical tradition, assigning the creation, order and destination of the world to a distant God beyond the world, does not fail to bring fore the question of the existence of the world.

It is therefore not surprising to find within this same tradition a constant questioning of the world and of our Being-in-the-world. One could say that the metaphysical tradition has in fact brought fore the question of the world and of its immanence with such insistence that the question never really deserted philosophical thinking. The tradition has therefore since the beginning sustained itself on its own reversal. The more one attempts to explain the world as the outcome of God's praxis – God's very productivity – the closer one draws God to the world; this being the case the only possibility for God to remain a Supreme Being would be for God to be completely alien to the world, so Supreme that no account of the world can, even accidentally, even by an odd trajectory, touch on him. God could be saved and thus save his divinity only as that which is farthest from the world. As long as God is at a distance, but still within concern, as Heidegger would say, still within the worldly horizon, then it is somehow fated to follow the destiny of the world until its own withdrawal within the world itself. The Supreme Being, which used to be the distance of the 'from a distance', privileged point of view on the world, has abandoned that position, closing the gap from the world, until no distance is left, not even a diaphragm, and the world and God become so bound up that one does not need to reference any supremacy or any beyond. As Nancy writes:

> the God of onto-theology was progressively stripped of the divine attributes of an independent existence and only retained those of the existence of the world considered in its immanence, that is to say, also in the undecidable amphibology of an existence as necessary as it is contingent.
>
> (Nancy 2007b: 44)

The places of the divine are now empty and have left space for what in Nancy's terms can be called the spacing out of sense. In commenting Heidegger's famous statement that 'Only a God can save us now' (spoken in September 1966 these were Heidegger's almost last words, unless one takes into account those spoken, by proxy, in Celan's *Todtnauberg*[6]), Nancy reminds us that 'every god is the "last one", which is to say that every god dissipates and dissolves the very essence of the divine' (Nancy 2008b: 27). The necessity of God leaves in this way space for the necessity of the re-affirmation of the sense of the world against (in front of) any given sense. A world where God has left its place vacant is a world that stretches itself out:

> divine places, without gods, with no god, are spread around everywhere around us, open and offered to our coming, to our going or to our presence [...] ourselves, alone, out to meet that which we are not, and which the gods for their part have never been.
>
> (Nancy 1991: 50)

Thus it is within this tradition that one should seek the crumbling away of the otherness of God and the becoming apparent of a world without principle or reason. If it is true, as Levinas also underlines, that 'the God of philosophers, from Aristotle to Leibniz, by way of the God of the scholastics, is a God adequate to reason, a comprehended god who could not trouble the autonomy of consciousness' (Levinas 1986: 346), then this deconstruction participates in the very construction of onto-theology itself.

The deconstructive gesture emerges as the search for a movement within that which rids itself of any principle and could be formalized as follows: there where the world occupies by necessity a space without Reason nor God, then what do we make of the necessity of its contingency?

The trajectory Spinoza follows in treating the question of the world and Divinity has already been examined. Spinoza's notion of divinity consistently departs from the Christian onto-theological tradition. Spinoza solves the problem of the relation between the immaterial God and the material world by abolishing the immateriality of God. What is more, Spinoza places at the centre of his system the denial of final causes and the necessitarianism, which drastically excludes the possibility of the creation of the world as an act of pure will. Spinoza says in the appendix to the first volume of the *Ethics* that God 'acts from the necessity alone of his nature', adding that 'things have been predetermined by Him, not indeed from freedom of will, or from absolute good pleasure, but from His absolute nature' (Spinoza 1949: 72). What has just been said stands in overt contrast with Aquinas' conclusion that God works not by necessity, but by His intellect and Will. Spinoza goes as far as to say that 'Nature has no end set before it, and [...] all final causes are nothing but human fictions' (ibid.: 74).

Before Spinoza, other philosophers working at the borders of the onto-theological tradition (whether on cosmology or on theodicy) had already reached similar positions. Giordano Bruno was the first philosopher to rework cosmological ideas starting from Epicurus and Lucretius' infinitist conceptions. Bruno's philosophy is thought to have influenced significantly the rationalist thinkers that followed him. As Koyré writes Bruno moves from Nicholas of Cusa's ideas, in particular from Cusa's idea of *contractio* according to which 'every singular thing in the universe represents it – the universe [...] each in a manner different from that all of other, by "contracting" the wealth of the universe in accordance with its own unique individuality' (Koyré 1957: 9).[8] Bruno argues for the immanency of God in ways that will have echoes both in Spinoza's *Deus sive Natura* and in Leibniz' idea of an intellect organising the world as the *best of all possible worlds*. Establishing a link between the material and the immaterial infinity of the universe, Bruno claims that God would be in need of the world as much as the world is in need of Divinity. Furthermore the relation between multiplicity and unity is worked out in a way that allows Bruno to argue that the unity of the universe lies within it and not beyond or above the universe itself, thus denying the existence of two distinct worlds. Divinity is then all in all and everywhere, not localizable beyond the world and not in a particular place. What is interesting for us is the conclusion Bruno reaches with regard to the fact that God cannot be placed in an 'elsewhere', due to the coincidence in God of spirituality and matter. The possibility for naming an elsewhere is thus foreclosed. Bruno defined his thinking as a new beginning, both for its cosmological insights and for the ethical implications that this could have, starting for instance with the question of Christology as mediation between the *ens perfectissimum* and the *ens creatum*. The 5th Dialogue of *Cause, Principle and Unity* starts with one of the interlocutors, Theophilus, saying:

> the universe is, therefore, one, infinite and immobile. I say that the absolute possibility is one, that the act is one; the form, or soul, is one, the matter or body is one, the thing is one, being is one [...] it possesses no outside to which it might be subject and by which it might be affected.
>
> (Bruno 2003: 87)

A few lines further down, the same character concludes that: 'the universe comprises all being in a totality; for nothing that exists is outside or beyond infinite being, as the latter has no outside or beyond' (ibid.: 89), something that will profoundly resonate in the ontologies of Spinoza, Malebranche and Leibniz.

The latter, commenting on God as Supreme Wisdom, will define God as existing everywhere as a centre, having everything present to itself immediately.

Leibniz' God works as the Reason of the universe. Although this Sufficient Reason is immanently present in the organization of the universe, it is not however to be found within things themselves. Even if Leibniz thus retains the supremacy of God and claims that things, lacking any perfection, do receive a sort of perfection from Him – through the idea of each monad as 'a perpetual living mirror of the universe' – the thought of a God less and less divine reaches with him a particularly advanced stage. God calculates and the world comes to be (*Cum Deus calculat fit mundus*), but calculation may have nothing to do with creation (at least as it had been thought of in medieval philosophy).

In particular when Leibniz writes: 'there is a certain urgency towards existence in possible things' (Leibniz 1975: 487), he seems to imply that the world might just as well happen out of its own fortuitous necessity, without any principle prompting it to change from possibility to actuality. It is perhaps with Leibniz that the idea of a world without principle emerges most clearly.

In the language employed by Nancy this would also mean that the world has no ground beyond its own taking place, our way of *in-habiting* it. The absence of principle is the absence of the world's premise. As Nancy puts it:

> if the world essentially is not the representation of a universe, nor that of a here below, but the excess – beyond any representation of an ethos or of a habitus – of a stance by which the world stands by itself, configures itself, and exposes itself in itself, relates to itself without referring to any given principle or to any determined end, then one must address the principle of such an absence of principle directly.
>
> (Nancy 2007b: 47)

It is crucial here to make sense of this 'without principle' that Nancy evokes, because it is this lack of principle that makes possible the world as a taking place of 'us'. To this effect Nancy writes:

> it is not a new idea to say that the world is without reason [...] We know quite well that it is found within Angelus Silesius ('the rose grows without reason'), but one does not always notice how it works within all the great formulations of the most classical rationalism.
>
> (ibid.)

By quoting from Silesius' *Cherubinic Wanderer* (1657), Nancy is here just partially disguising a reference to Heidegger's *The Principle of Reason*. Lending an ear to the lack of reason(s) with regard to the world means approaching once more, from a different angle, the question of the sense of the world. This operation also lets the various Heideggerian filiations of a thought on the world emerge more clearly.

More than 300 years ago Leibniz wrote *nihil est sine ratione*, speaking out for the first time in the history of Western thinking the principle of reason, which had, Heidegger says, slept within the inner structure of philosophical thought. As Leibniz repeats in *Principles of Nature and Grace*, the principle of reason identifies the very question of philosophy.

Within modernity, Heidegger says, one finds the unconditional demand for sufficient reasons, perfect cognition as the stretching out of complete rationality. In the thirteen lectures on Leibniz Heidegger aims to shows how the very Reason that was in the process of taking the place left vacant by the Divine principle was already showing its own limit, undoing itself and opening up to the lack of principles.

Heidegger opens the series of lectures by saying 'what the principle says is illuminating. When something is illuminating we understand it without further ado' (Heidegger 1996: 3).

And yet the principle can be read according to (at least) two tonalities. The first one reads the principle as '*nothing* is *without* reason' and addresses exactly the demand for the completeness of a foundation. The principle of reason becomes in the rationalist tradition that which decrees the existence of a being, of what may or may not count as an object of cognition. Therefore, if heard in this way, the principle is a statement about cognition as that which transforms the world into an object. The principle expresses the essence of being human as an 'I that relates to the world such that it renders this world to itself in the form of connections correctly established between its representations' (ibid.: 119).

Heidegger tries to also lend an ear to a second timbre, a second tonality where the principle is read as 'nothing *is* without *reason*'. Here it is the word 'is' that becomes decisive. The principle of reason can in this way be read as a statement on beings and in particular on the Being of beings. However it is thanks to this second tonality that names Being that the former becomes true in the first place. As Heidegger points out: 'as the fundamental principle of rendering sufficient reasons, the principle of reason is thereby true only because a word of being speaks in it that says: being and ground/reason: the same' (ibid.: 125).

If understood in this way, then the principle of reason speaks of the belonging-together of being and reason/ground. Being and ground/reason: the same.

The word *ratio*, though, does not explicitly evoke Being. The belonging together of Being and grounding must therefore be read within the tradition of Western thinking (the *Geschick* of Being, Being's destining) there where ratio translates the Greek *logos*. Thought from within the *Geschick* of Being, the belonging together must then be heard in its Greek formulation: τό αυτό (εἶναι) τε καί λόγος (ibid.: 106).

It is in the word *logos* that the belonging-together emerges more clearly. *Logos* names being because it names what lies present as the ground for everything that lies-present. In Heidegger's words:

> Logos names this belonging-together of being and ground. It names them insofar as it, in one breath, says: 'allowing to lie present as allowing to arise', 'emerging-on-its-own' [...] and 'allowing to lie present as presenting', laying a bed of soil, 'grounds'.
>
> (ibid.: 107)

Logos names being in terms of an *allowing to occur*. Named this way, according to the word logos, being is the ground from which everything arises. This also means though that Being – as that which grounds – remains itself groundless; every foundation would degrade Being to a being. Being is then that which cannot be appropriately founded and thus remains immeasurable. Heidegger calls it the abyss. Being is abyss insofar as being is ground. The leap into which, Heidegger claims, our thinking has stepped with the principle of reason consists in this reconfiguration of the immeasurable nature of Being. Being as the a-byss is then the limit of our thinking; that from whence something commences emerging as what it is. The principle of reason thus stakes on us a demand: to consider the lack of any principle as the only possible principle.

Therefore the second tonality establishes for the first time the possibility to think Being not according to beings (in particular to an ultimate being, *causa sui*), but qua Being: Being as that which cannot be accounted for by another being, not even the highest ultimate cause.

It is at this point that Heidegger introduces a leap: if Being is ground, then it means that Being is not grounded, it is an abyss. Being as abyss therefore does not repose on something present; instead, what Being reposes on is the 'play'. This play is what cannot be properly thought, since our manner of thinking does not allow us to think it. The play cannot be thought thoroughly because our way of thinking provokes us to think it again in terms of ground. If we try we end up reducing it to something present, 'we take the play as something that is' (ibid.: 112).

The play is instead determined as the dynamic of freedom and necessity and is not to be understood in terms of an object for cognition or representation. This play is without a why. It is the active nature of the play itself – its playing – that shrivels away the 'because'. This play is 'the world that worlds and temporalizes, in that, as κόσμος, it brings the jointure of being to a glowing sparkle' (ibid.: 113). The play is αἰών, according to Heraclitus' Fragment 52, 'ever-being' (ἀεί – ὄν), non-appropriable and non-finishable. The mystery 'in which humans are engaged throughout their life, that play in which their essence is at stake' (ibid.).

This play is the world without principle. It is κόσμος not as the fulfillment of complete rationality, but as the singular circulation of sparkles of sense, sense's non-identical movement. The juncture of the world without principle is the rendering of the abyss on to us, the continuous rendering of essence by the singular crossing of existences. 'Us' in a world without principle indicates precisely this: the tuning in with the crossing of essences opened onto an abyss. A world that plays is a world that constantly puts the essence of the human at stake – thus bringing the sense of the human forward always in sparkles of sense, before or in excess of an ultimate meaning. This is the world as the field of existence. As Heidegger writes 'it depends on us, so it is said' (ibid.: 128).

Within the formulation of Leibniz' *Principle of Reason – Nihil est sine ratione* – as the claim for an all-encompassing Rational Ground, Heidegger reads the belonging-together of ground and being. The abyssal character of Being now emerges. Being, which is now not accounted for by an ultimate cause (God), reposes instead on 'play' as the *engagement of essence in the work of undecided existence*: the world not as a rendered reason, but as the venture of existence. Being as abyss discloses being as play, where essence is continuously put at stake. This play is the work of the world, its becoming κόσμος beyond any pre-established order. It depends on us, 'whether and how we, hearing the movements of this play, play along and accommodate ourselves to the play' (ibid.). This play is excess, the world is in excess of itself; its essence is continuously submitted to existence.

What is a world that worlds then? It is a world that has itself as the space of its own principle, this space being constituted as the lack of any principle, as the consistent space where any reference to a beyond falls inside the a-byss, falls then within itself. This is precisely the mystery which Nancy evokes: 'the absolute mystery of spacing itself, according to which there is a "world," from that dis-enclosure that is preceded by no enclosure of Being' (Nancy 2008b: 161). The world has no principle outside its space.

What seems to change in a decisive manner from Leibniz to Heidegger and Nancy is the *eminent* character of the world. In Leibniz, beyond the principle of reason lies a God that *at least* is calculating. In *On the ultimate origination of the universe*, for instance, Leibniz writes: 'the reasons for the world are concealed in some entity outside the world, which is different from the chain or series of things, the aggregate of which constitutes the world' (Leibniz 1977: 86).

In Heidegger's text one finds another decisive leap, triggered by the definition of the principle of reason as that which shows the play of 'the world that worlds' (the world as the rendition of the abyss on to 'us'). In Leibniz the world is still placed within a chain of causality. Leibniz still employs the scholastic term *eminenter*, which stands for a movement through which a cause is more perfect than the effect it produces. When instead cause and effect are of the same nature, we would say that the effect is contained *formaliter* (formally) in the cause. The world, as cause of itself, as its own revolution, is the cause that contains – *formaliter* – its effect.[8] To put it in a different language: 'the world [...] is a fact without reason or end, and it is our fact' (Nancy 2007: 45).

A world that springs from the principle of reason, without a why, growing in excess of the demand of foundations, this is the world of bodies. A world that is configured differently from the world as cosmos – the world the God creator and cause had delivered – but also differently from the world as earth explored and mastered by a conqueror. The latter would in fact be the world of a complete rationality or at least of the possibility of a completion operated by reason, by representations permeated by reason. The world is not the property – 're-presented and presented to the faculty of representation' (Heidegger 2003: 61) – that finds its unity in the mastering subject. The world without principle therefore also requires a disengagement from a '"conquest of space" conceived if not in terms of kosmotheoria, at least in terms of kosmopoiesis, mastery and possession of the universe and thus mastery and possession of its reproduction by and for the subject "man"' (Nancy 1997b: 40).

This world is the world of the density, of the space between bodies; its truth, its very articulation being that of the spacing out of bodies, of their incommensurable distance. This density releases the question of the world as a question of singular sharing: 'sharing singularity means to configure a world, a quantity of possible worlds in the world. This configuration allows the singularities to expose themselves' (Nancy 2007b: 46).

The world as the exposition of singularities, necessity of their being-with. This necessity though always brings with itself a fortuitous quality. It is the movement of singularities at the heart of being-with that informs this necessity and it is the lack of principles announced by necessity's fortuitous character that makes up this world. As Nancy reminds us necessity can too easily be entangled once more into necessary significations (there is a glory proper to necessity). At the opposite there is nothing necessary about this world, its existence happens and could easily not happen at all. The stress should therefore be put on fortuity rather than necessity or contingency, the latter too associated to a promise of harmony and order. In *Adoration* Nancy promotes the discourse of fortuity: 'fortuity responds to discontinuity of singularities and of places – space/time – according to which it makes itself singular' (Nancy 2010: 21). It is to this fortuity that we must adhere, precisely there where no adherence can be guaranteed once and for all, precisely in the absence of ultimate causes and celestial guarantors.

The *with* or the question springing from the Heideggerian *Mitsein* has to be analysed as moving from a space, a space articulated by bodies, by extended beings. The world is the space just described as that which can no longer be addressed, that which no longer has an address. It is in this fashion that the world can be the space that belongs to the ones who inhabit it. One must pay attention to the fact that no other space would be able to resist this formulation. The only space where one can articulate a discussion on 'us', on me *with* you, is this world that allows no discussion on its principle. As Nancy writes:

> the world is not a unity of the objective or external order; a world is never in front of me or else is not my world. But if it is absolutely other, I would not even know, or barely, that it is a world.
>
> (Nancy 2007b: 45)

Singular existence is played out at the taking place of the world, but only inasmuch as the taking place of the world is all a matter of my singular existence.

The extension of the world, which has overcome any possible shape and epitomical city, is the distension towards all the sharing out that our existences are. To put it in other words, the existence of the world is nothing else than the *distance* – the play of the distances – we take from one another. The configuration in which something happens between 'us' finds its articulation in this touch in distance, it is the very *touch of distance*.

To say that the world is worldly amounts to saying that a world makes sense, whilst at the same time the sense of this world circulates, never leaving our borders but also never resting on them, circulating around and among us.

The sense of the world is a sending ('le sens est toujours le sens d'un chemin', writes Derrida in a text devoted to Heidegger [Derrida 1989: 142]) from one side of the world to the other, a sense that, although it never stops traversing the world, lacerating its texture, never falls outside it. This sense is the play of the world that worlds, the truth of the without principle. The principle of reason as read by Heidegger says that one can apprehend the world as that whose sense has no principium, no appropriable beginning and no absolute rendered reason. Instead the sense of the world continuously crosses out the possibilities for its own completion.

We experience the world and our experience is (and not represents or gives) the sense of the world, in that the world is a suppression of any sending out, of any sense residing somewhere else than in the world itself, but it is also a suppression of any resting of sense on a grasped and granted ground. What is worldly about the world is that it is our taking place, not as an otherwise than the world, but rather as that which makes the world what it is, the *promise of sense*.[9]

The trajectory of this reflection leads us to the core of the question, to a triad, to three quotations, one building upon the other and producing a sort of climax, that one is now ready to understand: 'the world is such for those who inhabit it', 'sharing singularity means to configure a world' and 'the world is our fact'.

Outside this configuration, the world is not a world anymore; rather it becomes what Nancy defines as a *glomus*, that is exactly its opposite, the dispersed juxtaposition of beings, a confused solidity. Glomus would here be the exact opposite of the word mundus, which originally stood for the pure. That the world is an ordered system is a definition that dates back to Pythagoras and his school. For our purpose the word 'world' resonates with a much subtler tone, as it means, simply, the age of man, but also this world as opposed to the afterlife.

The very long analysis of the world – touching mainly on Nancy's reformulation of Heideggerian motifs – brings back our initial question, the question that concerns 'us'. Two points should have emerged:

- the world happens as the taking place of a *us*;
- we take place as a being-in-the-world or as a being-world.

Double postscript

The film opens with a peasant (wearing the most traditional straw hat) walking in front of the camera until he comes to occupy the entire frame. Far behind him a reproduction of the Tour Eiffel interrupts the row of skyscrapers filling the horizon.

In the following shot a woman on a train answers her mobile phone: 'I am going to India, has Fenzghuo bought food?' The camera then follows a little train as it passes in front of the Arc de Triomphe and indulges for few seconds on the Pyramids, whilst a voice-over recites: 'See the world without ever leaving Beijing.'

Guards wearing uniform ride their horses, moving quickly from London to Rome and from Notre Dame to Manhattan ('haven't the Twin Towers been destroyed?' says someone, half-astonished, half-indifferent).

The shot of the Eiffel Tower, aligned next to contemporary skyscrapers overlooking a lake in a foggy and sultry morning, recurs for the whole duration of the film, up to the point of becoming its trademark. Title cards appear every now and then: 'Paris in Beijing suburbs', 'Tokyo in Beijing suburbs'.

This is the only way in which one can picture a world without principle (the title of the movie is in fact *The World*[10]). The only way this world lets itself be represented is by repetition, by duplication, by an infinitely extending pleonasm, which can collapse, all of a sudden, whenever a passage appears too brusque (as it is the case with the Twin Towers) or doubles finally encounter their double. Once exposed as this redundant duplication the world represented loses completely and absolutely its sense and is once again abandoned to the absence it comes from.

Cinema as philosophical model

In his extensive and far-reaching analysis of cinema Gilles Deleuze identifies a cinematographic mode he calls the 'cinema of bodies'. As with many other categories Deleuze forges in his reading of cinematographic works, the 'cinema of bodies' answers those philosophical questions that inhabit the heart of cinema (and to which cinema itself does not always answer).

It has already been said that cinema will be treated as a mirror to the philosophical discourse here developed. The link between the two is the question of the world. In the introduction it was said that the world of bodies recalls and demands the same kind of philosophical exploration as the cinema of bodies. This is so not only on the level of the forces constituting it, but also with regard to its coming to presence. As the world essentially happens and happens between us, so cinema 'contributes to free a motion, which is that of a presence in the process of making itself present' (Nancy 2001c: 16).

Cinema takes place at the crossing of this double demand: the world as being without reason – delivered to the exposition of singularities – and always caught in a process of happening by letting free.

According to Deleuze modern cinema re-establishes our belief in the world. This is configured as the belief not in another world, but in this world here, the one in which we live. According to Deleuze 'the cinematographic image showed us the link between the man and the world' (Deleuze 2005: 166). This belief, this speaking with terms that belong to (or appear to strictly emerge from) the realm of faith, may seem in apparent contrast with what has been said earlier on drawing on Nancy and Heidegger. However this belief points to the world as the lack of any principle, the world of the without reason, or what one would have to call the world of bodies. Deleuze adds: 'belief is no longer addressed to a different world or a transformed world. Man is in the world as if in a pure optical and sound situation' (ibid.). Belief can replace knowledge only if it becomes a belief in this world and in this world as it is, since the link between 'us' and the world, or between 'us' and the sense of the world, as a sense that calls forth something beyond this world, has broken. The belief of believers would instead be a belief in a world that precedes or jumps beyond itself, a belief that navigates the rim of the world without really touching on this world. Where believers, when asked about the world of today, claim the need for recovering a lost enchantment, the world's detachment from an ultimate sense, the belief of the non-believers demands that they think of a world 'moving of its own motion, without a heaven or a wrapping, without fixed moorings or suspensions' (Nancy 2001c: 44).

This is the belief that modern cinema gives us: a belief not falling from the sky – cinema speaks also of the silence of God[11] – but arising from the bottom of our bodies, from our feet as it were. This belief, outside any restoration, must be discovered in the spelling of the word 'world' itself. Cinema gives us the world so that we can give it back, so that we can enter its existence and reopen the simultaneous presence–absence of its significations.

Modern cinema presents us with this truth, the collapse of the other world: 'what is certain' – Deleuze says – 'is that believing is no longer believing in another world, or in a transformed world' (Deleuze 2005: 167). It is through the mode of evidence that cinema affirms belief as possible solely in this world or, to be less ambiguous, belief as possible only if addressed to this world that belief itself takes part in. In this way modern cinema opens inside itself the world whose sense is withdrawn and must be recreated, as opposed to a world where sense is always projected.

Deleuze analyses the shift between classical cinema and modern cinema, identifying on the one hand an organic regime of sensory motor images, and on the other a crystalline regime of time images. To put it in other words: classical cinema is kinetic whilst modern cinema is essentially chronic.

It is important to dwell for a whilst on the powers of the false, a term that Deleuze borrows from Nietzsche and that so prominently dominate the crystalline regime. Deleuze starts by tackling three categories: description, narration and storey. A crystalline description detaches itself from an organic one by the relation it initiates with its object. In fact, in crystalline descriptions the object is both created and erased in order to generate series of other descriptions 'which contradict, displace or modify preceding ones' (ibid.: 146). The kind of cinema these descriptions lead to is a 'cinema of the seer', a cinema that the agent is no longer able to dominate; rather, the agent, who necessarily does not possess enough qualities to be called an agent anymore, is plunged in pure optical and sound situations. The abovementioned redefinition of descriptions in the new context of a crystalline regime leads to a number of consequences. Whilst the organic description kept the real recognizable by mean of what Deleuze calls *consistency* and *continuity* – thus expressing functional associations and triggering the localization of relations and the actuality of links between imaginary and reality – the crystalline severs all actual and tangible motor linkages. What one finds in crystalline description is a play between imaginary and real leading to a confusion of roles, to indiscernibility of the two positions. Real connections and localizable relations cease to boast their own domain; instead they propel, are triggered and merge with eminently virtual situations.

The cinematographic image is delivered to both realms, the virtual and the real, and this results in a loss of control over them, their crossing and passing over having been uncertain since the beginning. What one thus ends up with is a constant crossing, a blending, which constitutes the image itself. If one were to analyse modern cinema by trying to trace the moment in which these crossings happen, one would inevitably fail, for the imaginary and the real, the real and the virtual, are in constant opening.[12] As Nancy puts it 'neither a "realist" nor a "fictional" phantasm, but life presented or offered in its evidence' (Nancy 2001c: 58).

This new status brings forth some necessary remarks on a second element constitutive of the two regimes: narration. Organic narration is to Deleuze true and truthful, because time remains necessarily chronological. What Deleuze means by truthful narration is that 'it claims to be true even in fiction' (Deleuze 2005: 123). Narrations proper to the different kinds of organic image develop out of sensory motor schemata to which the agents react in order to identify and intervene in a particular situation. For instance, the two schemas of the action-image Deleuze traces in *Cinema 1*, the small form SAS and its correspondent large form ASA, are both depending on qualities and powers actualized in a concrete and specific space-time. Both structures are delivered over to the reaction to real situations, and that reaction takes the shape of real actions. The structure itself, with its circular shape, implying a movement backwards to its initial point of emergence, already invites a reading on the basis of discrete and concrete actions.

In crystalline narration, on the other hand, sensory motor schemata tend to collapse, leaving no reaction to characters, because characters face pure optical and sound situations. Structures like the ones one finds in the action image cannot possibly take place in the crystalline regime, where the anomalies of movement become essential, substantial and constitutive of the image. Whilst the organic image tended to push the anomalies to the realm of the accidental, binding them to its essential continuity, the crystalline regime revolves around spaces that lack a proper spatial definition. In a similar fashion the world evoked as 'world of bodies' is the place of a taking place, thus a purely spatial definition will not suffice to exhaust its features.

Spaces defined in this way lead to non-localizable relations, which assume the form of direct presentations of time. Hence anomalies, the ab-normal, become the necessary element in the presentation of time, and movements are therefore necessarily false movements. It is interesting to see here what happens to montage as, Deleuze says, 'it becomes a mean to decompose relations in a direct time-image in a way that all the possible movements emerge from it' (ibid.: 126). Within such configuration, narrations do not try to absorb the imaginary and virtual into the real by reducing it to actuality and localization. In fact, quite the opposite happens: whilst in the organic image fiction was true even when pushed as far as possible from real – fiction was as it were fiercely true – here it becomes essentially false, the false being its dominant creative power.

To be more specific one could add that the prevailing quality of narrations now turns out to be their power to establish themselves as essentially false, without losing, as it were, their credibility. Saying that does not amount to saying, Deleuze warns, 'to each fact its own truth', as if it were a matter of estab-lishing a kind of relative system in which acts and facts find their innermost truth and coherence. This is by far a more radical movement, which finds its principle in the play between two poles of the false: 'simultaneous incompos-sible presents' and 'not-necessarily true pasts' (ibid.: 127). Cinema abandons the problem of truth. It moves beyond the problem of truth and untruth, imposing what one could call an existence, a play that moves on the discontinuity between these two poles. As Nancy writes: 'this existence identifies itself as thought and that means that this existence relates to a world: set down, felt, received as a singular point of passage in the circulation of meaning' (Nancy 2001c: 44).

Between cinema and the world one cannot establish a relation of analogy. Cinema does not represent the world; it does function as the world's mirror. In cinema experience is not reduced and then incorporated. Instead the impossibility of capturing it under the regime of truth liberates once more experience's evidence as undecidability.

However, one is not confronting a system of variable content; rather, what is at stake is to determine the false as cinema's productive power. To this effect Deleuze writes: 'the truthful man dies, every model of truth collapses, in favor of the new narration' (Deleuze 2005: 127). There is one far-reaching consequence to this new regime of narrations, which retains its value in the present discussion and has to do with the relational model established by falsified narrations. What is of particular importance here is to stress the fact that the model of freedom touches on the model of identification.

Deleuze writes: 'contrary to the form of the true, which is unifying and tends to the identification of a character [...] the power of the false cannot be separated from an irreducible multiplicity. "I is another" has replaced Ego = Ego' (ibid.: 129). This point skims over the whole question: *what happens between us*. In particular it offers a model to think about 'us'. The false exists only in a set of relations, where mastery over the situation cannot be seized once and for all, but keeps circulating.

Once cinema has entered the mode of existence as opposed to the mode of the truth, then the question is posed to our gaze. Cinema starts pressing against it and demanding that a respect is enacted in our gaze. It impels us to give back the sense of the world that has been opened inside the image. It is then a matter not of receiving the world and its senses but of deciding over the real as given to us by cinema. This decision passes through our way of looking as a way of articulating the evidence of the world. The image under the regime of existence cannot simply be accepted; it must be done again, recreated. Revault d'Allonnes speaks of insignificance and non-evidence of reality as the lack of guaranteed significations: 'modern cinema is seized here by the possible and sudden evidence of sense [...] at the opposite in classic cinema we face a world of assured, established and permanent sense' (Revault d'Allonnes 1994: 18).

Therefore metaphors are avoided, unless those come from within the world itself and only when they express the play, the absence of an ultimate sense.

This evidences set in front of us by cinema correspond to a disclosure of the world. The world is delivered and therefore separated from its character of mere given. Evidence would stand for the fact that the indeterminate totality of the world is presented to us as a sparkle that extinguishes itself. That the world is given and given as a whole would not make sense if it were not for the continuous singular evidence that on one side exposes it and on the other discharges both the world's wholeness (the world's grip on itself) and its givenness (the world's eternal resemblance to itself, or what one could call representation). The absolute referentiality of the world is interrupted so that referentiality keeps happening. Understood in these terms, the being of the world is thus the 'discontinuity of what keeps happening' (Nancy 2001c: 44), wholeness gathered only in indefinite evidences.

According to Deleuze what one now has is this: falsifying narrations free themselves from the system of actual, localized and chronological relations; the elements are constantly changing according to the relations of time into which they enter and the terms of their connections. Narration is constantly being completely modified. We witness the emergence of purely cinematographic powers. The agent dissolves into an 'I as another' structure. My gaze becomes the agent, not only what sees but what participates.

There is something of a doing in my looking, a mobilizing of the world, an agitating and an organising. Adopting a truly Heideggerian tone Nancy remarks that 'presence is not a mere matter of vision: it offers itself in encounters, worries, concerns' (ibid.: 30). Presence is always coming to presence, passage: the technique of exposing and bringing forward reality.

It is because of the active role of my look – which engages with the real, with the image as what carries the real – that Nancy can play on the words *regard* and *égard*, on the coming together of look and regard: 'looking is regarding and consequently respecting'. Nancy notes that 'the word respect also comes from regard (respicere): it is regard towards ... guided by attention, by obser-vance or consideration' (ibid.: 38, translation modified). Our gazes disclose the real without trying to master it. 'Looking just amounts to thinking the real, to test oneself with regard to a meaning one is not mastering' (ibid.), this is what a respect for the real means in a cinema that works under the mode of existence. Inevitably this implies engaging other gazes, becoming intimate with otherness at a distance. 'A common task, that is to say not at all collective, but a task imposed on *us* all *together* [...] to say *us* exactly there where this possibility seems to vanish sometimes into a "one", sometimes into an "I"' (Nancy 2001a: 116). Relationship is the effect produced precisely across this distance.

What remains, Deleuze writes, are bodies, forces without any linkage with/to a centre, forces confronting each other. For Nancy it is a matter of a cinematic metaphysics: 'cinema as the place of meditation, as its body and its area, as the taking-place of a relation' (Nancy 2001c: 44).

Under the mode of existence – differently from the mode of the truth where the character could be judged according to external criteria – every being, and the world itself, has to be judged with regard to the life which it involves, and only with regard to this: a world without principle/reason; sense as a rebound from one end of the world to the other.

The power of the false reestablishes then the belief in the life this world 'here' involves, the life as the taking place of this world.

One finds cinema in a completely new situation, responding to a radically different definition. If previously the fitting definition was 'art of looking made possible and required by a world that refers only to itself and to what is real in it' (ibid.: 18), now cinema becomes 'a matter of life as it happens and passes'. The relation between cinema and the world becomes the sharing of an intimacy crossed by a distance and therefore never absorbed: 'the evidence of cinema is that of the existence of a look through which a world can give back to itself its own real and the truth of its enigma' (ibid.).

Deleuze too describes this proximity in distance: 'there is a point of view which belongs so much to the thing that the thing is constantly being transformed in a becoming identical to point of view' (Deleuze 2005: 142). The point of view – in Deleuze's lexicon – or the look/gaze – in that of Nancy – are always working in this proximate distance, whose measure is the passing of an existence. This distance, as it will be articulated more clearly in the following pages, is exactly what allows not just the relation between cinema and the world to rest entirely on the real (which is therefore not alienated but confirmed and reopened in images), but also the relations within the cinematographic image – almost inside, in the silver nitrate – to take the real into account as his ultimate horizon: 'the reality of images is the access to the real itself, with the consistence and resistance of death, life' (Nancy 2001c: 16). This does not amount to attributing to cinema a constructive relation to the world, as if what is real is real just because the camera poses its gaze on it or makes it a particular point of view in a series; quite the opposite, this indicates that the existences variously produced in and by cinema identify themselves always in relation to the world taken as a point traversed by sense. Right distance: cinema engaging itself with a world whose evidences never surmount those of cinema.

The power of the false, as traced by Deleuze is exactly this: it is not a matter of truth anymore, but of existence. It is not just about images and the laws of their accordance. It is about images 'as opening onto what is real and insofar as they alone open onto it' (ibid.) and this opening goes all the way into the givenness of the world.

There is still a last point in this reconstruction of the Deleuzian argument in which one inevitably is to find the world: the storey.

The storey concerns the subject–object relationship and the development of this relationship. The new kind of storey no longer refers to an ideal of the true, which constitutes its veracity, but becomes a storey that simulates, or rather a simulation of the storey: objective and subjective images lose their distinction, but also any possibility of identification is abandoned, substituted by a new circuit where they contaminate each other.

The shift is not as much between fiction and reality as in the storey itself, because the storey affects both: 'what cinema must grasp is not the identity of a character, but his objective and subjective aspects. The real character when starts making fiction' (Deleuze 2005: 145).

This is the ground on which cinema poses questions to thought, or better where cinema starts enacting questions that have thought, thinking, as their primary references.

The question of thought, Deleuze says, concerns cinema as long as the image no longer follows the rule of the sensory motor schemata. When the sensory-motor break appears, cinema is then able to reveal a link between man and the world. This is the moment where the belief in the world – that particular kind of belief I have mentioned few pages earlier – draws the limit. Cinema, as seen in crystalline narrations, gives up metaphors and metonymies, 'because the necessity which belongs to relations of thought in the image has replaced the contiguity of relations of images' (ibid.: 146). The reconfiguration from organic images to crystalline ones, then, is such that cinema not only ceases to be true, but leads to a limit, that which, by mean of a traversing, marks a surfacing. This limit is structured on two main points, on two ends, and imposes a thinking that moves from leftovers. As Nancy puts it:

> Cinema stretches and hangs between a world in which representation was in charge of the signs of truth or of the warrant of a presence to come and another world that opens onto its own presence through a voiding where its thoughtful evidence realises itself.
>
> (Nancy 2001c: 56)

What remains is: on one side, a belief in the world, a belief nevertheless entirely immersed in this world, as a point of view on itself, an immanent belief; on the other side this belief is articulated by bodies, forces, whose most proper quality is their being relational.

Contrapuntal close-ups

Deleuze defines the cinema of bodies as that cinema where characters are fundamentally reduced to their bodily attitudes and the plot is undone in favor of those attitudes. Deleuze identifies in John Cassavetes the author that more than any other draws the limit, which means the emergence, of such a cinema. To this effect Deleuze writes: 'the greatness of Cassavetes' work is to have undone the storey, plot, or action, but also space, in order to get to attitudes as to categories which put time into the body, as well as thought into life' (Deleuze 2005: 185).

In fact the cinema of Cassavetes responds to a precise concern. By no means was it accidental that he was to develop a cinema of bodies. Speaking about *Faces* (1968) in *Cahiers du Cinéma*, Jean Comolli develops the definition of 'alcoholic form':

> Characters define themselves gesture by gesture and word by word as the film proceeds. They are self-creating, the shooting is the means whereby they are revealed, each step forward in the film allowing them a new development in their behaviour, their time span coinciding exactly with that of the film.
>
> (Pierre and Comolli 1986: 327)

When Cassavetes says 'when you cease to know the way home, things go wrong. And then you get detoured. And when you can't find your way home, that's when I consider it's worth it to make a film' (Carney 2001: 161), he is putting forward the entire program underlining most of his mature works. In Cassavetes' films actors are persons and are judged as such. In the same interview with Carney, Cassavetes says 'a person in our picture is judged more as a person than as a performer – from the point of view that they have to add something as people' and adds 'the mistakes that you make in your own life, in your own personality, are assets on the film' (ibid.: 166). This is something that Deleuze had not failed to understand, as when he says that Cassavetes' originality lies in having addressed the question of film as

> interesting oneself in people rather than in the film, in the 'human problems' more than in the 'problems of the mise-en-scène'; so that people do not pass over to the side of the camera without the camera having passed to the side of the people.
>
> (Deleuze 2005: 149)

Deleuze understood that Cassavetes was one of those directors walking within the distance that brings the cinematographic image to the point where what is at stake is not fiction or reality, but rather their continuous crossing (a sort of double-crossing).

Deleuze seems to pay a debt to the long-sighted analysis published by Comolli just after the first European screening of *Faces* in Cannes: 'Cassavetes does not use cinema as a way of reproducing actions, faces or ideas, but as a way of *producing* them [...] We start from scratch, the cinema is the motor and the film is what causes event to happen (Pierre and Comolli 1986: 326).

What Cassavetes strove for was a cinema that could tackle the 'right distance', taking the risk to approach the image not as a given, but as the outcome of the interruption of lives and contacts. Deleuze realised that Cassavetes' imagination as a filmmaker pointed at creating an 'indirect discourse operating in reality', pushing further the powers of the false. The philosopher saw that the director was concerned with getting to people, to others (or even, in a formula, probably not far from Deleuze's lexicon: getting to people as the other of cinema, although this other is not, in any way, beyond cinema, but rather its very evidence).

It is possible to list two ways in which Cassavetes – whose directorial style was forged around a feeble presence behind the camera, balanced by a strong presence on the stage – accomplished his plan to make movies on people who cease to know their way home.

The first one rests on the analysis that Deleuze devoted to him and to the cinema of bodies. The second might be interpreted as an exacerbation of the set of gestures identified by Deleuze in relation to the cinematographic device of the close-up.

With Deleuze one could say that Cassavetes maintained his promises by interpreting cinema mainly as a cinema of body. Cassavetes would approach the cinematic by undoing the plot and exposing characters to the experience of the camera. This means that characters do not present themselves through the internal consistency implicit in or delivered by the plot; quite the opposite, they come to the screen by opposing themselves to that coherence. Characters are constraints, barriers placed in front of the camera, turning the camera movements upside down, or even moving the camera in an uneven way (most of Cassavetes movies were shot with handheld cameras).

The confusion a movie like *Faces* creates depends exactly on this. The character must struggle with the storey and with the presence of the camera to get there, to see his birth on the screen. Once dialogues and situations migrate from the script to the screen, what takes place is an operation of undoing, as if the script were banging into bodies, literally failing to flow. The script is open enough so that the bodies can twist it. Among other examples, one could mention Gus's love night in *Husbands* (1970), where the two bodies engage in repeated sequences of twists and re-positioning, as a consequence of which the hotel room they are occupying seems at times to enlarge and at other to compress. In *A Woman Under the Influence* (1975) the scene where Mabel confronts the doctor and her husband Nick shows the erratic and frantic movements of the woman turning a familiar setting – the living room of the house – into an uncharted space.

As Comolli says, with Cassavetes one always starts with nothing, that is to say that one starts with a complex set of exposures, but with no time and no spaces, with characters with no inner experience; one has bodies exposing one another: 'cinema of bodies: the character is reduced to his own bodily attitudes' (Deleuze 2005: 185).

With regard to the second strategy the point to be made here relates to how the presences on the cinematic screen trigger a particular kind of relation. Once more one needs to restate that initial remark: Cassavetes' aim was to make movies on people, on people who cease to find their way home (it would take another kind of reflection to show how this happens). Cinema of bodies then, but also a cinema that should engage with 'us'.

Although Deleuze spends a considerable amount of pages on Cassavetes, there's no mention of the American director in the study of the close-up. For the sake of clarity, here one needs to quickly revisit this analysis. Deleuze, quoting Eisentein, defines the close-up as 'the face'. The face acts on two poles, as reflecting surface/quality and intensive series/power; although the two poles do not occur by closing one another out, preventing the other from appearing, they always realise themselves by letting open a possibility. The criterion of distinction revolves around the following point: 'we find ourselves before an intensive face each time that the traits break free from the outline, begin to work on their own account and form an autonomous series which tends toward a limit', on the contrary 'we are before a reflexive or reflecting surface as long as the features remain grouped under the domination of a though which is fixed or terrible, but immutable and without becoming, in a way eternal' (ibid.: 91–2).

Deleuze's concept of 'the face' does not apply solely to the human visage, but to any image that could be said to occupy these two poles: 'each time we discover these two poles in something [...] we can say that this thing has been treated as a face' (ibid.: 90). Opposing the idea of the close-up as the upsurge of the partial object, Deleuze turns to Balász to say that the close-up 'abstracts it [an object] from all its spatial–temporal co-ordinates. That is to say, it raises it to the state of an Entity' (ibid.: 98). What is more, the close-up allows us to abandon the three ordinary roles of the face: individuating, socializing and communicating. 'The close-up has merely pushed the face to those areas where the principle of identification ceases to hold sway […] The close-up suspends individuation' (ibid.: 102). In Deleuze's opinion it is Bergman that has pushed this suspension, this nihilism, of the face to a limit.

Cassavetes operates a very different gesture with regard to the close up. Whilst he does erase the face (or objects standing for it) he does so not simply to prevent identification, rather to add a condition, a co-essential condition to it: the face is offered always as co-belonging.

Faces in particular is a film where the close-up is used to the point of violence, that is to say to the point where it violates the smooth flowing of the film. In fact there is nothing smooth about *Faces*; rather, the apparent simplicity of the plot is continuously interrupted and then proceeds not from but in the interruptions themselves. Exactly by interrupting the plot, the close-ups establish almost a register that precedes the storey. Whilst the film depicts a rather stiff social situation, characterised by individualism, the social constraints of marriage and a rather well-known collection of middle-age middle-class repressive norms, self-deceptions and betrayals, what is liberated in the series of successive close-ups is a distance that sends for a different model of being-with.

A first set of succinct remarks is needed to open the way for the discussion:

- like Bergman, Cassavetes operates an erasure of the face. He does so in that, surpassing the face as entity, surpassing the poles of quality/powers, he places the face there where it shouldn't be: there where everything else is expected, where all the others should be, all that which takes place off the frame. Saying that amounts not to affirming the face as a bearer, an icon, as if it were a sort of visual synopsis, a herald or promise, but exactly to taking it as that which testifies for the dispersion of the evidence, that which goes as far as saying: there's no movie here, this is not fiction but rather the dispersed presence of a reality which a look agitates. *Faces* is a film of dispersed (and agitated) presences, which, perversely, find their peak of dispersion in the play of close-ups. The close-up is constantly trapped in this leap towards an outside of itself as if it were there to declare its impossibility, the impossibility of recollecting in itself any meaningful statement.

- The faces in *Faces* do not just suspend individuation. This suspension triggers the circulation of sense within the film: the sense of the film as situations rendered by a sending toward, rather than by a meaningful closure; the sense of the film as materiality on and through which looks encounter one another. In other words, *Faces* is a film where no one is allowed to stay alone; conditions, locations and positions open into absences and at the same time these absences make the happening of relations most evident. Close-ups link one presence to another; they do not lead anywhere as they are there to underline the importance of what the spectators cannot see, the distance required by relation. Close-ups show what is beyond their reach; they carry this beyond in and carry away what falls inside the frame.
- Cassavetes managed to put in the close-up the openness of a long shot by accumulating one close-up after the other. Once the face appears, it appears as the excluded and the intruder at the same time. Close-ups serve to allow the characters to stay together and to prevent one character from standing out, from being singled out. Therefore what is at stake in Cassavetes' use of close–ups is the impossibility of affirming the face, as this always come as the presence of what lies outside the frame.
- Cassavetes' close-ups work towards establishing a mode of relation without relation, a model where what is at stake is a coming of the relation without this having to be announced. The relationship here is realised in the action and is not then the substratum that channels, motivates and directs the action. In this also resides the great vulnerability of the faces of the film. The measure of this relation is itself incommensurable.

Pan-orama and dis-tance

At the very beginning of *The Evidence of Film* Jean-Luc Nancy writes: 'capturing images is clearly an ethos, a disposition and a conduct with regard to the world' (Nancy 2001c: 16). It is interesting to see here how the relation ethos/world comes back. What is Nancy expressing here? The capturing of images exposes the world's standing on itself and opens our standing in it. Capturing images is a way of exposing the world and a way in which the world exposes itself.

Cassavetes' use of the close-up manifests an ethos, a particular disposition and conduct. The close-up is not just a device thanks to which the director arranges the internal structure of his work; rather, it becomes an offering oneself to the world, a particular way of happening in the world and of the world going *through* the image. Here the close-up becomes the way to make remarkable the world in its evidence and to open the world to itself.

Cassavetes' *habitus* revolves around an attempt to provoke us, shaking the ground that binds 'us' together, exposing the actors to our looks. What the director demands on our part is to abandon both an all-encompassing gaze (objects of the film are signified regardless to their singularity) and an absorbed one (the objects of the film replace reality by providing an overarching vision of it). Not then to direct our attention to a *panoramic* perspective, but to remark our distance from the film and a respect of the distances within the film.

As the word indicates, panorama, from the Greek πάν – ὁράω, means to see everything, or better said, to strive in order for everything to become visible, apparent, for everything to surface and occupy a place in front of us.

The concept of pan-orama should here work on two levels. On one side the panorama is what allows us to gain an overview, a general gathering in front of our eyes, a gathering where presence melts into a plurality that forecloses any singularity appearing and anything appearing as singularity. This is panorama as whole, totality. One the other side the panorama also gives to the eye the opportunity of seeing not the whole, but each and every thing, every tiny detail. In this scenario things come from an infinite distance and one descends into them apprehending their porosity, grasping their granular, corpuscular texture. Things become permeated by our sight.

It is interesting to note how in *Faces* no character is devoted enough space so as to be *alone*, to transform into *the* character. The shot-reverse shot composition, which would wrench the individual out of the context, is almost abandoned. At the same time one never has the impression of receiving a general overview, or a visual synopsis, whilst the film remains nonetheless an extremely choral composition. Bonitzer is right when he notes that the camera in Cassavetes accompanies a 'system of crises' (Bonitzer 1985: 8).

Cassavetes aims to play in between the uprising of the main character, a detail that one is forced to take as everything, whilst escaping at the same time the possibility to present everything inside the frame. Cassavetes interrupts Bazin's classification, since he is neither a director who believes solely in the image, nor a director who simply documents reality. Rather, his gesture is something like a play with distances.

As Raymond Carney stresses: 'Cassavetes works to resist the individual effort to isolate himself' (Carney 1985: 98) and also, one could add, to prevent the individual performer from elevating himself above the in-common into which he is immersed. So much of the personal point of view is privileged that we almost forget that there are *others*. However the result is the opposite of what one expects: the individual is not allocated enough space and enough time to control the visual area, to wrap the frame around himself. As Carney notes the character 'is everywhere put back into a series of relationships' (ibid.). One could therefore say that *Faces* starts with us. The being-in-common, our being *us*, is never given; rather, it is something that takes place beyond any construction and takes place in this world here as that set whose holding together constantly reframes its given significations. Characters do not put themselves to work to reach as it were a kind of communality; quite the opposite, the picture is almost always about disintegration, it shatters its own solidity, it is not an oeuvre; it holds nothing of a per-forming.

Cassavetes starts with 'us' by orchestrating the close-ups mainly in a contrapuntal way. As cinema lacks a similar concept, one has to borrow it from music: close-ups are independent but harmonically related. They are independent in that they appear not as intimately chained to the series they – at least because of a temporal succession – belong to, but as always interdependent; they are not there to identify anything or to underline one's role, gesture, words, *face*, but to introduce another close-up that will generate a different movement, focus on a different articulation. Cassavetes seems to try to reply to the demand to "say 'us' otherwise than as 'one' and otherwise than as 'I'" (Nancy 2001a: 116).

Carney notes this as well: 'Cassavetes intercuts and edits together close-ups of over forty interrelated glances, responses and adjustments of position' (Carney 1985: 99) and this works as a constant reminder of simultaneous presences. In this way Cassavetes starts with 'us', 'us' becoming almost a white noise, which never falls into complete silence.

By means of contrapuntal close-ups, Cassavetes is able to oppose to the double signification of the pan-orama, a play of distance, or more properly a dis-stance. He never allows us to see the whole, or every detail, of a given situation. He plays in between these two categories of the panorama. Distance written as dis-stance (in which also resonates this-stance) should be thought here as that standing, posture, taking place, which is also a habitus, an ethos towards something or someone, which by means of the prefix *dis* indicates a movement outside, a difference that is constitutive of one's own place. Dis-stance works here as the impossibility of closing oneself from others by pushing them at an irreducible distance. Every distance is always a happening outside, towards, an occupying a place by trembling. Distance as self-standing passes and traverses every other self-standing, since the beginning, even before the film starts, but in particular in the span of time in which the film, rather than separating us from reality – constantly delivers us back to the world. Distance is impossible if not as an approach, not out of an intentional humanitarianism, but as that gesture which I cannot, by any means, completely limit.

Cassavetes' contrapuntal close-ups and all the faces of *Faces* bring fore this evidence of distance as a dis-stancing, a bringing towards, a going out, the irreducibility of a being-with. Distance is here the opening of my stance to the other; my stance is always already a standing out, something I cannot fully appropriate nor withdraw within. I am always already delivered to this opening, which is also the taking place of the sense of the world, the sense of the world as the singular difference of a passage, or as Nancy puts it in his discussion of the multiplicity of the arts:

> the sense of the world is only given by dis-locating at the origin its unique and unitary sense of 'sense' in the general zoning that is sought in each of the many differential distributions of the senses [...] There would be no world if there were no discreteness.
>
> (Nancy 1996: 19)

Cinema can then say something about *what happens between us* because the world and cinema do not stand in an analogical or mimetic relation. The world on the screen is still the world. Although things are not available for use, nonetheless their evidence sizes the circulation of sense. Nothing is manifested on the screen if not the sheer existence of the world, its being 'remarkable'.

Cinema shows a discontinuity in the world and this discontinuity opens up a place for 'us': we are at the crossing between the indistinct world and the evidence delivered by cinema.

The world in cinema becomes remarkable: it becomes the 'disclosure of a look in the middle of ordinary turbulence' (Nancy 2001c: 22). This turbulence is the movement of the everyday, the Heideggerian *Bewegtheit*. On one side the world on the screen holds on us the same obvious grasp as in the everyday; on the other the fact of it being placed at a distance – made evident – submits it to the unseen, as that which needs to be marked once more. Its sheer existence is once again weighted down by sense.

Cinema does not support the signification of the world; instead it shows the obvious fact of the world, that is also the *not-yet-signified*. Within this obviousness the abyssal sense of the world becomes evidence. Obviousness and abyss indicate the fact that the world is common, sharing itself in constantly creating itself as world.

That a model of truth is replaced by one of existences shows a world whose sense constantly reopens its references (its 'sense') and is sustained on possibilities to be realised, meanings to be taken up, discontinuities not yet sublimated.

On the screen the reality of a world without principle is mobilised, which also means that it necessarily calls us to engage in what is there delivered. Cinema does not seal the sense of the world by drawing world-pictures, nor does it replace the world with pure appearances, the play of fantasies. The world exposed by cinema is one in which the absolute accountability of sense is continuously handed over to 'us' to be readdressed. It is in this way that cinema precisely constitutes the crossing of the question of the world and the question of 'us'. Cinema makes evident a constellation where the world is a set of relations in constant disclosure; this disclosure is operated in the distance 'us' as being-with takes from its inscription in a closed horizon of sense. As Nancy puts it:

> the common, having-in-common or being-in-common, excludes interior unity, subsistence, and presence in and for itself. Being with, being together […] are precisely not a matter of being 'one'.
>
> (Nancy 2001: 154)

The opposite of this is what a world-view would entail or promise: sociality finally assured once and for all, grounded around a tension that makes sense unavailable. The reference in this case would not be to our happening together, but to the transformation of the togetherness in the essence of what has always happened. This means that 'us', instead of existing on the register of deliverance across otherness (what has been here called its 'happening'), is returned to the register of an autonomic charisma, where everything is immanent and within which everything is already resolved. This scenario founds itself on the same structure and proceeds in the same way as the juxtaposition of the crowd, where the dispersion is not a singular exposure of sense, but the collapse of sense by disengagement. The world remains the task and the responsibility of 'us', as long as 'us' always opens its own presence and makes it remarkable. 'Sense is the singularity of all the singular ones, in all senses simultaneously […] the sense of the world is thus in each one as totality and unicity at once' (Nancy 1997b: 68).

'Us' happens only in the world as long as it does not close the world within a natural intimacy. Cinema unlocks this intimacy by showing and ex-scribing the uncertainty of what we have always already seen, between us.

Separations

Dialogues and disputations

At the end of the last chapter the question 'What happens between us?' found articulation in the discussion of the concept of the world, once this is freed from its reliance on an external substance.

It has been argued that a deconstruction of the onto-theological tradition positing the world as dependent on a substance or essence external to it would allow for the first time the appearance of the world as *that which exists*. The process described made it possible to trace the emergence of the world as that which is always at stake in our Western tradition, though hidden under the determinations of a substance. A related movement highlighted the idea that a certain conception of God was to identify God itself with the notion of the world. This could happen by way of a shift that became increasingly evident (though it is not simply a matter of chronological development here) at the beginning of the rationalist tradition, in particular with those thinkers – Bruno, Spinoza and Leibniz – who hold God as an intelligent principle rather than as a creator, Demiurge or architect. The account of this deconstructing process reopened the question of the *creatio ex-nihilo*.

The analysis of the world then has been considered as a step in view of a more detailed analysis of the question 'what happens between us' and of its various figures. If it has been argued that 'we are the world' it is now time to engage with the measure of this world, namely with 'we' and 'us' and 'with'.

It has been argued that Nancy and Levinas do not occupy completely distinct poles with regards to the argument on the body, if only because they both attribute great importance to it whilst coming to discuss ideas of otherness. Both thinkers read the body as opening of the singular moment of existence.

The body signals the arising of singularity and simultaneously illuminates the horizon of sharing and otherness.

However it should be repeated that they tackle the question of the body for almost opposite reasons: in Nancy's case the body opens up the question of Christianity and forces Heidegger's silence to speak, breaking through both the self-deconstruction of Christianity and Heidegger's elusion of certain elements of existence. On the other hand Levinas writes under the impulse of freeing philosophy from Heidegger's geopolitical strategies and pagan tones. Levinas adopts the notion of position as early as *Existence and Existents* in order to make room for separation, living from… and the emergence of responsibility from the anonymity of existence.

The three elements that will be considered here as separating Nancy and Levinas are:

- the idea of the world;
- the syntax used to identify the relationship with the other;
- the notion of an element beyond the terms of this relationship.

The pattern encompassing the following line of reasoning relies on one constituent motif: the breaches that Nancy and Levinas engage with are possible within a Heideggerian perspective. It is within Heidegger, which also means in his absence, within his *unthought*, that one can meaningfully join the two sides and follow them through thoughtful dialogues and acrimonious disputations.[1]

One should obviously not forget that this same rule is, in the end, a Heideggerian formulation:

> what is unthought in a thinker's thought is not a lack inherent in his thought. What is un-thought is there in each case only as the un-thought. The more original the thinking, the richer will be what is unthought in it. The unthought is the greatest gift that thinking can bestow.
>
> (Heidegger 1968: 77)

Accordingly, the following discussion is not meant to determine only the resonances between Nancy's and Levinas' thinking, but should also provide insights as to the originality of Heideggerian thought. The movement of thinking in this case should be grounded on absence and the methodology must be that of clarity for 'one thing is necessary for a face-to-face converse with the thinkers: clarity about the manner in which we encounter them' (ibid.).

We are the world

It has been said that Nancy follows Heidegger rather faithfully in understanding the disclosure of the world and the world's mundane character as the very springing forth of the question 'What happens between us?' This question does not hold on to anything but the world as world, as a system of relations or references, into which we are always and already immersed. It has been repeatedly emphasised that this 'always already' should not trigger the idea of the world as a Pascalian *cachot*; quite the opposite, it composes the very plane where sense, in particular the sense of the world itself, can be and can remain open.

The opening towards others is then an event taking place not as much 'in' the world as that inside which would then be in correlation to an outside, but *as* the world. The fact that singularities open towards each other is the fact of the world and is our fact. The dependence of this constellation on the structure of the Heideggerian Being-in-the-world and in particular on the care Heidegger takes in defining the 'in' not on strictly spatial grounds has already been determined. The world is not a container, but rather the place of a specific kind of transcendence, which constantly has in view a reopening of existence beyond acquired significations. The world – as it has emerged from a deconstruction of metaphysics, or, to give the term a more precise connotation, the deconstruction of Western onto-theology – is stripped bare of any principle that would not in the end return to the world itself, to the transcendence of the world towards itself. Sense, as long as one shows it to be that which does not rest on determined significations, beyond unity or oneness, takes place as world. Following Heidegger, Nancy states that 'we have already come into sense because we are already in the world; we are in the world because we are in sense. One opens the other' (Nancy 2003: 11).

In Nancy's view the idea of an outside of the world is conceivable only if one again refers this outside to the world, the outside as the differential character immanent to the world. It is not that the world so conceived holds a secret that one can disclose or reveal or occasion the unraveling of its very secrecy. As Nancy writes, 'the whole of being is its own reason; it has no other reason, which does not mean that it itself is its own principle and end, exactly because it is not "itself"' (Nancy 2000: 86). The outside is always already this differential trait, wherein the world cannot conceive of itself as identical, dignified or vilified by the acquisition of a meaning. As long as the world is the plane of this disclosure, then it is that which lacks a principle; it neither refers to a beyond nor signals or points towards it.

The world is neither the '*creatum*' nor the evidence or manifestation of an '*ens perfectissimum*' but that which holds itself as its own difference. To say that the world is a difference, to say that its structure involves a pulsation, implies also that one is at times able to envisage this difference. One could refer to these moments when the difference shows itself – which means that the difference has already moved the world somewhere else – as the irreparable. This notion in this case indicates that the world is never simply ready-at-hand or a given: it is that which remains constantly different from itself. As Giorgio Agamben writes: 'at the point where you perceive the irreparability of the world, at that point it is transcendent' (Agamben 1993: 105).

The world then does not simply *contain* the references that compose the correspondence between its surface and its depths; rather these references form an outside that is nonetheless never beyond the world itself. The world is then that relational totality (but never closed, never complete, never entire) from which one starts all the relational work. Every decision thus takes place as an opening of the world; every sense makes sense as a migration from the world back to the world. If the notion of a multiplicity of worlds would not be already overloaded, one could say that sense is that which goes from one world to another, though never reaching for an elsewhere to this world here.

The analysis of the ready-at-hand, which marks the first steps of *Being and Time*, emphasises that the relational characteristic of the world is what is – at each and any time – at stake. Saying that amounts to expressing the fact that the world is not the outside of an inside, the outside of God or the outside of subjectivity, the externalization of an intimacy. It might still be right to say that the world is an expression, provided that one pays attention to term *expression*. Expression means seeking the *ex*, seeking the movement towards an outside. The world is the expression in its most productive meaning: an *ex* that is at any time gambling with itself. It would be a mistake then to reduce it to a pure juxtaposition of beings, which find themselves chained to one another. Relation must mean something else because Being-in-the-world defines not a bare proximity, but the event of disclosing this proximity, of opening up the sense of this proximity and sense as the possibility of proximity. Heidegger always thinks of the world in terms of involvement (the discussion of the ready-to-hand as opposed to the metaphysical present-at-hand could already bear witness to this). Heidegger's concept of world does not merely give priority to subjective projections; it constitutes the ontological underpinning of every mode of engagement with things, including theoretical encounters. The world is then defined by significance and involvement, a connection that is at times only implicit and at others unequivocal in Heidegger's text:

the context of assignments or references, which, as significance, is constitutive for worldhood, can be taken formally in the sense of a system of Relations [...] the phenomenal content of these 'Relations' and 'Relata' is such that they resist any sort of mathematical functionalization; nor are they merely something thought, first posited in an 'act of thinking'.

(Heidegger 1962: 121)

Before moving forward with the discussion it is necessary to pay attention to the first point announced in the introductory remarks: what can develop from within Heidegger's notion of Being-in-the-world? This question somehow demands to return Levinas to Heidegger, to read as it were Levinas from within Heidegger's thinking. This does not amount to reducing Levinas to a plain reformulation of Heidegger. Levinas himself remarked more than once his debt to Heidegger, although this was always counterbalanced by an 'irreversible abomination'. Heidegger's abomination animates long passages in many of Levinas texts. The very development of Levinas' philosophy could be said to maintain throughout a link to the question of impossible forgiveness. As he writes in a Talmudic commentary: 'if Hanina could not forgive the just and humane Rab because he was also the brilliant Rab, it is even less possible to forgive Heidegger' (Levinas 1994: 25). In a lecture delivered in 1987 Levinas stated once more his 'admiration inspired by a philosophical intelligence among the greatest and the irreversible abomination attached to National Socialism, in which that brilliant man was somehow able to take part' (Levinas 2006a: 179). A number of commentators have been reassessing the extent of this ambiguous debt. Peter Gordon writes that

to argue for an enduring continuity between Heidegger and Levinas is not to condemn Levinas. It is, quite simply, to challenge the notion that Levinas is capable of effecting this separation without recourse to the very philosophy he opposed.

(Gordon 2008: 203)

Whilst explicit contentions with Heidegger are more evident in Levinas' preparatory texts (mainly in *On Escape* and *Existence and Existents)* than in his mature works, Heidegger's influence never really ceases to play a role in Levinas' thinking. As Manning puts it, 'Levinas' own philosophy is both a heavy borrowing from Heidegger's philosophy and also a constant argument against it' (Manning 1993: 29). Jacques Rolland, in his introduction to *On Escape*, is even more explicit in pointing out that

what is taken over from Heidegger without contestation is a certain comprehension of philosophy, by virtue of which one problem will be considered as

philosophical par excellence in as much as it confronts us with the ancient problem of being qua being.

(Levinas 2003b: 6)

A matter of hyphens

In *Being and Time* Heidegger explains that the 'compound expression "Being-in-the-world" indicates that it stands for a unitary phenomenon' (Heidegger 1962: 78). To such questioning of the world Levinas opposes a completely different trajectory:

> in contradistinction to the philosophers of existence we will not found the relation with the existent respected in its being [...] on being in the world, the care and doing [...] Doing, labour, already implies the relation with the transcendent.[2]
>
> (Levinas 2005: 109)

Levinas omits the hyphens and speaks of philosophers of existence, but here he is explicitly arguing with Heidegger. Being in the world offers yet another thematic understanding of the Other, one that forecloses the access to Infinity; the thematization always seems to bring with itself a closure that cancels the Other out. Levinas thus proposes an approach, which he names metaphysical relation, that avoids linking up a subject with an object. Husserl and Heidegger are coupled here in the accusation of having mistaken the relationship to the Other in the world as that of an object facing a subject. Levinas argues that the world is already a way of confining the Other within the Same. It is then a matter of seeing how this confinement takes place and what kind of reading allows Levinas to impeach Heidegger with the above-mentioned accusation.

Levinas writes in *Existence and Existents* that 'existence is not synonymous with the relationship with a world; it is antecedent to the world' (Levinas 2003a: 8). Levinas' concern here calls attention to a kind of involvement with the world that translates in attachment to things. For Levinas this would be opposed to separation and purity, 'absence from the immediacy of possessing [...] Judaism as an irreducible modality of being present to the world' (Levinas 1994: 153). The problem here lies therefore in the kind of involvement with the world. Levinas seems to always take attachment as the mastering or cognitive recognition (thematization or substantiation), the panoramic apprehension of every fold of the world. This preoccupation returns in a number of texts. Whether he addresses it as the attachment of the other to things ('in the world the other is [...] never separated from things' [Levinas 2003a: 30]) or as the other's apprehension as object ('in the world the other is an object already' [ibid.: 31]) or affirms that 'it is one thing to ask what the place of the world in the ontological adventure, and another thing to look for that adventure within the world itself' (ibid.: 35), these remarks contain the same implicit concern: in the world, including the Heideggerian formulation of the concept, the Other is absorbed within the Same.

However when Levinas announces 'we will not found the relation with the existent respected in its being […] on being in the world' (Levinas 2005: 109) he removes the hyphens from Heidegger's compound expression and this gesture seems to bear important consequences. By lifting the hyphen and translating Being-in-the-world for *being in the world*, Levinas loses that which is most dear to Heidegger, namely the definition of Being-in-the-world as an existential. By way of this erasure Levinas disperses the existential dimension and reduces the Heideggerian expression to its constitutive pieces. One should be careful in undertaking such operation, as it seems that the consistency and novelty of the *Sein-in* is lost as soon as the tightness between its constitutive terms is loosened. Without the hyphens one is left more or less with the denotations of 'in' and 'world' that Heidegger sets out to refuse. Once the terms of the expression are made independent, the tone changes: they no longer collaborate but tend to withdraw, moving back towards the accepted meaning of 'in', a container, and 'world', a given that contains. Some splendid pages are devoted to food, enjoyment and dwelling in Levinas, but they all take their cues from the removal of the hyphens, so that the reflection on the 'in' as a *having that has the character of a being*, the in as *ethos*, fades out. The expression 'being in the world' does not do justice to the Heideggerian effort. It is true that Heidegger as well starts with separated terms, for the analyses of 'in', as derived from *innan, habitare, diligere*, and of the 'world' as existential must first be set free from their traditional (in the literal sense of the term, as referring to a thinking tradition) meaning. Nevertheless, as the analysis advances the two terms cannot be pronounced separately any longer, for this would mean delivering them back to the tradition, thus stripping them of their fecundity.

It would then be necessary for Levinas to reformulate the two terms 'in' and 'world'. Separating the terms in the compound expression Being-in-the-world, thereby returning them to their substantial position after they have been carefully composed, does not suffice to silence their articulation, as if by tearing them apart one were triggering an elastic movement which then binds them together with more strength. As Alweiss writes, 'the hyphens between the words being-in-the-world are crucial for they emphasise Dasein's dis-location: this essential interdependency between Dasein and the world' (Alweiss 2003: 79).

Levinas, in short, seems to rely on a definition of the world that Heidegger explicitly refuses. A great deal of the claims Levinas advances relies on the definition of the world as the totality of entities that can be present-at-hand within the world. This is the idea of the world that has prevented, according to Heidegger, the world from becoming an element for philosophical discourse. The notion of the world as a totality present-at-hand, or as the given, prevents us from unveiling the world. If the world has never entered philosophical discourse, covered as it was by the corrective definition of totality, then Levinas' critique cannot really be addressed to Heidegger; rather, it sounds more appropriate when addressed to the very same 'enemies' Heidegger engages against. With regard to the question of the world therefore Levinas might be therefore much closer to Heidegger than he seems.

It is nonetheless necessary to investigate the Levinasian strategy, the route he travels in order to reach 'beyond the world', in view of transcendence, as that which is already implied in the relation with the existent.

Desire-in-the-world

It is worth summarizing the structure Levinas formulates in order to explain why he will not find 'the existent respected in its being in being in the world' and the transcendental relation that, according to him, every doing already implicitly assumes.

The argument develops from the intention to explain interiority and the central part of *Totality and Infinity* is largely devoted to explain this idea.

Levinas' style precludes the possibility to draw a schema of its development; his writing deliberately resists accepted procedures. In one of nine Talmudic commentaries Levinas describes Moses' wisdom as 'the objective style of a thought that fails to embrace the forms of rhetoric' (Levinas 1994: 181). The constant negotiation between Judaism and Greek philosophy that Levinas' writing is committed to produces 'a sermon without eloquence' (ibid.). However it is still possible to see the emergence of a number of frames and trajectories from Levinas' analysis.

Man's relation to the world, an exteriority not alien to man himself, takes its first step as enjoyment. Our apprehension of things in the world is envisaged under the mode of enjoyment, the satisfaction, in happiness, of necessary needs. The notion of enjoyment is worked out thanks to the concept of *living from*.

Enjoyment, 'the very pulsation of the I', 'a quenching', is the very fact of living; men move into it by the simple fact of living. It is, Levinas says, different from the Heideggerian disposition towards Being, for it always exceeds Being. It is both an accomplishment and an opening, as its order is disclosed in the incomplete nature of a being. As the very pulsation of the 'I', enjoyment, or better the independence and sovereignty that this produces, is also the place where subjectivity originates. Again it can't go unnoticed here the critique of Heidegger's Being-in-the-world. As Thomas, among others, remarks 'for Levinas, to live from something is neither to act on it in an everyday immersion in the world, nor to act by means of it, utilising the world as tool or implement' (Thomas 2004: 57).

The instantaneous enjoyment, by which man recollects himself and becomes familiar with things in the world, is then completed by the concepts springing from dwelling: habitation and possession. These concepts elevate the independence already achieved in enjoyment to a more mature level. Habitation and possession again should not be intended the Heideggerian way but as the separation of a being, which recognises itself as both needy and happy, able as it is to overcome indigence, the nudity, and finds in itself the encounter with the Other. Levinas calls this movement *separation*, that which is necessary for the constitution of the idea of the Infinite and, later on, for that of Justice. As Levinas writes: 'enjoyment separates by engaging in the contents from which it lives. Separation comes to pass as the positive work of this engagement [...] To be separated is to be at home with oneself' (Levinas 2005: 147).

As mentioned earlier, one can find within Levinas' works a series of statements that lead to the same conclusion, albeit moving from different angles and premises. Levinas' structure of enjoyment and the effects this has on his understanding of the world can therefore be analysed by examining a series of quotations.

When Levinas writes that 'it is one thing to ask what the place of the world is in the ontological adventure, and another thing to look for that adventure within the world itself' (Levinas 2003a: 33), he is suggesting that it is not by investigating our attitude towards the world that we can understand something of that world. One could translate the statement by saying that by being in the world, by being immersed in things, we cannot account for it, as our experiences of things prevent us from understanding the relationships enacted therein. This reproach is again clearly directed against Heidegger. However in *Being and Time* Dasein is precluded a picture of the world as it finds itself in it. Every possibility is laid down *as* world, the latter being not just the taking place of possibilities, but the very possibility of these possibilities. Thus in saying what the world is, the starting point of the ontological adventure, one should not look for an account of the totality of existents, but for the conditions of possibility of relations which constantly open up such a totality (to the point where the very term totality becomes superseded).

The ontological adventure starts exactly by questioning what ontological status one can assign to the world. The two questions then are not at all different, as Heidegger writes in *On the Essence of Ground*: 'Dasein is not Being-in-the-world because and only because it exists factically; on the contrary, it can only be as existing because its essential constitution lies in Being-in-the-world' (Heidegger 1998: 11). If one questions the existence of the world, its place as it were, one finds that the world is not a place, that means it is not something 'within' which, as a site, the ontological adventure takes its first steps; rather, it is the access into or plane of disclosure for Dasein's possibilities, there where Dasein faces questions as to the possibilities and modes of existence. In other words, the world is the moment at which Dasein confronts its own in-decision, this is a moment that never passes, it is never past, rather Dasein is constantly crossing it. As Dreyfuss writes in his volume devoted to the first section of *Being and Time*, Dasein's submission to the world belongs essentially to its Being, therefore 'Being-in-the world is ontologically prior as the ontological condition of the possibility of specific activities' (Dreyfus 1990: 107). This indicates that even when Heidegger stresses practical activity, he does so in order to describe a more fundamental involvement with the world, a concerned absorption with the world that could not emerge from a subject–object understanding of intentionality.

If the world is primarily 'the structure of all possibilities', then ontology cannot start within it, as the world neither has a within nor contains the ontological adventure; rather, it exists *as* the ontological adventure, that means as an existential ontological concept for which no substance (no *what*) or set of qualities could successfully account.

In *Basic Problems of Phenomenology*, whilst discussing the schemata of ecstatic temporality, Heidegger explains that 'self and world belong together in the single entity, the Dasein. Self and world are not two beings, like subject and object [...] but are the basic determination of the Dasein itself in the unity of the structure of being-in-the-world' (Heidegger 1982: 297).

Levinas' interpretation seems then to rest on the question of the within or better of the with-in. If one were to write them separately one would see that *with* in this case would address a relation, whilst *in* again would address the way in which one exists (in the transitive) this relation. Thus the question would now be translated as: *it is one thing to look for the ontological adventure within the world and another thing to look for that adventure as the with-in the world is.* The world is the set of relations that traverse it and the way one traverses these relations. The consequence of this is that, as Dreyfus writes, 'as being-in-the-world Dasein must take a stand on itself and must be understood in what it does, uses, expects, avoids' (Dreyfus 1990: 147). To an extent the relation between Dasein and the world is such that the distance necessary to draw a picture of the world is never secure, the question of the world is asked 'in ignorance, by one who does not even know what led him to ask' (Kierkegaard 1985: 9).

Levinas, however, is at the same time looking for a way to be in the world that would break with the imperative of existing, what he calls *ontologism*. This theme, which moves from the implicit understanding of Being as overwhelming plenitude, is developed for the first time in *On Escape*, an early text where Levinas' main concern is 'getting out of being by a new path, at the risk of overturning certain notions that to common sense and the wisdom of the nations seemed the most evident' (Levinas 2003b: 73). The analysis of pleasure, need and nausea will find a more thorough development in *Existence and Existent*, where Levinas writes that 'to be in the world is this hesitation, this interval in existing; to be in the world is precisely to be freed from the last implications of the instinct to exist' (Levinas 2003a: 21).

The questions that arise here are: in what way does this differ from what Heidegger says? Does Heidegger say something different when he points out that the world is open before our thematizations?

Totality and Infinity indicates that the possibility to return the world to the singular life freed from the 'instinct to exist' is achieved through enjoyment, the great missed chance of Heidegger's existential analysis. For Levinas the concept of 'enjoyment – ultimate relation with the substantial plenitude of being, with its materiality – embraces all relations with things' (Levinas 2005: 133). Levinas operates a shift in emphasis by redefining, as Harman describes, 'the "ontic" realm as the zone where ontology stakes its genuine claim' (Harman 2002: 241).

Enjoyment is the positive event by means of which Levinas tries to break with Being-in-the-world as concerned absorption, 'attempting to describe a subjectivity in relation to a world that does not fit into the ontological categories of Dasein's being-in-the-world' (Thomas 2004: 64). The moment of separation triggered by enjoyment allows the emerging of separated subjectivity, disengaged from immersion, departing from the world of work and tools, as Heidegger describes it. According to Levinas things are grasped primarily in the love of live, 'the primordial relation of man with the material world is not negativity, but enjoyment and agreeableness of life' (Levinas 2005: 149).

Three further questions impose themselves at this stage:

- Levinas sees in enjoyment both a 'primordial relation' and the ultimate moment of the utilization of tools.[3] In spite of this, before apprehending things in enjoyment, should there not be something akin to a disclosure that allows us to envisage the fact that we will enjoy those things, or at least that one can intend those things as the ones leading to enjoyment? How can enjoyment render things accessible? It seems that Levinas at least has to acknowledge the fact that things are disclosed – they come to be pres-ent, they rejoin themselves – and then enjoyed. The world presents itself to us as the relational encounter of singularities; in the multitude of entities, each entity is defined each time as being what it is. This disclosure of singularities, the fact that Dasein works out its conduct as Being-in-the-world, does not rule out enjoyment or sincerity.
- Does the enjoyment Levinas refers to completely escape the logic of the *in view of...* that he so vigorously criticizes? Namely, does the kind of beyond-utility, beyond grasping and beyond themes that Levinas seeks to attain prevent the unleashing of things for Dasein's own sake? Whilst it is true that one never finds in *Being and Time* the word 'enjoyment', or terms like pleasure and happiness, as Harman points out in commenting on Levinas' sincerity, 'Heidegger obviously realised that the invisible system of reference only tells half of the storey' (Harman 2002: 241). In particular one should consider whether the analyses of *Zeughaftigkeit* do not in fact lead there, albeit in an implicit way. Does the pleasure that one derive from food not always imply feeding oneself? The same goes for building a house and for labour in general. Surely building a house does not stop at finding a shelter, but at the same time a house is not simply decoration, carpets and wallpapers. Whilst one should not overlook the aspirational side of our relation with things, nevertheless one should assume the fact that they introduce themselves not firstly and only as aspirations. It might be true that 'enjoyment embraces all relations with things', but at the same time it is not true that all relations with things lead to enjoyment, not

even in the sense Levinas attributes to the term enjoyment. One cannot expose oneself to enjoyment unless one has already entered, exposed oneself to the referentiality that allow us to stick to things, by letting them be, without ever exhausting them. One should then start thinking of enjoyment as the non-exhaustion of the referentiality proper to the world, for the referentiality is always prior to enjoyment, although enjoyment can ultimately come to pervade and justify and validate it.

By saying that doing and labour already imply a relation with transcendence Levinas suggests a movement beyond the mere use of things and towards what he names 'desire' (defined as that which does not exhaust itself in apprehension, but produces a movement that reaches beyond itself and 'desires beyond everything that can simply complete it' [Levinas 2005: 34]). One should pay attention thus to the fact that in Heidegger's text the dimension of *usability* is often linked to the description of moods. In particular in Section 18 and then in Section 28 onwards Heidegger refers to a more poignant comprehension of the worldly nature of the world. Does this *more* not refer to a letting be that also assumes on itself the possibility for Dasein to be affected by intraworldly beings? Heidegger says it explicitly:

> to be affected […] becomes ontologically possible only in so far as Being-in as such has been determined existentially beforehand in such a manner that what it encounters within-the-world can *'matter' to* it in this way.
>
> (Heidegger 1962: 176)

If Levinas' critique can be translated to read that things experienced in the world are present and then clothed with a meaning, so as to be enclosed in themes, Heidegger replies by bringing fore the notion of 'involvements'. This designates a grasping of things different from thematization, at least not in the mode according to which Levinas seems to understand thematization. It is important to pin this down at this moment, for the discussion ultimately leads to the question of sense as that which allows something to be comprehended, entrance into a referential system. As Heidegger writes, 'the context of assignments or references, which, as significance, is constitutive for worldhood, can be taken formally in the sense of a system of relations' (ibid.: 121–2). This last passage suggests the idea that the sense of things has to be grasped beyond their pure presence, or even their pure readiness or mere consumption. Rather this sense must be disclosed in terms of relations, a referring back to the density of referability, where access to things is always somehow deferred and things never offer themselves in their bare presence. As Heidegger writes:

in interpreting, we do not, so to speak, throw a 'signification' over some naked thing which is present-at-hand, we do not stick a value on it; but when something within-the-world is encountered as such, the thing in question already has an involvement which is disclosed in our understanding of the world [...] The ready-to-hand is always understood in terms of a totality of involvement. This totality need not be grasped explicitly by a thematic interpretation.

(ibid.: 190–191)

Levinas might then be mistaken in thinking that Heidegger is simply trying to privilege the practical; in fact, he rather attempts a description of involvement that escapes the traditional model subject–object.

It is not only in the phenomenology of enjoyment though that Levinas points his finger against Heidegger's presupposed understanding of the world as the world of work. In the discussion of possession Levinas once more makes explicit that his intention is that of providing a different horizon from which to understand the world. When he writes that

the doctrine that interprets the world as a horizon from which things are presented as implements, the equipment of an existence concerned for its being, fails to recognise the being established at the threshold of an interiority the dwelling makes possible.

(Levinas 2005: 163)

he is again reducing Heidegger's propositions to the primacy of readiness-to-hand, concluding that 'it is not the world that makes things possible' (ibid.).

As already pointed out, Heidegger does not argue that the primacy of theoretical cognition should instead be accorded to practical activity. As Dreyfus puts it, Heidegger is rather attempting to drift away from 'the traditional relation between self-referential mental content and objects outside the mind' (Dreyfus 1990: 62).

Being and Time does not establish a priority of readiness-to-hand to presence-at-hand. Rather, what Heidegger proposes is that theoretical contemplation does not allow one to take hold of aspects of the practical mode of activity, which is particularly relevant for Dasein's worldliness. As Mulhall points out:

overlooking our worldliness, we overlook something ontologically central to *any* form of human activity, theoretical or otherwise; and if this notion of world grounds the possibility of theoretically cognizing present-at-hand objects, it cannot conceivably be explained as a construct from an array of purely present-at-hand properties and a sequence of value-projections.

(Mulhall 1996: 42)

Heidegger reads in Being-in-the-world the overcoming of intentionality when the latter is understood according to the subject-object articulation. Given that Being-in points to the structure of transcendence, his aim is to argue that what remains unresolved in the relation between a subject and an object is precisely the relation itself. As Giorgio Agamben points out for Heidegger the subject–object relation is 'less original than the self-transcendence of Being-in-the-world' (Agamben 1999: 187).

Heidegger is quite explicit on this: 'one of the main preparatory tasks of *Being and Time* is to bring this "relation" radically to light in its primordial essence and to do so with full intent' (Heidegger 1984: 130). Dasein is always already open to the world. The kind of opening at stake in Being-in-the-world is a mode of Being before any knowledge and subjectivity. This means that Dasein is already open to entities in the world, without making them the objective correlative of intentionality or of an appropriating subjectivity. Thus for Heidegger the problem is not which type of intentionality gives us the best account of things; the attempt is that of moving beyond traditional intentionality.

Levinas is here drawing near Husserl and Heidegger right there where Heidegger's effort to differentiate himself from Husserl is greatest. Dasein can have a world; in fact, the very possibility of being open to the world, prior to knowing it, means that Dasein is not merely an intraworldly being. If it were so, Dasein could not properly be-in-the-world, but only be contained or present in it.

Heidegger writes that 'an entity "within-the-world" has Being-in-the-world in such a way that it can understand itself as bound up in its "destiny" with the Being of those entities which it encounters within its own world' (Heidegger 1962: 81). To have a world does not mean to overcome it by encompassing it: to have a world is a mode of Being, by means of which Dasein is open to Being prior to knowledge. Being-in-the-world is an existential, one of Dasein's way of Being. As existential Being-in-the-world is thus an *a priori* character of the Being of Dasein and as such it has an 'active' form. Categories on the other hand simply indicate a series of properties, attributes or qualities we can use to identify things.

The distinction between existentials and categories proves here to be particularly important. Heidegger puts it like this:

> all *explicata* to which the analytic of *Dasein* gives rise are obtained by considering *Dasein*'s existence-structure. Because the being-characteristics of *Dasein* are defined in terms of existentiality, we call them '*existentialia*'. These are to be sharply distinguished from what we call 'categories' – determinations of

Being for entities whose character is not that of *Dasein* [...] *Existentialia* and categories are the two basic possibilities for characters of Being.

(ibid.: 44)

To put it concisely, existentials always refer to Dasein, they always respond to the question of *whom*, whilst categories respond to the question of *what*. Somehow Heidegger here seems to invoke the notion of necessity, for something has to exist in a particular way if it has to be Dasein.

Oddly enough at times Levinas seems to turn to Heidegger, albeit not explicitly, in order to criticize Husserl, as he had already done at the beginning of his philosophical adventure. As Derrida notices in *Theory of Intuition* Levinas turns his back to Husserl and grounds his analysis on a reading of *Being and Time* (Derrida 2002: 108). Not by chance, the critique revolves mainly around the concept of the world and in particular around the notion of the world understood not as a totality of perceived or present objects, but rather a 'centre of action'. Levinas says that Heidegger goes further than Husserl in that he thinks the world not as given over to the glance, but 'in its very Being as a centre of action, as a field of activity or of *care*' (Levinas 1995: 119). Even if, as Derrida says, one cannot be sure whether Heidegger would have retained the definition of the world as a 'centre' and as a 'field of activity', nevertheless one should notice that Levinas here acknowledges the referential quality of the Heideggerian world. This gesture, to read Heidegger in opposition to Husserl, also resurfaces at times in *Totality and Infinity*, leading to a quasi confusion within the Levinasian critique of Heidegger. Some remarks – a series of moves of rehabilitation through which Heidegger, kicked out from the door, gets into the discourse through the window – appear to be contradictory. One still finds in *Totality and Infinity* a peculiar accent, a concern that seems to lead back to Heidegger. After having detached himself from the idea of Being-in-the-world, Levinas expresses himself in these terms: 'the world I live in is not simply the counterpart or the contemporary of thought and its constitutive freedom, but a conditioning and an antecedence' (Levinas 2005: 129). One is not too far from Heidegger here: what suddenly resonates is the idea that the world *is* prior to any acknowledgement (and possession). The idea that the world is disclosed beforehand, primarily, anticipating its thematization, or the fact that 'if the world can, in a way, be lit up, it must assuredly be disclosed' (ibid.: 130), is a motif that Levinas had already used in his writings from the 1930s. Even when his discourse moves overtly against Heidegger, it still draws lines that intersect from within the Heideggerian horizon.

There are significant examples that could add consistency to these comments. Before moving on to discuss elements and things, Levinas repeats once more that

> the world I live from is not simply constituted at a second level after represen-
> tation would have spread before us a backdrop of a reality simply given, and
> after 'axiological' intentions would have ascribed to this world a value that
> renders it apt for habitation.
>
> (ibid.)

It is crucial here to show that in understanding the relation with the Other as separation, metaphysics, desire of infinity, Levinas needs a world that is not immediately thematized, but disclosed, and as such open as the always already open. This, it seems, can be found only in Heidegger's work. The fact that Levinas wants to stress the structures of enjoyment and happiness, labour as *living from...* does not place his discourse in the apparent antithesis he attempts to reach.

Levinas' understanding of the world cannot do without the Heideggerian critique of Descartes and of presentness-at-hand. Only in this way can it be effective and only in this way can Levinas introduce desire in the world. In order to overcome the subject–object relation, as it has been constituted up to Husserl and reinforced by Husserl himself, Levinas necessarily turns to Heidegger. It is true that one can show that the register of enjoyment is absent from Heidegger's lexicon. Nonetheless one should also ponder that all the 'negative' connotations that Heidegger deploys in describing Dasein's involvement with the set of relationships the world is must be specified not as negative in the sense of a lack of, or as the dialectical antithesis of a positive movement. At the opposite these terms should be intended as possibilities. The series of 'not' indicates conditions of possibility. Heidegger himself takes care to specify this in many passages. Whenever one finds a privative expression one should always be reminded that those aim to convey something positive. To this effect Heidegger writes: 'in such privative expressions what we have in view is a positive phenomenal character of the Being of that which is proximally ready-to-hand' (Heidegger 1962: 106). The series of 'not' do not necessarily foreclose positivity, desire, want, aspiration, hope, enjoyment; they are not necessarily forces of anonymity or figures of negation. Quite the opposite, this emphasis on 'possibility' suggests perhaps the emergence of *powers of existence*. One should then consider their function as that of opening conditions of possibility. When Heidegger says that 'if it is possible for the ready-to-hand not to emerge from its inconspicuousness, the world must not announce itself' (ibid.), one should read in these two instances of 'not' the very method to approach the *in se* of the world and of things in the world. Heidegger makes it clear, years after the publication of *Being and Time*, in a passage from *Letter on Humanism*:

> the reference to 'being-in-the-world' as the basic trait of the humanitas of homo humanus does not assert that man is merely a 'worldly' creature understood in a Christian sense, thus a creature turned away from God and so cut loose from 'Transcendence' [...] in the name 'being-in-the-world', 'world' does not in any way imply earthly as opposed to heavenly being, not the 'worldly'; as opposed to the 'spiritual'. For us 'world' does not at all signify beings or any realm of beings but the openness of Being [...] with the existential determination of the essence of man, therefore, nothing is decided about the 'existence of God'.
>
> (Heidegger 1978: 228)

The discussion of enjoyment previously undertaken calls for one more question. Levinas writes 'in the ontological adventure the world is an episode which, far from deserving to be called a fall, has its own equilibrium [...] to call it everyday and condemn it as inauthentic is to fail to recognise the sincerity of hunger' (Levinas 2003a: 37). This passage deserves to be analysed in light of the Heideggerian concept of the *fall*. Levinas seems to imply that enjoyment and sincere happiness cannot find their place in the Heideggerian treatment of the world because fallenness precipitates Dasein into bereavement and ruination. Therefore the mode according to which enjoyment and sincerity take place, that of the everyday, would be *a priori* disqualified or, as Levinas says, inauthentic.

As King points out, though, what Heidegger means by falleness is not the situation of something

> fallen perhaps from a state of grace into corruption, but the *movement* of falling. This movement, moreover, is not one of the accidents that can befall Da-sein in his factical existence but is one of the basic ways in which Da-sein can-be-in-the-world.
>
> (King 2001: 88)

Falling should then be understood as an existential structure of Being-in-the-world. Dasein already finds itself falling: an ontological motion, but without nostalgia. Heidegger writes:

> in falling, nothing other than our potentiality-for-Being-in-the-world is the issue, even if in the mode of inauthenticity [...] On the other hand, authentic existence is not something which floats above falling everydayness; existentially, it is only a modified way in which such everydayness is seized upon.
>
> (Heidegger 1962: 224)

Heidegger is explicit in maintaining that fallness does not designate an irrevocable existential distortion and that falling contains no assertion as to a possible corruption of what is properly human.

The concept of fallness then does not necessarily imply a curse, a 'condemnation', as Levinas seems to read it. Terms like 'average understanding', 'idle talk', 'everyday' do not address a judgement; rather, they constitute sites where Dasein's decision towards its essence (that is its existence) takes place. As Nancy puts it, it is precisely in adherence to existence that Dasein's interest towards itself is disclosed. Rather than being the world of banality, of the general, the everyday is adherence to existence itself, 'the taking-place, of the each time according to which existence appropriates its singularity' (Nancy 1993: 89). Therefore it is not simply in deserting the everyday that we 'attain another, more "authentic" register of existence' (ibid.).

The inauthentic should then not be thought of as the 'decline into an inferior form' (ibid.: 99) or the negative reduction of the authentic. As Agamben explains whilst discussing the concept of love in Heidegger's thought, 'authentic existence has no content other than inauthentic existence; the proper is nothing other than the apprehension of the improper' (Agamben 1999: 197). From the two works just mentioned, it emerges that when Heidegger talks about the inauthentic, one should be extremely careful in deriving from this any sort of judgement.

Recalling Nancy's elaboration of the question of the world one could say that the world as such emerges out of the withdrawal of Gods and constitutes itself as the spacing of sense. The world refers to itself and networks with itself; 'in short, it has started to comprise a co-existence' (Nancy 2003: 305). As one can see then Nancy's reading is close to Heidegger in linking the question of the world to that of Being-with and otherness. The reference to co-existence appears every time the question of the world is at stake. What need to be traced is precisely how the two questions unfold together, how one shapes the other and finally how both are intersected by the question of sense. One could attempt one provisional formula, expressed in three modes: the world is the co-existence of sense; co-existence exposes the sense of the world; sense circulates as the co-existence of the world. This co-existence is not a simple juxtaposition of things: as Nancy puts it,

> it refers to everyone and to no one, the circulation of a sense that nothing either retains or saturates, a circulation found in the movement between places and beings, between all places and all beings, the infinite circulation of a sense that will end up having its entire sense in this with.
>
> (Nancy 2003: 306)

To say that 'you are absolutely strange because the world begins in its turn with you' or that 'the world is the generic name of this ontological curiosity' (Nancy 2000: 6) means inscribing in the world the problem of Being-with or, better said, it means taking the world as the only plane in which these questions become meaningful. It is by way of an access to sense as sense of the world that one can gain an entrance into otherness, the sense of the other. 'Co-appearance, then, must signify that "appearing" (coming into the world and being in the world or existence as such) is strictly insepa-rable, indiscernible from the *cum* or the *with*' (ibid.: 61). In Nancy's thinking the Heideggerian structure that links Being-in-the-world, sense and Being-with is not simply respected in its incipient moves, but exploded in its conclusions.

What appears at the end of the analysis is that where Levinas understands Being-in-the-world mainly as instrumentality, a being-near-things which tend to turn the world into a category, Nancy reads it in terms of the abandonment to possibilities – offered and unleashed: this is what 'in the world' is taken to be. Therefore rather than being an abstract constraint, the world is the very site where the enactment of sense as the opening beyond a principle becomes possible, the play of specificity.

Whilst for Levinas the world forms part of that system from which one needs to find a way out, through nausea, insomnia, desire, enjoyment, eros and fecundity, Nancy sees the breaking away as the world itself. As Eric Sean Nelson writes 'individuation as the break of indifference can take place because Dasein's neutrality is already broken by the facticity of its existence' (Nelson 2008: 133). The world is open to the facticity of singular existences in a way that makes it the open par excellence, the very factical breach constantly re-opened.

Two versions of originary otherness

Levinas formulates his notion of originary otherness as an explicit reaction to Heidegger's Being-with. As mentioned earlier on Levinas' strategy is deliberately complex and the interpretative effort finds itself constantly resisted. The following argument will therefore proceed by separating what in fact in Levinas constitutes one single movement. The question of Being-with (the refusal of Heideggerian Being-with), the I–Thou (relation to the Other person) and the question of Illeity (the third term, God, Justice) will be treated deliberately as distinct moments.

The argument will start discussing Levinas' rejection of the notion of Being-with as articulated by Heidegger in Section 26 and Section 27 of *Being and Time*. It will then move on towards a questioning of the I–Thou relation, as the preferred field for the emergence of the ethical; here particular emphasis will be addressed to the concept of symmetry developed by Martin Buber. Finally the last step will be devoted to the theme of Illeity, the Third term. Appearing as early as in *Existence and Existents*, the term remains at times ambiguous, for it contains references to God and explains at the same time the resolution of the mutual convocations between the *I* and the *Thou* in the ethical relation, what Levinas names *justice*.

A number of these considerations will appear again at the end of this work, in relation to the thinking of Jean-Luc Nancy, who proposes a treatment of Being-with, which seems to go in the opposite direction of the one undertaken by Levinas. The aim will be to show how the two, moving as mentioned on radically different paths, propose the ethical not as a set of norms, but as absolute demand that compels the human from beginning to end. Levinas proceeds by introducing what he terms metaphysical desire and the links this establishes with a third term that does not take part in desire or in relation whilst nonetheless judging it and adjusting the measure of one's responsibility to the other human being. On the contrary, Nancy resolves the ethical problem through a more apparent Heideggerian twist: ethics is not to be found outside ontology, but is rather ontology's central problem. The ethical can follow only from a reformulation of ontology that would take into account a *co*-existential analysis, an ontology that takes the world of bodies as its starting point. Whilst Levinas then attempts to move beyond ontology and beyond philosophy, Nancy on the other hand goes at the very bottom of it, at its core (the overcoming of philosophy as a consequence is produced as a releasing of philosophy's limit). According to Levinas one reaches ethics by stepping into otherwise than being, whilst Nancy finds it at the core of Being as the co-essentiality of with and Being.

Perhaps one is not that far from the question Heidegger poses to the thinking of Being in *Letter on Humanism* when he writes that

> if the name 'ethics' in keeping with the basic meaning of the word ethos, should now say that 'ethics' ponders the abode of man, then that thinking which thinks the truth of Being as the primordial element of man, as one who eksists, is in itself the original ethics.
>
> (Heidegger 1978: 235)

Levinas seems to dismiss the notion of *Mitsein* entirely, in view in particular of what Heidegger was 'in 1933, even if he was that for only a short period' (Levinas 2006a: 98). One should not be too quick, however, in assessing this opposition. As discussed Levinas proves on several occasions to be fully aware of the debt one is to pay to Heidegger if one is to philosophize these days. One should always keep in mind a certain ambiguity, a sort of conscious resistance on Levinas' side to the seduction of Heideggerian thought. It is within this ambiguity, on the edge of seduction, that one could situate the questions here at stake. On the one hand it is apparent that Levinas rejects a great deal not just of the Heideggerian perspective, but of the tradition that Heidegger deconstructs (and in so doing reinstates); on the other hand, and this might be less evident, it is still from within Heidegger, a certain Heidegger at least, that Levinas finds his own solutions.

Levinas poses a number of reasons for not articulating the question of otherness in terms of Mitsein. Already in *Time and the Other* he devotes half a page to the refutation:

> the other in Heidegger appears in the essential situation of Miteinandersein, reciprocally being for on another [...] the proposition *mit* here describes the relationship. It is thus an association of side by side, around something, around a common term and, more precisely, for Heidegger, around the truth. It is not the face-to-face relationship, where each contributes everything, except the private fact of one's existence. I hope to show for my part that it is not the preposition mit that should describe the original relationship with the other.
>
> (Levinas 1987: 43)

Levinas will confirm his concerns in a very similar manner in an interview, almost forty years after *Time and the Other*:

> In Heidegger the ethical relation, *Miteinamdersein*, the being-with-another-person, is only one moment of our presence in the world. It does not have the central place. Mit is always being next to [...] it is zusammensein [being-together], perhaps zusammen-marschieren [marching-together].
>
> (Levinas 2006a: 99–100)

Gathering together the elements from these two passages, Levinas' critique could be said to rest mainly on two points:

• the merely propaedeutic role of the *with*, which remains in a subordinate position;
• the fact that the *with* simply states a juxtaposition, a *being next to* that does not involve responsibility.

The *with* does not only fall short of the ethical command, it also constantly runs the risk of embodying a violent movement: a crowd walking side by side, the vicious rustling of a march. One can find here a reference to the question of destiny and to the theme of the people. Levinas finds in Heidegger a distorted geographic constellation, a prevalence of the People, of some people: 'there are texts in Heidegger on the place of man in Central Europe. Europe and the German West are central to him. There is a whole geopolitics in Heidegger' (ibid.: 101).

Levinas' main contribution to contemporary philosophical debate lies in having (re)discovered the question of the Other, in having opened a way, at the very limit of Western thought, through which the Other comes to be seen as that which is always in a position to overcome and overhaul the possibilities of the 'I'. Levinas understands the Other as the non-phenomenon opening up the way to Infinity, opening dialogue and language as the question of responsibility, beyond the confines of knowledge and understanding. *Ethics as first philosophy* is this very welcoming of the Other, an act which precedes any approach by the Other, any request or demand for hospitality, kindness, generosity. The relation with the Other is a relation with Infinity, with that which cannot be contained, a relation where the *I can* finally surrenders.

In order to reach the said conclusions, Levinas often turns to Martin Buber in order to elaborate notions such as 'relation' and 'meeting'. 'In the beginning is relation' (Buber 2007: 22), Buber wrote. Levinas explicitly acknowledges Buber as the thinker who has opened the originality of the ethical register:

> the discovery of that order (the ethical relation) in its full originality and the elaboration of its consequences, and, if one may designate them this, its 'categories', remain inseparable from the name Buber, whatever may have been the concordant voices in the midst of which his own made itself heard.
>
> (Levinas 1997b: 41)

In associating his name to that of Buber, Levinas is not just referencing a specific tradition of Jewish thought and mysticism; he is also delineating a path following which one would from time to time find oneself outside the philosophical tradition of the West. Reading Levinas one perceives, in pages that are among some of his most inspired, the constant attempt to breach out of the history of Western philosophy, without completely leaving that tradition. Buber seems to offer Levinas this very possibility. Mysterious powers and the magical emerge quite frequently in Buber's major text *I and Thou* (a text which references Western thought only through few fleeting mentions of Kant and an almost ironic rephrasing of Spinoza). Buber seems to resort to a different background, to what one could name *traditions of the otherwise*.

It is not simply this leap outside philosophy though that draws Levinas and Buber close. Levinas' refusal of the notion of Mitsein draws consistently on Buber's conception of relation, the primary importance of relation as meeting, in the form of an *I* uttering a *Thou*. Whether Levinas tries to express the encounter with the Other, to formulate the concept of Illeity, to express the surfacing of Justice or to argue with regard to the State, he seems to always bear in mind, or start from, a one-to-one situation. The same fact that he uses the Face as the concept that unleashes the 'power' preventing a return to the Same could be intended as a telling sign of the fact that facing – whether one takes it as a shock, a breach, the exposure of gentleness, or the condition of responsibility prior to decisions – constitutes the situation *par excellence*, excluding all others, or including, which is to say submitting, all others within itself.

Levinas finds in Buber a model that allows him to reformulate the Husserlian subject–object relation without having to turn to Heidegger, as he had done in *Theory of Intuition*. Buber provides Levinas with the resources to start freeing the Other from the Same. Levinas will initially structure his thesis around the bursting forth of a meeting, the encounter with the Other as ungraspable. Moreover, as in Buber, one finds in Levinas the motif of language as holding primarily onto a dialogical nature, thus always being readable in the form of the address, a sending to the other human being.

With regard to the subject–object relation, Buber locates the *I–It* relation in a different realm from the dialogical relation *I–Thou*. Whilst for Heidegger Dasein, whether it encounters things ready-at-hand or is solicited to and by other human beings, is always caught in the understanding of the Being that is at stake for it, for Buber the two spheres, the world of things and the world of other human beings, do not cross. Analytically they have an independent life. Buber opens his work with the following words:

> To man the world is twofold, in accordance with his twofold attitude. The attitude of man is twofold, in accordance with the twofold nature of the primary words which he speaks [...] The one primary word is the combination *I–Thou*. The other primary word is the combination *I–It* [...] Hence the *I* of man is also twofold.
>
> (Buber 2007: 11)

From the outset Buber distinguishes the appraisal of things from dialogue, the meeting with a partner or a friend, the turning towards the unknown neighbour. He maintains though that even when one addresses things, the *It*, one is still addressing an interlocutor, one is nonetheless in the midst of dialogue. Buber places this realm at the threshold of mutuality and describes it in the following terms:

it is part of our concept of a plant that it cannot react to our action towards it: it cannot 'respond'. Yet this does not mean that here we are given simply no reciprocity at all [...] In the sphere we are talking of, we have to do justice, in complete candour, to the reality which discloses itself to us.

(ibid.: 95)

However it is important to underline that for Buber even the *It* is primarily the calling forth of a relation: rather than simply facing objects, an *I* calls them forth, insisting not on their presence, but on the relation that can be established with them. It is from within this relation and as this relation that a world of things exists. Its existence springs from dialogue, from an interrogation. The constitution of the *I* is always bound to the uttering of a composite mode, it is to be found in the midst of a relation. The existence of subjectivity as such, the *I* alone, is considered to be impossible. Prior to dialogue the subject has, so to speak, nothing to say. It is closed in a taciturn autonomy.

Buber's philosophical architecture thus rests on speech as dialogue and on dialogue as the opening up of relations constituting a meaningful plane. This structure is displayed in a more explicit way when Buber describes the relation with other human beings. In *I and Thou* Buber writes: 'if I face a human being as my Thou, and say the primary word I–Thou to him, he is not a thing among things, and does not consist of things' (ibid.: 15). To say that the other human being escapes the direct grasp of things amounts at saying that I am not in relation with a set of quality, but primarily with a response that comes directly to me and to no one else, a response that follows my addressing one and a single person. Every utterance of the 'Thou' singles out another 'Thou', who is also an 'I' readdressing me in the same way. It is therefore impossible to encounter another human being without addressing that person as an active and responsive interlocutor, as part of a dialogue in which I will always have to question myself as a Thou. I can try, Buber goes on, to exclude some quality of the human being I am facing, but in doing so I would be losing him, placing myself outside the relation. Every time I attempt to draw something particular, a quality, out of a Thou, I am already stepping outside, Thou flies out of my reach. Therefore there is no experience of a Thou: experience is a mode that is not given in my relation with the other man. This relation will always be commanded by his light, nothing else exists if not through the light cast forth by our dialogue, by our unending calling and responding. In Buber's words:

I do not experience the man to whom I say Thou. But I take my stand in relation
to him, in the sanctity of the primary word. Only when I step out of it do I
experience him once more. In the act of experience Thou is far away.

(ibid.)

It is not only experience that is ruled out in the encounter with the other
human being, so is any intentionality that aims to draw the 'Thou' close, that
would bring him within my sphere, subject to my manipulations. Certainly,
it is through an act that 'I' addresses the 'Thou', but this act is not an act of
my will, one action among others: rather it has something of the unknown,
an unconditioned reflex, an impulse I follow with my whole being. My very
being is completely engaged in a leap towards the Other. This unconditioned,
absolute leap gives Buber's notion of the meeting its force. The meeting is
presented as a drive: urgent, compelling, undeniable, boundless. No agency,
no subjectivity, meet its requirements. No idea of the 'I', no self-consciousness
or extrapolation suffices to account for the encounter with another human
being: the vanishing point of this relation terminates right at the feet of
infinity: 'only when every means has collapsed does the meeting come about'
(ibid.: 17).

Buber elaborates the meeting according to three main conditions:

- the meeting is that which happens outside the sphere of experience: 'Only
  when every means has collapsed does the meeting come about' (ibid.);
- the meeting is that which – in relation to the Thou – belongs to no space
  and no time; it unleashes itself as the uncontained: 'The world of Thou is
  not set in the context of either of these (space and time)' (ibid.: 32);
- the meeting is that which sets forth the world as destiny and man as free
  man, free in that he is in need (and awaiting) of this destiny: 'he intervenes
  no more, but at the same time he does not let things merely happen. He
  listens to the course of being in the world [...] in order to be brought [...] I
  said he believes, but that really means he meets' (ibid.: 49).

With the notion of meeting Buber also crafts a refusal of abstraction. His
philosophy is very much bent towards life and the living man. 'You and me',
'real living', 'actual man', 'our life' are recurrent turns of phrase. Buber employs
them to inscribe the first section of his volume in a concreteness that reverses
philosophy's negligence for the 'province of the lived'. Within this lexicon Buber
inscribes also what he names objective speech, that register that 'snatches only at
a fringe of real life' (ibid.: 21). Objective speech is able to express only 'shadowy

solicitude for faceless numbers', without thus taking the meeting into account and therefore foreclosing the way to God and the infinite.

Buber addresses the very deficiencies that Levinas is trying to overcome in his attempt to restructure the order of philosophical priority. The proximity between the two thinkers could be said to revolve around two core points:

- the subject–object relation: Buber understands it in terms of a bursting forth – his preferred expression is *meeting* – in which a degree of reciprocity is always possible. Although Levinas will then distance himself from Buber by the adding the crucial concept of *asymmetry* to the meeting, in this he is still closer to Buber than to Husserl or Heidegger;
- language: the primary dimension of language is not the naming of things or the expression of Being, but the triggering of relations. The relational tone of language and the primacy of the dialogical mode structured around few original words (*Grundwort*) allows man to meet the world and the Thou as an I that utters the relation.

Whilst Levinas will subsequently argue against Buber that his characterization of the I–Thou as mutual, reciprocal and symmetrical does not allow him to enter the properly ethical field, the mode of relation 'discovered' by Buber allows Levinas to move, to an extent at least, beyond Being-with.

Between Buber and Levinas there are nonetheless consistent differences. For Levinas what triggers the relation with the Other is not as much my uttering a Thou, although this dialogical irruption constitutes an important moment, as my responsibility for him. Responsibility does not need to be triggered by any particular event; rather, it lies always there, before any encounter, before experience and before any actual, concrete, eventual call. Levinas often refers to Dostoyevsky in order to elucidate this more clearly: 'We are all guilty of everything and everyone, towards everyone, and I more so than all the others. The superlative degree of guilt does not refer to any personal history' (Levinas 1997b: 44). From this Levinas argues that the relation to the other cannot reside in reciprocity and symmetry. Quite the opposite, it rests on the original difference, neither mediate nor immediate, that proceeds by a-symmetrical confrontations. This might sound surprising given that the privileged mode of this relationship is the face-to-face (one-to-one). However, it is exactly because the face-to-face is played out within a situation that never manages to include itself – I can never really see the face I am confronting – that Levinas can name this relation *ethics*. Whilst Buber establishes an intimate reciprocity, Levinas founds his thought exactly on the overcoming of reciprocity, on 'the dissymmetry of inter-subjective space' (ibid.: 45).

The main difference then lies in the emphasis Levinas places on the ethical as the primal term. In particular the word *responsibility* draws the line between the two. To this effect Levinas writes: 'in my own analyses, the approach to others is not originally in my speaking out to the other, but in my responsibility for him or her. That is the original ethical relation' (ibid.: 44). However, it should be mentioned that despite the idea of original asymmetry, Levinas often seems to resort to figures of intimacy. In his attempt to distance his ethics from Being-with, Levinas often seems to relapse into Buberian relationships. Within Levinas' writings one often encounters the pair and the couple, though this is presented often as an open couple. Through the reversal there operated, Buber's teaching remains for Levinas the first resource against Heidegger.

Since the beginning it is this reversal of terms that motivates Levinas' refusal of 'with': 'Being before the existent [...] is freedom before justice [...] The terms must be reversed' (Levinas 2005: 41). Levinas' intention is then that of reversing the terms of the question: the face to face would be more original than the 'with', for the 'with' would still refer to an understanding of sociality communicated through unity. In this view individuals would be aggregates undertaking an always latent process of fusion.

Levinas' concern for the exclusivity of the face to face pushes him to reduce the 'with' to the cornerstone of a logic devoted to mastering the crowds, directing their trajectories to a single-minded destiny. Levinas seems to fear that by placing the with as the primary mode of relation one would be then obliged to surrender to the Same; Being-with would then be Being-within-the-same.

However, contrary to what one might think, one does not find in Levinas' texts many references to the Heideggerian 'with', neither to Being-with nor to Being-with-each-other (*Miteinandersein*) and in general very few explicit mentions of Sections 26 and 27 of *Being and Time*. In *Time and the Other* Levinas writes:

> it is the collectivity which says 'us', and which, turned toward the intelligible sun, toward the truth, experience, the other at his side and not face to face with him [...] Miteinandersein also remains the collectivity of the with, and its authentic form is revealed around the truth [...] we hope to show, for our part, that it is not the preposition mit which must describe the original relation with the other.
>
> (Levinas 1987: 43)

It is the subordination of the Buberian I–Thou convocations that motivates the first movement of Levinas' criticism. It is the submission of the ethical explosion to Being-with that Levinas moves against, since the latter, as Michael Lewis writes 'by invoking "being" neutralizes the asymmetry of a relation that can be accessed only from within that relation itself. Any view from the outside betrays the relation' (Lewis 2005: 8). The reference to marching, the translation of Being-with as Marching-together, is also present in more elaborate works. Levinas fears that by placing the with as the primary mode of relation one would be then obliged to surrender to the Same; Being-with would then be being-within-the-same, an holistic ending Levinas cannot accept.

One fundamental misreading seems to motivate Levinas' position. As Derrida points out, Levinas is taking Being-with as a 'derivative and modified form of the originary relation with the other' (Derrida 2002: 112). Whilst Heidegger explicitly says that 'with' belongs to the existential character of Dasein, Levinas appears to evoke what is an existential possibility under the traits of a category.[4] This has a number of consequences:

- it means to interpret Being-with as instrumental intersubjectivity, the plural readiness-at-hand of actual individuals. As Heidegger says though: 'the kind of Being which belongs to the Dasein of Others, as we encounter it within-the-world, differs from readiness-to-hand and presence-at-hand' (Heidegger 19962: 154). In this way the 'with' is reduced to an incident of solitary Da, and – as Lewis puts it – 'being-with is taken to be little more than a placatory appendix to a description of what is ultimately a solipsistic ego' (Lewis 2005: 18).
- Levinas seems to underline an undifferentiated equality at the heart of Being-with, overlooking the fact that the equality that makes co-existence possible (*Mit-dasein*) rests on the being-open of entities to one-another. This openness prevents the constitution of a pure subject (therefore also of a pure sociality, which Levinas names philosophy of communion), to which world and others would be added.[5] This is confirmed not only by Heidegger's argument that the being-there-too (*Auch-da-sein*) is not a simple Being-present-at-hand-along-with, but also by the fact that the with constitutes a relational difference, where every and each Dasein discloses the world as a with-world. Whilst Levinas seems to highlight a kind of constraining empathy, Heidegger explicitly refutes this. As King suggests, differently from Husserl, 'Heidegger avoids founding his solution on empathy (Einfuhlung), because it assumes that the other is a "double" of oneself' (King 2001: 75), whilst the access to the world others provide can be understood just as *absolute curiosity*.
- Levinas underscores that Being-with remains confined within the limits of the They, therefore taking the They as the purely negative moment of banality. The They, although it constitutes the moment of indifference

(Dasein does not recognise its absorption), must also mean, in Jean-Luc Nancy's words, 'the site of disclosedness' (Nancy 1993: 89).

Whilst one can, as Jean-Luc Nancy does, advance the critique that Heidegger's question of the with as co-existential to the Da basically leaves open just two possibilities – a crowd with no proper names or a People forged around the destiny of its Proper Name – one should nevertheless be careful not to mistake Being-with for a category. What one would rather reproach Heidegger for is that Being-with often seems to float on the surface of the analysis of Dasein, never becoming as fundamental as, according to Heidegger's announcement, it should be. Nancy addresses this unfulfilled promise by saying:

> In his analytic of *Mitsein*, Heidegger does not do this measure justice. On the one hand, he deals with the indifference of an 'uncircumspective tarrying alongside' and, on the other, an 'authentic understanding of others' [...] Between this indifference and this understanding, the theme of existential distantiality immediately reverts back to competition and domination.
>
> (Nancy 2000: 82)

This legacy and this lack is something that Heidegger does not attempt to resolve even in his later writings. Levinas seems therefore to duplicate this Heideggerian gesture (*Fürsorge* is mentioned just a couple of times in *Totality and Infinity*).

By taking Being-with as a category, not an existential possibility necessary to Dasein, but an occasion of its world, Levinas can criticize the fact that by calling into question Being in the compound expression Being-with, Heidegger describes a relation that refers constantly to an element outside of itself. Brought into play in these terms, Being would thus overshadow the asymmetry necessary for the relation to be ethical. The approach of the Other would then be reduced to or mediated by the relation to an overarching totality, which assumes the Other as part of itself. If Being-with though is taken as an existential possibility (necessary if one is to identify something as Dasein), then Being in the Heideggerian formula should be understood as a singularity not reducible to anonymous totality.

From this it follows that the other invoked by Being-with is precisely the other whose otherness remains intact (as it remains intact his possibility to disclose a meaningful world). As Lewis aptly puts it, 'Being is the uniqueness of a Being, the singularity of an entity before and beyond any wider horizon of meaning which might subsume it and render it comprehensible' (Lewis 2005: 8). The shared world, the world-with, is always made available as singular opening of sense. Therefore even when Dasein is alone, even in complete solitude,

Being-with does not cease being Dasein's existential possibility. As King writes 'even when Da-sein thinks he does not need the others, when he withdraws from them and has nothing to do with them, this is still only possible as a privative mode of being-with' (King 2001: 75). Dasein's access to the world is always made available and guaranteed by an access with-others. It is precisely the *with* that allows Dasein's double disclosure: the movement towards the world cannot be separated by a movement towards otherness. The first already discloses the second. Being-with should then be taken as that which exposes a logic of separation rather than companionship, differentiation rather than fusion.

Once Levinas has turned Being-with into a category, his work 'against' ontology begins. One could read it already in the following passage:

> from the start I repudiate the Heideggerian conception that views solitude in the midst of a prior relationship with the other. [...] the conception seems to me ontologically obscure. The relationship with the Other is indeed posed by Heidegger as an ontological structure of Dasein, but practically it plays no role in the drama of being.
>
> (Levinas 1987: 44)

Here Levinas is pointing out that Being-with remains nothing more than a missed chance, since 'it plays no role'. He is not going as far as to say that the notion forecloses access to alterity, but at this point it already seems to him 'ontologically obscure'. From here on though Levinas' argument becomes sharper, meant to highlight not just an obscurity, but also a real darkness at the heart of Mitsein, a darkness that makes it impossible to retain the alterity of the Other. Heidegger is then seen as participating in a long tradition:

> beginning with Plato the social ideal will be sought as an ideal of fusion. It will be thought that, in its relationship with the other, the subject tends to be identified with the other, by being swallowed up in a collective representation, a common ideal. It is the collectivity that says we, that, turned toward the intelligible sun, toward the truth, feels the other at its side and not in front of itself.
>
> (ibid.: 45)

If one takes Being-with as a categorical, then one defines Being-with purely as indicating the human being as a social animal.

Nancy shows a possibility to understand Being-with differently. His argument addresses a dynamic opposite to the one Levinas seems to detect: 'we do not have to identify ourselves as "we" [...] we have to disidentify ourselves from every sort of "we" that would be the subject of its own representation' (Nancy 2000: 71). If one formalizes Being-with in the way Levinas does (*zusammen-marschieren*), one entangles Being-with in significations that are, if not foreign, at least posterior and eventual and that tend to reduce Being-with to the truism 'man is social'. All attempts to thematize the 'with' in 'Being-with' simply take one of its occasions – 'being-next-to', 'marching together' – and make of that the exact definition. The question that should be reopened at this stage is: what does it mean to say that Being-with is an existential and not a categorical and what does it then mean to co-exist?

To begin with it is possible to offer two negative arguments, namely to indicate at least what co-existing is not. On the one hand, co-existing cannot simply be the co-appearance of a series of entities alongside each other. A chain of human beings, slaves chained and sold at the market, does not make co-existence (and not even co-appearance). On the other hand Being-with cannot be a universal destination, the common ground on which to build the People. This second connotation would in fact lead to the violence Levinas' philosophy wrestles against. What one has to revert to is something different: it is the logic of the 'with' thought immediately alongside Being, something that would go beyond ontology if ontology stops at the thinking of Being (thus excluding the co-extensive 'with') or that would change ontology (by pushing it to a place it has not yet been able to occupy, namely taking the *with* acutely, as Being's most intimate problem). What needs to be thought is an *originary with*. This also permits thinking the origin as the difference at the heart of the origin, for 'the with is strictly contemporaneous with all existence, as it is with all thinking' (ibid.: 41). What the *Mit* in *Mitsein* invites one to think is the exposure of our being-many; that is to say plurality as such, which does not mean plurality disentangled from the one. The two terms have now to take a new undertone. In the word plurality one should now hear the plurality of existence, and in the word one, the one-to-every-other, simultaneously many and each one. Alterity, in its inner structure, is made possible by the way the many confront the singular always as an each-one, never simply as crowd; each one even when alongside and not in front of each other. There is though nothing fortuitous here: this register of positions, simultaneity and being-alongside, does not fall back into the crowd, it is a being-together founded on separation. Being-with makes separation possible: 'together only if separated' (Blanchot 1999a: 20).[6]

The concept of distance used to describe Cassavetes' work becomes particularly relevant here. Being-with exposes this contrapuntal logic whereby the singular is called an 'each-one' each time it exposes itself to the many. In this process the 'each-one' is not constructed (and then destructed by society), rather it is exposed to its own being-social, it finds itself as the singular as long as plural. Again, this is not the constructivist formula according to which the individual understands how to behave in society by looking at others. Quite the opposite, the singular apprehends nothing and loses nothing, it simply happens to be among others, and this happening is the very essence of its existence. In discussing the work of Cassavetes, Deleuze for example points out that: 'linkages, connections, or liaisons are deliberately weak [...] sometimes the event delays and is lost in idles periods, sometimes it is there too quickly but it does not belong to the one to whom it happens' (Deleuze 2005: 205). Further, Deleuze also says that: 'the characters can act, perceive, experience, but they cannot testify to the relations which determine them' (ibid.: 211).

The close-up activates identification in order to offer the identified singularity to the plurality that this identification exposes. Identifying the singular in this case would be at the same time to open up and gaining access to the plurality. Cassavetes makes clear that the regime of identification is inseparable from a regime of distancing, of even minimal spacing, sharing and circulation. The movement in the close-up is not directed from one to many, but passes both types and *rests* in this passing and therefore never really rests on anything. It takes place between us, between the each-one and the many.

The attention paid in every close-up to the singular and the repetition of this gesture for other singulars, without ever letting one be the only One, is not just a cinematic gesture responding to the attempt to achieve a choral composition. The close-ups do not simply aim at establishing a common ground. They respond to the effort to reach the eventual trait of our being-together. Being-together: explosion of singularities exposing each in its own way an access to the plurality they also are.

By using the close-up in a contrapuntal way, by cutting several close-ups one next to the other, Cassavetes (dis)organises the composition: the close-up makes sure that sociality, our being-there-together, is purely happening and is sustained only by the fact that it is happening. The communality of the social situation is sustained not by the choral fellowship of the many, but by the displaced appearances of each one. Sociality is not reduced but exploded in these situations, exploded because what makes it solid, what prevents it from dissolving all of a sudden, is that everyone poses a distance which can't be reduced if not in view of a betrayal of sociality itself. Many authors have identified a sense of 'destruction' at work in Cassavetes' images.

Kouvaros speaks for instance of 'a tension between composition and annihilation at work in the very construction of the image' and of a filming technique that tends to 'to eat away the characters, showering them in too much light or losing them in a deliberate underexposure' (Kouvaros 2004: 149). Jousse puts it in terms of elusiveness when he says that 'the aim of Cassavetes's cinema is to show the streams which surround a person, a constantly moving rhythm between beings and things which is beyond the self, elusive' (quoted in Kouvaros 2004: 117). As already noted, Deleuze often insists on this point. With particular reference to *The Killing of a Chinese Bookie* (1976) and *Gloria* (1980) he argues that locations can abruptly change coordinates as empty spaces can be filled all of a sudden, creating the effect of an 'event which exceeds its actualization in all ways' (Deleuze 2005: 125).

Sociality in Cassavetes never rests on an obligation, a principle: it always takes an adverbial form – and it is in this sense that all his films are utterly 'social'. Contrapuntal means exactly this: that the simultaneity is not simply the appearance of subjects, but the appearing of distinct subjects, whose coming together is for them neither the reception of an extrinsic property – an accident – nor the giving of intimacy – the unleashing of an *a priori*. Contrapuntal is the distance of one from the other when those ones are together. This is barely presentable, if not *as* the time it takes from one cut to the next, from one close-up to the next, the non-consequential appearance of one face after the other.

This situation is not presentable because it cannot be reduced to one single vision, this is what makes the *with* appear and withdraw at the same time. To some extent one could say that those are not images, or barely so, if the image is what detaches itself completely and lies in a temporary isolation; these images never completely disentangle themselves from the multiplicity of other images. The process of extraction that the image necessarily propels is never completely accomplished. This is why one can speak of Cassavetes' films as having an alcoholic form: filming is never simply the attempt to render a narrative or a silent act of witnessing; rather the camera flings the mundanities of day-to-day life towards a constant crisis whereby we are no longer sure how things come together or what the proper order of things is; the everyday is taken as a portion of eternity. Characters appear, become solid, as long as they always have the possibility to revert their presence into an absence, into circulation. The fact that those films tend to be long and almost exhausting for the viewer, the fact that the action is followed always almost in real time, spanning across a short period of time, a matter of days or even hours, depends on the fact that there is no need for any reference external to the film itself. The realism of Cassavetes' films lies in the fact that they avoid resemblance, they resist it; likeness can't affirm itself because the film does not institute a relation with something beyond itself. Rather than delivering the film to the real, the film sucks the real in. Things are left without 'the time to corrupt themselves nor the origin to find themselves' (Blanchot 1999d: 258). Realism is here not an attempt to reproduce a status quo or to draw the image close to it. The real should be taken here according to the coordinates that Blanchot suggests: 'that with which our relationship is always alive and which always leaves us the initiative, addressing that power we have to begin, that free communication with the beginning that is ourselves' (Blanchot 1999c: 418). The birth of the film rests on no other resource than what is happening in front of our eyes, and what is happening is the impossibility of a presence that is not also making itself present and is therefore always on the verge of becoming the instinctual flow of time. Cassavetes seems to say: we are always there, but this is given not as a condition or agreement, but as the affirmation of something that lives just as this affirmation. In a paradoxical formula what those films say is: there is no reason for being-here-together, therefore we are-here-together.

If plurality is then not a mere multiplicity and the one is not the only one – subject, Man – then what needs to be thought is a different exposition of Being. One has to do with a reversal of the philosophical priority, but a reversal that is of a different kind from the one sought by Levinas. Not Being and then its correlations, but Being as correlation, exposing a logic that in one stroke names both 'together' and 'singularly'.

One immediately hears at this point the protestation raised by Levinas, for whom Being would already mean the finite totality, which forecloses access to the Other. This position can nevertheless be challenged. To the Levinasian objection that the unity of ontology addresses a finite totality precluding access to the Other, grasping the Other in order to betray him, Nancy replies that in fact the unity of ontology must be taken as the distancing, the in-between of its singular-plural articulations. The apparent encompassing totality of Being is here dispossessed of its powers, since Being becomes simultaneity, simultaneously singular and plural, which means also *with* itself, without ever recovering itself. 'Being does not coincide *with* itself unless this coincidence immediately and essentially marks itself out according to the *co*structure of its occurrence' (Nancy 2000: 38). Where Levinas affirms that the recurrence to Being is a threat posed to alterity, Nancy insists that alterity lies at the heart of Being. In a footnote to *Being Singular Plural* Nancy in fact writes that: 'Levinas testifies to this problematic in an exemplary manner, but what he understands as "otherwise than Being", is a matter of understanding as the "most proper of Being"' (ibid.: 199). The displacement operated by Nancy here could be read as the very reverse of the operation that Blanchot attempts in the *Unavowable Community* (Blanchot 1988), where Nancy's concept of community is rephrased in Levinas' terms, so that, as Leslie Hill writes, 'Nancy's skepticism towards Levinas is discreetly rebuffed by Blanchot's infinite skepticism towards Nancy' (Hill 1997: 201).

Nancy's argument can be reconstructed in this way: if one is to reread the Heideggerian Being-with, the problem of otherness cannot be posed simply with regard to the Other as the Other concrete human being, the problem must be posed at the heart of Being itself, concluding that Being is Other, by being with itself. This configuration presents itself as even more originary than the ontological difference, or better the ontological difference at this point becomes the question of the with: difference between Being and Being.

If the critique Levinas moves to philosophy – to always and only conceive the Same, perennially returning to itself – is grounded on the understanding of Being as the One, then any mention of Being would return philosophy to a standstill. The languishing position in which philosophy rests signals its inaptness to detach its sight from the splendor of the system. Being as an indeterminate and abstract predicate, 'seeking to cover the totality of existents in its extreme universality' (Derrida 2002: 175). To think Being would then always mean to think the Other as a category of Being itself. Levinas addresses this comment to philosophy in general, but he has Heidegger in particular in mind. It is though from within Heidegger that perhaps the criticism could be probed. If the critique rests on the fact that Being reduces the Other, then learning to think Being as the other (and not the Other than Being) could reverse the terms: not the Other in being, but being-as-other. Being-as-other means understanding the plurality at the heart of Being itself, the impossibility on Being's side to recover itself, or opening the possibility to understand the solidity of being (being-one) starting from being-with-one-another. If Being is not solid, neither a state nor a quality, but graspable only in the action of being with, then the Levinasian critique loses much of its force. As Nancy points out in a text on love – one of the few explicit debates with Levinas' thought – 'there is the "each time" of an existing, singular occurrence. There is no existing without existents, and there is no "existing" by itself' (Nancy 2003: 270). What Nancy is pointing out once more is Levinas' misunderstanding of the Heideggerian emphasis on Being as the thinking of a generality. The Being at stake here is rather a

Being that is both multiplied and singular, hard and cut across. Being-with – co-essential and constitutive of Being – takes place as the cutting across of a singular occurrence.

The togetherness offered by Being-with is thus one that always takes itself as a problem. In Nancy's intentions co-existence should be not as much the side-by-side or the taking others into account as the fact that we constantly, on an everyday basis, do not accept juxtaposition and that we open the sense of our being-together, of our otherness, reopening in this way sense at large.

One could envisage here an argument against the capitalization of the word Other. If otherness is understood as an originary situation, attached to the question of the world, made patent primarily in the unleashing and circulation of sense (without otherness there would be no sense), neither missable nor appropriable, then the 'Other' would be misleading. The mode of Being-with requires an access to the originary other that considers no appropriation and no loss. It is composed according to a logic that accepts only the exposition of others as always already coming. On the other hand the 'Other' demands a making, a welcoming that is in the end still a construction, the sight turned towards eternity. The Other becomes a fixed eternity, 'the exalted and overexalted mode of the propriety of what is proper' (ibid.: 13).

At this point one might be surprised to find Levinas – at the end of his remarks on Buber – saying that 'the Da of Dasein is already an ethical problem' (Levinas 1997b: 48). From this brief statement, an almost neglected remark, an abandoned note, one seems to see a *'poros'*, a reopening of the aporia. If the Da of Dasein is ethical, this is because the Da of Dasein is always already a Mit-da, a there-with. The Da of Dasein is an ethical problem because my being there always already implies the opening of and towards *an other there*. The consequence of this opening, this necessary displacement from my own Da – displacement which is also access to my there, to the possibility itself of occupying – is something we all have in common, regardless of the position we occupy. The fact of being there is that which we have in common. The ethical stature of this statement is perhaps Heidegger's left-over, the un-thought, an unrepeatable and inexhaustible gift, with which Levinas – after having been shaken – shakes philosophy.

That the 'Da of Dasein is an ethical problem' might suggest that the 'having to be' that Heidegger indicates as the task of Dasein should be understood as a 'having-to-be-with-others'. *Having to be* then imposes to justify one's own Being-with, understanding this Being-with not starting with one's own position, but moving from the fact that this position is a dis-position with regard to another Da. Therefore the ethical dimension of Da, and also its understanding, any form of understanding, even one beyond knowledge and theory, would start from the *with*, not as companionship this time, the light of solidarity shining on the darkness of the thrown subject, but as the irreducibility of being-there-with to the simple being-there. *With* instructs us on what has to be justified: drawing the trajectory and sustaining the momentum of this justification. On the one hand one receives the impossibility to jump back (though this back should not suggest the idea of a return, rather of a defense) into one's own Da, without finding this Da already displaced; on the other, the access to other Da*s* is an *always, but not yet*, a reinvention of positions one can never take for granted.

This logic is that of an irresolvable togetherness whose ethical dimension rests on inaccessibility. Irresolvable because, as already said, one cannot imagine a way out into the absolute properness of an origin (even a limit concept as that of solitude would in fact invoke the very heart of the with and its logic; Heidegger: 'Only can be lonesome, he who is not alone'), and inaccessible because it makes itself accessible only as the eventual form of a displacement.

It is this analytical shift that allows Nancy to say that the 'ontological disposes what the ethical exposes' (Nancy 2000: 99). The Heideggerian invitation expressed in the *Letter on Humanism*, 'think about the essence of action' (Heidegger 1978: 213), very much lays down the guidelines here.

Challenging the well-known criticism that Heidegger does not have a position with regard to ethics, Nancy attempts to read Heidegger's thinking itself as a 'fundamental ethics' (Nancy 2003: 174). The work titled *Originary Ethics* is devoted precisely to this task. Many of the motifs presented in this work are in fact recurrent themes in Nancy's reformulation of concepts such as *world*, *sense* and *with*.

Fundamental ethics will not lay down a body of principles, nor specify a particular conduct – it is an ethics without archetypes and without even the possibility of man to identify completely with his polis. An originary ethics instead responds to the demand of philosophy to think of the essence of action as action of sense. Therefore the ethical interest here will not be merely theoretical or speculative. The question of an ethics should then be posed starting from the particular engagement with existence that is Dasein's stake and responsibility. Dasein's comportment is that of being essentially preoccupied with existence, therefore with the re-opening of sense. The accomplishment of this opening has to be deferred, necessarily, since an ultimate opening meaning also an immediate closure; the appropriation of the beginning already promises the teleology of the end. This is, Nancy says, what the finitude of Dasein, on which a fundamental ethics must rest, calls us to think: 'unaccomplishment as the condition for the accomplishment of action as sense' (ibid.: 178).

This means that such an ethics does not rest on values and does not produce ideals. It announces simply the making sense of existence, the taking up – *hic et nunc* – of existence as the rigourous call to explore possibilities for making sense. Existence, conduct and disposition of sense, is both the moment of inscription of this ethics and the putting back into question of ethical assumptions. One could try at this point a provisional conclusion: to position the possibility of such an ethics, one should pay attention to the fact that Dasein is at any time that which engages with its own existence, this engagement signaling already an absolute responsibility towards making sense. Given that the *making* in making sense is always a matter of primarily opening the circulation of sense (meaning a co-existence that does not rest or present an already given evaluation of sense), this leads us to the problem of being-with and of responsibility towards others. In this way the being-with gives the measure of the measureless opening of sense. If it is true that no ethics can exist without measure, the measure of fundamental ethics is this absolute responsibility to the everyday experience of being-with. Contrary to Levinas there is no altruism here, unless altruism is taken to mean an an-archic intrusion of the other in everything that has to do with the opening of sense. As Nancy puts it 'the other is going to be essential to opening, which is essential to sense, which is what is essential in the action that makes up the essence of being' (ibid.: 181). The approach then to the humanity of the other human being (this expression inevitably recalls Levinas' work on the humanism of the other) will be directed always against and towards the excess that any definition produces. To put it differently: what needs to be answered about the humanity of the other lies in the impossibility to respond *exactly* to the question. As Lewis says, there is almost an equation in Heidegger's work between thinking and ethics, and Nancy himself seems to respect this: 'what counts as "thinking" is anything which does not remain oblivious to the void or simply, as Levinas might say, to the excess of the totality, "infinity"' (Lewis 2005: 100). The act of questioning works to install ontological difference right at the heart of totality and therefore to unsettle the very composure of this totality. When Nancy argues that 'saying "man" will always mean letting ourselves be conducted by the experience of a question that is already experienced as being beyond any question to which a signification could respond' (Nancy 2003: 194), he expresses the logic of a questioning that acts sense out, for it does not let itself be absorbed by any determination. This acting out of sense always has in view the singular, the singular event of being, 'an element within a field which cannot be encompassed within one's own view of that field, but which rather has a gaze of its own and thus stares back at the viewer' (Lewis 2005: 192).

Therefore the question is 'that of making-sense-in-common, something quite different from making common sense' (ibid.: 195). Provisionally one could then argue that ethically reaching to the other means then:

- to act sense out, as opposed to acting on a reserve of available senses;
- that this acting of sense is a sharing of finite existence; it means to enter the sharing that sense is, a sharing that exposes a plural singularity to its own existential finitude.

It is a matter precisely of unleashing the wonder, the power as it were, of this inaccessibility, of saying with Blanchot 'I recognise that you are as unknown to me as you are familiar. It is a wonderful impression' (Blanchot 1999a: 55). But of also asking, at the heart of this logic: 'Are we together? Not quite, are we? Only if we could be separated.' To finally conclude, beyond every conclusion, with astonishingly poignant brevity: 'United: separated' (but with a subtle voice, just about to be lost, or just about to reemerge, the woman replies: 'we cannot be separated, whether I speak or not' [ibid.: 21]).

How to read then Blanchot's description of the *third relation*, how to keep to his words, and to this man without horizon, affected by this most terrible, but without terror, relation. Blanchot provides a guideline to the task when he writes in *The one who was standing apart from me* 'He had put me to my task by creating a void around that task and probably by letting me believe that the task would be able to limit and circumscribe the void' (Blanchot 1999b: 265).

Blanchot's third kind of relation is 'not a relation from the perspective of unity or with unity in view, not a relation of unification' (Blanchot 1993: 71). This is then a relation where the presence of the other does not return us 'neither to ourselves nor to the One' (ibid.: 70). This is a relation that maintains itself in the interval, it is a relation of interruption, of the impossibility of finding the way home, of distance: a relation that rests on *the strangeness between us*. Blanchot is also very cautious in using the term Autrui (the other person, in Levinas' lexicon), 'Autrui is not the word one would want to hold onto' (ibid.). Moving from similar concerns as Derrida and undertaking an analogous examination, Blanchot questions the status of the Other. Whilst Derrida wants to 'examine patiently what emerges in language when the Greek conception of heteron seems to run out of breath when faced by the alter-huic' (Derrida 2002: 159), Blanchot sets off to discuss the linguistic adventure of Autrui.

Without much introduction, in the midst of the discussion, moved by a slight terror, confessing without hesitation a 'feeling of fear', right there where one has to come to terms with the unknown, or maybe precisely because it is too late, because one is already trembling under the pressure of having just passed the threshold, without being attentive enough to its resistances, without being cautious enough not to walk on that spot where the alibi of all relations is finally exposed, Blanchot solicits everyone to think: who is Autrui? He does so by clinging on to the provenance of the word and its proximity to the third term, *Lui*, Him or He. Autrui is not a word one can use without much caution. He concludes that by asking 'Who is Autrui?' one already distorts what one means to call into question, for Autrui cannot designate a nature; it does not indicate a certain type of man.

In conclusion: 'we have to do with a non personal punctuality oscillating between no one and someone' (Blanchot 1993: 71). In a relation of this kind one is also not too sure who the other is: a presence in abeyance.

Ambiguity of the Third

What will be proposed here is that the Third, developing in a philosophy of Illeity, is on one side a necessary term for the ethical relation, since it allows the very idea of the face-to-face to be developed, and on the other it takes the form of a return to neutrality, to an order that evades the relationship.

The ambiguity between what Critchley calls 'the alterity of the il y a and the alterity of Illeity' (Critchley 1996: 112) prompts the question whether Levinas ever completely overcomes the bad experience of neutrality.

By the time Levinas reaches the breaking point of his philosophy, the peak perhaps of his attempts, Illeity has become the very concept from which the emergence of Justice is discussed. If one can see in this 'philosophy of the He', as Derrida has called it, the resolution of the Face of the Other 'that resembles God', at the same time the Third seems to undermine the face-to-face relationship with the Other, by reintroducing a density beyond the relationship itself.

The third term keeps swinging between two poles: God and the Third Man, absolution and companionship (understood as the constitution of a common ground). Whilst the Third constitutes a necessary development of Levinas' philosophy, it interrupts the absolutely ethical relationship – the face-to-face

– and reduces the radicalism Levinas had introduced. To say that the face is not an allegory, not a symbol or metaphor, but that which exceeds and breaks visibility, resisting and exceeding phenomenology, and then claiming that the face of the other resembles God, or even comes from Him, poses a number of radical challenges.

Levinas is careful in explaining that the resemblance just mentioned does not fall within *mimesis*: 'the God who passed is not the model of which the face would be an image' (Levinas 1986: 359). The resemblance comes instead as respect for the Infinite: man resembles God because man is in the trace of God, not because he presents God's icon. Resemblance between the Other and God means that God can and must be heard in the voice and in the face of the Other, 'He at the root of the You' (Levinas 1998: 69). As Levinas repeats, it is not God who makes the revelation – He does not cast it – but the one who receives it (and receives it without having demanded it, by inhabiting the trace of God). This reversal of the order – according to which doing comes before hearing – this 'secret of angels' repeats the receiving of the Torah. As Levinas writes in a Talmudic commentary: 'the truth of the Torah is given without any precursor, without first announcing itself in its idea (like Malebranche's God), without announcing itself in its "essay," in its rough draught' (Levinas 1994: 46). In a passage from *Of God Who Comes to Mind*, Levinas writes that 'His (God's) absolute remoteness turns into my responsibility' (Levinas 1998: 69).

Nevertheless, if the face resists phenomenology, should its very epiphany not prevent any reference to a higher order, an order that comes to illuminate it? In the course of an homage to Levinas, Jean-Luc Marion formulates the question in this way: 'if the face does not properly give itself to be seen in the same sense as does an object or a being, how does it come to me, or reach me at all?' (Marion 225: 2000).

The answers to such questions might come only from the analysis of the third term itself. More specifically one has to be attentive to the way in which the Third orders the relationship and inscribes in it an externality, the very outside that the hypostasis of the Face seemed to have foreclosed from the very start. One can see the contradictory traits of the third term in Levinas' writing by undertaking an analysis of the different connotations it undergoes within his thinking.

In *Existence and Existents* the third term oscillates between the neutrality of Being, *there is*, and the third man, who makes possible my relation to the Other. As neutrality of Being, the third term is simply the space of horror, the space through which Macbeth and Phaedra wonder aimlessly.

The attempt in this case is to shed light on Heideggerian anxiety, fear of Being, the horror perceived in confronting the rumbling of neutrality, 'the impersonal, nonsubstantive event of the night [...] like a density of the void, like a murmur of silence [...] like a field of forces' (Levinas 2003a: 59). What Levinas wants to underline here is that Being as conceived by Heidegger can turn out to be that which makes us feel the burden of existence, that impersonal field confronting which one feels one's own impotence. With the expression *there is* Levinas aims to convey anonymity, that which 'like the third person pronoun in the impersonal form of a verb, designates not the uncertainly known author of the action, but the characteristic of this action itself which somehow has no author' (ibid.: 52). This indicates the place from which there is no escape, where suspension is closed off, where impersonal events like 'negation, annihilation and nothingness' dominate. The *there is*, neutrality over everything neutral, third term embracing the erasure of contradictions, is the locus where our existence strolls without aim. Levinas will employ this theme again and again, up through his very last texts. In the concluding pages of *Otherwise than Being*, for instance, Levinas writes:

> essence stretching on indefinitely without any possible halt or interruption, the equality of essence not justifying, in all equity, any instant's halt, without respite, without any possible suspension, is the horrifying *there is* behind all finality proper to the thematizing ego, which cannot sink into the essence it thematizes.
>
> (Levinas 2006b: 163)

The question one would want to pose is whether, despite Levinas' struggle against neutrality, the Third term does not still lead to the appearance of an externality with respect to the face to face that seems to impeach the immediacy of the ethical appeal.

This is, though, only the negative side of Thirdness. Thirdness acquires also a positive meaning. Thirdness names what is other in the Other, whilst at the same time granting access to Justice.

The motif of the third is intimately bound to the notion of the trace. It is in fact as trace that the positive meaning of the thirds is inaugurated. It is important here to fix some points, in the way of a preliminary commentary.

Levinas introduces the notion of Thirdness to overcome a certain intimacy implied in the Face-to-Face relation, the kind of intimacy for which he reproached Buber.

What is other in the Other cannot simply rely on proximity, the radicalism of the Face can be pushed even further by relating it to a term external to the relation itself.

In order to further bury alterity into an ungraspable otherness Levinas associates it with the passing of Infinity. This passing holds the character of something that will never come to an end, it is a passing that will never come to reside on a substance. Understood in this way, as the passage of Infinity, the third renders available a process by which the presence of the Other becomes absolute, for it absolves itself from the kind of presence an object would have, immediately put under siege by sight, grasping hands, thematic understanding. Levinas' aim here is clear: to bring the Other outside the Same, making its return to the Same impossible, drawing Ithaca too far from Ulysses. Once the Other is taken as absolute, the Same cannot advance enough to reach it.

In this configuration the Other can only be caught in a passage, and it will be precisely this passing that guarantees its irreducible otherness. Alterity resides now on the imperative of a passing, its mode being the opposite of representation, its order being that of disorientation, unsettling of intentionality.

A first consequence of what has been said so far is that when one comes to Illeity one can no longer discern Levinas' program on man from that on God. The intervention of Illeity, its passage transporting the Other to an order impossible to consciousness and intentionality, inevitably calls for an explanation of the concept of God. The discourse on God (which is not just the discourse on the divine, as God is here an 'overwhelming semantic event') will be inextricable from a discourse on the other human being. 'There can be no "knowledge" of God separated from the relationship with men' (Levinas 2005: 78), Levinas says.

In *The Trace of the Other*, then, Levinas writes:

> from its infancy philosophy has been struck with a horror of the other that remains other – with an insurmountable allergy. […] It is for this reason that it becomes philosophy of immanence and of autonomy, or atheism. The God of philosophers, from Aristotle to Leibniz, by way of the God of the scholastics, is a god adequate to reason, a comprehended god who could not trouble the autonomy of consciousness, which finds itself again in all its adventures.
>
> (Levinas 1986: 346)

Here Levinas associates the refusal of the Other that remains Other, the great refusal of philosophy, philosophy's primal gesture, with the disappearance of God (what Nancy calls the gods' withdrawal).

It becomes clear, here more than anywhere else, that Levinas binds together a project on the other human being with a project on the radically Other, God. A reversal of the philosophical priorities, from the Same to the Other, from hearing to doing, goes together with the emergence of God outside of reason. God as Third term – that which allows the reversal of terms – must be understood in and as an overcoming of reason. This overcoming will be dynamic and will result in a trace – sign of infinity – that does not withdraw completely, but does not make itself evident either, being completely foreign to this kind of play.

To name the trace means here to name something that does not conclude the transcendence by inscribing itself in what is immanent; rather it is by remaining an open transcendence (unmemorable) that it acquires its meaning of trace, a non-graspable relation. God must then be placed beyond the reach of reason. Once God is installed again within the realm of reason – doing after having explained – it becomes part of a movement through which philosophy aims to regain its own solidity.

By accepting this, Levinas says, philosophy engages in a logic that rests on a reassuring inertia: the Other, 'within reasons'; God as well, but only 'within reasons'; everything can be done, but only once everything has been pre-empted through knowledge.

At the same time though one must be careful not to intend Levinas' reversal of terms just as a resuscitation of the 'religious'. Whilst it is true that Levinas finds in the relation with the Other the dimension most proper to the religious and that this relation is at times divinized – for the Other and God are somehow inseparable – on the other hand he warns that 'everything that cannot be reduced to interhuman relation represents not the superior form but the primitive form of religion' (Levinas 2005: 79). Therefore when Levinas uses the term 'religious' he does so not in order to align his discourse to the apparatus or the manifestations of various religions – phenomenology or anthropology of religion – but to disclose something beyond these. 'The sentence in which God comes to be involved in words is not "I believe in God"' (Levinas 1998: 62), God is rather marked as that which in religions stands back as the ungraspable, the desire for the 'tenuous ark that ties us to the inaccessible' (Nancy 2008b: 8). Furthermore the God Levinas has in mind does not resemble the one of theology, apprehensible by knowledge (in analogy) or via its modes and attributes. Following the contradictions emphasised by Derrida's reading one could in fact say that this God is still very close to the tradition of negative theology, in particular in sentences like: 'the direct comprehension of God is impossible for a look directed upon him' (Levinas 2005: 78) or 'in the impersonal relation that leads to it the invisible but personal God is not approached outside of all human presence' (ibid.). These formulas strangely echo Angelus Silesius: 'What God is one knows not [...] he is what I, or you, or any other creature, before we became what He is, have never come to know' (quoted in Derrida 1995a: 52).

It is important to notice that by naming the alterity of the Other as he does – passage, desire, Infinity, trace, the imperative of the Third – Levinas further detaches the relation with the Other from the subject–object relation. The reference is to a past that allows no memory, a past impossible to awaken, an eternity too remote to be recalled in the present. This time from which the face comes is the time of absolute absence.

In leaping towards the Other it is not enough to follow its trace; one needs to respect this trace as that which does not obey rules, but on the contrary asks me to change my own rules.

That is also the reason why the Other in his non-phenomenal splendor remains enigmatic. Another work that attempts a development of the idea of Illeity bears the significant title *Phenomenon and Enigma*. Here Levinas insists on the irreversibility of the temporal dimension, which alterity inhabits and in which it comes to signify: 'we hear this way to signify – which does not consist in being unveiled nor in being veiled, absolutely foreign to the hide-and-seek characteristic of cognition, this way of leaving the alternative of being – under the third person personal pronoun' (Levinas 1987: 71).

The reference to listening, an intending, a lending an ear to, is not just incidental, for Illeity, the word Illeity, is not just a name, but also a voice, a command whose demand I follow even before having accepted it. The voice comes from an unbridgeable gap in time, and it is precisely this gap that allows me to lend an ear to it, to be respectful. As voice Illeity approaches me and turns me towards the Other, without me being able to change direction, to divert or to escape it. It commands me to a desire for the Other that cannot be inscribed in what is contemporaneous, even if the Other is the closest by. This desire divests me of contemporaneity and moves me to a longing of a completely different nature. It is a desire that does not grow simply by getting close to the other man, but by following the Other in what is most remote about him. As Levinas writes:

> desire, or the response to an enigma, or morality, is a plot with three personages: the I approaches the infinite by going generously toward the you, who is still my contemporary, but, in the trace of Illeity presents himself out of a depth of the past, faces, and approaches me [...] I approach the infinite by sacrificing myself.
>
> (ibid.: 73)

Following the Other into this depth I will encounter at the end of the approach his presence as transcendence, not a transcendence that resists presence, but rather a transcendence cutting across presence. One could say then that for

Levinas *the presence of the Other rests on his transcendence.* The presence of the Other, coming from the depth of a time I cannot even calculate, signifies without appearing – it signifies by visiting, but this visitation is not a phenomenon I can inscribe into my light, as if it were a matter of incarnation. Coming from the absolutely absent, the other visits me in what is disincarnate, interrupting phenomenology and impeding its movement.

From this it follows that together with Illeity is also introduced the motif of distance, of a great distance, the absolute distance, absolute in that it absolves itself from the immediacy of space.

It is important to remark that it is within and because of this distance that the Other comes to touch what is in my innermost intimacy. Namely it comes to subvert and substitute the order of my consciousness. As soon as the Other visits me from this distance I am at stake, for I am indebted to allow his being-without-horizon to appeal to me. The other is Other as Illeity, in the trace of Illeity, what eludes my presence, like a *verbosity infinitely withdrawn in an instant of laconism.*

A few words should be spent more explicitly on the role that the word God (with Levinas one is called to avoid using the *divinity* of God or the concept of the *divine*), this word at the very limit of the dictionary, this 'beast' as Blanchot puts it, plays whilst discussing Illeity. Movement of infinity, indivisible, inmultipliable, each time singular in its voice, retaining all the infinity of its absence even in the personal order, showing itself through its absence (the trace); those are some of the ways Levinas retains to articulate the word God.

Levinas often gives the impression of overlaying the two terms, Illeity and God. To put it differently: Illeity is God inasmuch as it intervenes as the inner externality of the face-to-face. This also motivates the fact that Levinas seems at times to bind together the approach to the Other as God and the approach to the Other as other human being. God is always already there in the face-to-face, the absence of his presence being entangled in the otherness of the Other.

In the process of rendering the Other absolutely distant, apprehended solely in the passage and in the trace of this passage, the Face – this face that is not an allegory but the visitation of a movement that does not belong to this world – is what makes transcendence come upon me. Musil seems to have glimpsed this when discussing the difference between common and great ideas. The latter triggers a movement of the self towards infinity, but provokes at the same time the opposite movement, according to which 'the expanse of the universe enters the self, so that it becomes impossible to differentiate between what belongs to the self and what belongs to the infinite' (Musil 1995: 114).

Once I am invested by the transcendental absolution of the Other, I am also in the presence of God, a presence always conserving the character of an absenting. God can and must be heard in the voice and in the face of the Other. Looking at the face of the Other, a look that is a glimpse because it immediately encounters the non-phenomenality of the Face, means that one is also witnessing the passage of God. As Levinas writes 'the other, inasmuch as he lends himself to thematization and becomes a phenomenon said, becomes something present and represented – but that by which he is other is precisely the Ille that eludes my presence [...] as an irrecuperable past' (Levinas 2006b: xxxiv).

Following the trace of the Other, welcoming his face as the encounter with that which withdraws in the absolute, I also withdraw *to* God. *Withdrawing to* God means that I grow less interested in my presence, in my own phenom-enology, and become enmeshed with a command falling upon me, without me being able to substitute that command with something else. *Withdrawing to* God would mean that I engage in a process whereby I substitute my subjectivity for something else. God calls me to this substitution by presenting the Other in his resistance to my grasp. God conveys to us, wrapped in an enigma, a most simple demand, that we realise that 'what we give others comes back to us'. This should not be taken according to the 'do ut des' formula, whereby to every action on my side would correspond a reaction on the side of the Other that would re-establish a just balance. In Levinas' understanding the equilibrium is always already broken, asymmetry is what establishes the ethical situation. To say 'what we give others comes back to us' means that I can acknowledge my subjectivity only in terms of substitution. I am a subject as long as I have substituted my ipseity with a movement (which holds something of a leap) towards the Other. This movement comes back to me in constituting my subjectivity as a 'for-the-other'. The act of giving to others is in the end the only thing that comes back to me; it is not a reaction from the Other, but the same act I started with. This coming back is possible since I am responsible for a responsibility for which I have never asked. I respond to a command coming from a voice so remote that in this absence I can hear at the same time God and the Other. Illeity silently slips into me. God performs this command not by setting up a structure in which I would be his interlocutor, as there is no correspondence between God and myself. Every correlation has been already warded off, for correlation would inevitably translate a command in terms of constrain or domination. 'Illeity – Levinas says – lies outside the "thou" and the thematization of objects [...] it indicates a way of concerning me without entering into conjunction with me' (ibid.: 12). I realise that 'what we give to others comes back to us' in lending an ear to Illeity, to God, but I hear this pronounced by me, it is in my own saying that I hear this. It is my subjectivity, once it has entered the play of substitution, that says so and calls me in cause in my own voice. I offer my own saying to my own consideration, I am involved in what I pronounce before knowing its meaning. What is at stake is then the acquiring of something one has never even been in need of, 'glory [...] commanding me by my own mouth' (ibid.: 147).

God thus is glorified when one of the terms in the face-to-face paradoxically inscribes itself in an order where the infinitely exterior becomes an inward voice.

A proximity so specified allows Levinas to make a distinction between his kind of commanding theology and both positive theology and the propositions of negative theology (with which it nevertheless retains a link). The triad *proximity*, *substitution* and *responsibility*, which I have summarised in the sentence 'what we give to others comes back to us', converts negative theology into an assertive form. This conversion structures itself around three constitutive moments: the absolute distance of the Other becomes proximity; in my own saying I am addressed by the passing of Infinity; substitution transforms the blurring of identity into the very excess in which I can find myself again.

God is therefore the very movement of Illeity, Illeity as dynamic – as opposed to the icon or the sacred, immobility – the passage through which the Infinite can be heard and becomes an insight for life. It is the moment when infinity forces us away from theoretical life. To put it differently: the Other and God can be approached in the same passing; what makes their passing what it is being the fact that my approaching never results in a reaching, but remains in the hesitation.

God is the passage[7] within which I can encounter the Other, but I cannot see the Other any better than by accepting the appeal (to me, only to me) as that which does not manifest itself, though I cannot avoid responding to it. As Levinas puts it: 'the infinite wipes out its traces not in order to trick him who obeys, but because it transcends the present in which it commands me, and because I cannot deduce it from this command' (ibid.: 12).

What has been said so far regarding God-Illeity and the approach to the Other, though, gives way to a series of questions. In particular it seems to allow for two ambiguities. Jean-Luc Marion indicates a first possible confusion: 'the face which appeals can be equally assigned to the Other or to God, thus avowing the indecision of its origin as well as the necessity of questioning both identity and individuation' (Marion 2000: 227). The problem highlighted here questions the overlapping between God and the Other and becomes even more stringent when the concept of justice is introduced. Marion rephrases his objection by asking: 'does the appeal come from the other person, or it refer me to the Other only from an other than the other person – no doubt God?' (ibid.: 228) It is not clear who is appealing and what is the aim of such an appeal.

A criticism linked with the question posed by Marion emphasises then a second perplexity. This calls attention to the fact that the absolute distance that Illeity as God takes on poses a challenge to Levinas, since it draws God and a neutral absence (that of the 'there is') extremely close.

As Blanchot discusses in *Our clandestine companion*, Levinas' philosophy does not manage to eliminate the presentiment 'that the infinite transcendence, the transcendence of the infinite, to which we try to subject God, will always be ready to veer off to the point of possible confusion with the bustle of the there is [...] absolute indetermination' (Blanchot 1986: 49). John Llewelyn points out this possible impasse when he writes 'Anonymous ilyaity recurs in pro-nominal illeity to the point at which the former may be mistaken for the latter. Between the one and the other there is a recurring alternation' (Llewelyn 1995: 204).

The possibility ascribed to the Third of introducing justice in the face to face and the ambiguity at work in the Third itself (ambiguity that revolves around the Third Man, God as Illeity and the neutrality of the 'there is') seem to return Levinas to the point he had primarily tried to avoid, namely the return of a neutral term. As Derrida writes: 'responsibility for the other human being is *anterior to any question*. But how does responsibility obligate if a third troubles this exteriority of two where my subjection of the subject is subjection to the neighbour?' (Derrida 1999: 32).

If it is the Third that commands me to justice and if this element cannot be disentangled from the confusion invoked by Blanchot, then justice appears as the site where the face to face has to accept some kind of overwhelming external force that concludes its trajectory. As a consequence the face to face falls prey to the same accusation Levinas had moved to Heidegger's Being-with, that of being simply a moment in view of something else. This something else would be in Levinas' case the reduction of the singular ethical encounter to a neutral justice fulfilled through the intervention of Illeity, behind which one could easily see the shadow of God as *ordo ordinans*.

The sky over justice: Return of neutrality

At this point one cannot avoid the question of justice any longer, for it is at the threshold of the demand for justice that something unexpected happens. In his *adieu* to Levinas Jacques Derrida calls it a perjury:

> if the face to face with the unique engages the infinite ethics of my responsibility for the other in a sort of *oath before the letter*, an unconditional respect or fidelity, then the ineluctable emergence of the third and with it of justice would signal an initial perjury.
>
> (ibid.: 33)

The question of justice calls for the motif of the Third to be addressed once more, this time moving from a different articulation. Where before the focus was on the Illeity of God, now it will be on the Third Man. As the study develops it will become clearer that the link already envisaged between the Other and God is also, and inevitably so, at work in the development of the idea of the Third Man. Hence one cannot completely separate God and the Third Man. The way the latter enters the face to face makes him somehow similar to the figure of the angel, if one generously sticks to the word in its Greek meaning: that which announces, but announces something just as long as it announces only itself, its own coming. This is the role played for instance by the young woman haunting Myrtle (Gena Rowlands) in Cassavetes' *Opening Night* (1977). She is not just the very non-phenomenon at the heart of the film, but the evidence of a chronic announcement, always investing the actress from within her own voice, her own presence. A similar angelic moment can be seen in *Love Streams* (1982), where a naked bearded man suddenly appears on a chair. As Kouvaros says these apparitions 'put representation into question', introducing 'a violent tearing of performative space' (Kouvaros 2004: 147). They not only take us by surprise, they impose on the spectators to bear witness to an unaccountable singularity, exceeding control and comprehension.

All the ambivalence of the Third Man comes from this act of pure announcement revolving only around itself.

The Third man develops in a twofold way: on the one hand the third man is the other of the other which calls me one among others, and thus breaks the intimacy; on the other he obliges me to a concern for everyone and therefore for myself. Therefore the Third Man founds a sort of contemporaneousness, a common ground. In *Totality and Infinity* Levinas had already announced the question of Others, by saying that the response triggered by the Other cannot remain simply 'between us', for 'everything that takes place here "between us" concerns everyone [...] even if I draw back to seek with the interlocutor the complicity of a private relation' (Levinas 2005: 212). The preferred being, clandestine and in love, is now open to humanity. A universality clinging onto a higher register breaks through. It does so by simply announcing its own arrival, announcing justice as non-postponable.

In Robert Walser's *The Tanners* the arrival of Kaspar disposes things from curiosity and chance, from the autonomous fortuity into which Simon and Klara live, to love and concern. This is the situation that manifests the insufficiency of personal happiness. Klara spends anxious words to describe how unbearable the solitary brilliance of her happiness has become. Justice needs the two, but at the condition that these two do not shut themselves up.

The community of lovers is not just, not because within it injustice would prevail, but because it lacks the means, being played as it is on the possibility of condemning to oblivion what lies outside it. Tristan and Isolde are beyond the logic demanded by justice, for they can still lose the world and the world can just as easily get rid of them, whilst their tie remains intact: 'the world has collapsed' and they are pulled in 'the place of the strange' (Blanchot 1993: 191). Lovers are foreign to the logic of justice; whilst they are not exactly unjust they always choose in favor of oblivion and against the rest of humanity.

Justice is available only to a society where there is no distinction between those close by and those far off. This erasure is made possible by the arrival of the Third Man. Upon his entrance the Third Man always speaks a prophetic word, which means it addresses a universality, though this address never takes universality as a theme (i.e. human race, biological genus, common functions). As Levinas puts it 'biological human fraternity, considered with the sober coldness of Cain is not a sufficient reason that I be responsible' (Levinas 1998: 71).

The analogy with the angel should appear now less anomalous. The Third Man's announcement does not announce an horizon, like humanity united by resemblance; rather, it announces its own coming, the very moment of its movement *into* the face-to-face and across it. The breaking through of the Third Man is straightforwardness: it takes the form of the announcement of its unicity, by way of which my own unicity is also underlined. This means that the Third Man does not come to establish differences within a genus; quite the opposite, by coming foreign to differences, he makes being-for-one-another a more urgent and problematic matter. The Third Man imposes a problem on the face-to-face. It has been said that the Third Man could be read in a twofold way. He makes me one among others by announcing himself in his forthright coming, thus he urges us to lower our intimacy, not towards a common cause, but for the sake of a wider command. As Levinas puts it: 'the entry of a third party is not simply a multiplication of the other; from the first the Third Party is simultaneously other than the other, and makes me one among others' (Levinas 2006b: 155). At the same time the Third Man imposes on me a concern for *everyone*. Given that everyone includes myself, the Third Man also announces in its coming my responsibility towards myself. Apart from removing the face-to-face from clandestinity, it introduces a concern for myself, concern that comes from the substitution of my identity in the for-the-other, 'my concern for myself is triggered by the third party; not the reversibility of the relationship with alterity, but its multiplication to the second power makes the ethical possible' (ibid.: xxxv).

Following the introduction of the Third Man then proximity becomes a problem. Within this new situation I cannot simply address the Other that confronts me in the face-to-face, but I also have to address everyone in the face of the Other and myself. Proximity becomes a problem because it no longer concludes my ethical commitment. It is not enough to receive the epiphany of the face, to address this proximity in order to be just – justice is revealed as the uneasiness of proximity. Proximity now becomes what simultaneously founds and obstructs the opening of the plane of justice. As Derrida puts it

> comparison is superimposed onto my relation with the *unique* and the incomparable and in view of equity and equality, a weighing, a thinking, a calculation, the *comparison of incomparables,* and, consequently, the neutrality – presence or representation – of being, the thematization and the visibility of the face.
>
> (Derrida 1999: 32)

As previously mentioned, close proximity, of which love is an exemplary situation, achieves the opening of a realm of respect, the relieving of the all-encompassing moment, but at the same time the closer the face-to-face becomes, the more it deepens the intimacy – even when this is played out in asymmetry and absence – the higher the barricade it erects against the Third and the development of justice.

Whilst the face-to-face binds me to the Other, and immerses me in his trace, it always threatens to leave the Third Man outside the door. This proximity has to acknowledge the angelic element, the prophetic word of the Third, the correction of the asymmetry that the Third Man provokes. There must be a flash of recognition: one must be able to recognise a positive obsession at the very heart of the face-to-face, namely all the others that sit on the opposite side of the face-to-face into which I am engaged.

Through the eyes of the one whose face I receive I must become able to see a plethora of eyes. They are all looking for me and I am commanded to substitute myself for them all. The Third therefore commands me to a concern for everyone, which is not meant to degrade my relationship with the Other in front of me, but imposes on me to see this relationship as problematic, as bound to fail despite the best intentions. The Third, Levinas says, is responsibility extended beyond intention.

One is here confronted with a double constraint, because if it is true that the Third introduces justice, at the same time it 'violates in its turn, at least potentially, the purity of the ethical desire devoted to the unique' (ibid.: 33), as if the solution would dissolve the very thing it tries to preserve. If it is true that the face-to-face is ethics itself, responsibility without decision, secret of angels, doing before hearing, then this should exclude all foreign order, confusion with neutrality. Levinas seemingly carries a battle against neutrality, to the point that one could be led to say that his philosophy is in the end the attempt to push neutrality to its own limit, there where neutrality is neutral even with regard to itself and its forces then collapse under a private inertia. Levinas' philosophy seems to move from a demand that holds neutrality as its most crucial preoccupation (Heidegger's anxiety, fear of Being, is the neutral par excellence). One might say that this is a way of considering *Totality and Infinity* and that the following works purely from the negative and critical point of view. Such reading would overlook their propositional vigour and the immeasurable density of their language and diminish the constellation of affirmative statements that are there constantly offered. What I am trying to say here is something different. The thesis here would be that *in the formulation of Justice there happens an inevitable u-turn, one which threatens to reintroduce neutrality at the very heart of the ethical.*

It has been said that the other is Other as long as its infinity is respected, which is to say that we do justice to the Other as long as we encounter it in the trace of God. Face-to-face describes respect for the absolute distance of the Other, his remoteness in the resemblance to God. A series of questions arise: does not God emerge as the bearer of Justice rather than the Other? If this is the case then the movement that would reconcile us to a just relation to the Other would be primarily a look directed to the Other as that which can lead us to God. God is Justice because it is that of the Other which escapes themes. Every time I try to reduce the Other to pure theory, it is God that comes to remind me of the respect for the absolute distance of the Other.

One could try to say this with other words: the resemblance between the Other and God is made possible by the fact that, as Levinas repeats, the revelation is not made by God, but by the one who receives it and receives it without having demanded it, by inhabiting the trace of God. Still, does not the fact that a revelation is possible indicate the need for an agent beyond the relationship, so as to make this relationship meaningful, this meaningfulness becoming the renewal of the singularity of the ethical experience?

Marion seems to advance a similar criticism:

> to evoke 'the wonder of the I claimed by God in the face of the neighbour' amounts to suggesting that the claim which refers to the face effectively goes back to God, in the fashion of some strange ethical occasionalism in which the effective cause (God) recovers and would always precede a simply occasional cause (the Other person).'
>
> (Marion 2000: 227)

By introducing God into the elicitation of Justice, does not the requirement become more important than the terms carrying Justice forth?

God appears sometimes close to a neutral overarching element, the lassitude of the there is. As Leslie Hill says in discussing Blanchot and Levinas, the reference to God in the discussion of justice 'has the potential of turning Levinas' account of the transcendence of the other into precisely one of those philosophies of the neuter' (Hill 1997: 175).

One can identify here two crucial elements: the face-to-face needs Justice, Justice is obtained by the intervention of an Illeity, a distance proper only to God; in turn this distance draws God close to an ordering entity, which can be preserved only if its neutrality is taken into account. In this double movement one can glimpse the risk that Levinas' project might fail to preserve the non-renounceable, asymmetrical command that makes possible the reopening of the philosophical horizon otherwise than Heidegger.

From these questions one can conclude that the neutral, against which Levinas moves his first step, is in fact taken as the guarantor of justice, which is – given that Justice makes room for the State and the law – the very achievement of the ethical experience. Exigency for justice seems to always come from above, from that which remains equally distant from me and from the Other. Therefore, in the accomplishment of justice, Levinas seems admits into asymmetry an impersonal reason, chaotic otherness, conceptual totality. In *Totality and Infinity* Levinas criticizes 'the obedience that no face commands' (Levinas 2005: 298), but the question of justice seems to bring this right back, for the obedience to which I am commanded if I am to be just responds exactly to a faceless entity.

Whilst it is true that the movement is from the Other to God, an inversion with regard to theology since it is not God that triggers my kindness, but the other that turns my sight to the sky, nonetheless God comes as the light – visible only as a shadow – that establishes a higher level. It is this luminous shadow that promotes the ethical beyond knowledge, justice. The ethical thus confirms itself as God because of this possibility of turning its terms to something that is not 'just' the face-to-face.

Can this discourse on justice avoid reintroducing not only the need for thinking about Being-with even before substitution, but also about what the *with* of Being is, as that which would prevent Being from transforming itself in an all-encompassing movement? Does not Levinas, by way of a series of odd moves, reach a position not at all distant from the one from which Jean-Luc Nancy advances his analysis in the first place?

If justice is what needs in primis to give the face to face its ethical dimension, how can it do so if the face to face is excluded from the accomplishment of justice? Is this not to impose on the order of the face to face a higher order, that of a purer, more distant Justice? This order would remain then the true achievement, the energy of ethics, though still a theory, whilst the face to face would be a mere, though crucial, step.

Levinas opens *Totality and Infinity* with a chapter entitled 'Desire for the Invisible'. Rather ironically this casts fore at the very end of *Otherwise than Being* the following question: in striving for justice, is it God the one I desire rather than the Other? Desire will then be directed to the Other in order to occasion the encounter with God. I choose the other in the absence of God. Once the other is called to merely fill a gap, is he still respected in its being? The reintroduction of neutrality seems thus to take the following structure: on one side justice is called to wrap up the ethical dimension of the face-to-face by intensifying it as the foundation of State and system; on the other hand, if justice is that which is possible only thanks to the emergence of the *He*, God, interruption of the face, how can justice be found at work within the face to face without the introduction of a neutrality, a superior gesture that elevates the face to face and in elevating it also consumes the face to the point where this loses every expression, the force of its epiphany? Justice at this point seems to be the very revenge of Neutrality.

The immeasurable face of the *with*

One could return at this point to the initial question: how does Levinas' philosophy of otherness challenge a formulation developed from within the work of Martin Heidegger? To put it in different terms: how could the measure of the 'with' resist the immeasurable face of the other?

The distance between Levinas and Nancy has been evaluated against those considered to be key stages in the development of the question of the other: the problem of the world, the I–thou relation and the reference in Levinas' thinking to the Third Term, Illeity.

As to the first concept, the line was drawn between Levinas' need for an escape from Heidegger's world and from Nancy's radicalization of the possibilities of the Heideggerian world (which is also to say the world as the site of the abandonment to possibilities).

The two other stages scrutinized contained a more direct reflection on the question of the 'with' and the reasons Levinas holds to dismiss it. It has been argued that Levinas fails to consider the existential character of the with, reducing it to a category, thereby offering a reading of Being-with as:

- a stage within a solipsistic trajectory;
- an element that expresses the logic of a grouping together, holding on to on one side the indifference of the crowd and on the other the overarching power of the destiny of Being.

It has then been questioned whether Levinas' criticism of the instrumentality of the Heideggerian world does not perhaps rest on a misreading. Levinas' reasons for finding access to the other outside the world would thus be challenged: if the world – as Nancy has it – is in fact not only the place of work, tools and attachment to things, but also the breaking through of possibilities, then Levinas' critique becomes less powerful.

The notion of world has been investigated in detail, as it seems to constitute a crucial moment of distinction between Levinas and Nancy. They both start with the Heideggerian formulation of Being-in-the-world, but where Levinas opens his line of reason by finding a way out from the Heideggerian world, Nancy places the opening of sense right at the heart of Being-in-the-world. This has important consequences as it also sheds light on the question of Being-with and in particular on the Mit of each Da.

Levinas subscribes to a common criticism attributed to Heidegger, which Nelson summarises in these terms: 'Heidegger's thought is inherently unable to think the social and the ethical' (Nelson 2008: 141). It has been argued that this is not entirely true. Quite the opposite, Heideggerian ethics – which Nancy calls 'originary' and Nelson 'ethics of facticity' – seems to also allow Levinas to make his claims, once it is understood that this originary ethics rests on impossibility to be reduced to a moral code.

Whilst it is true that Heidegger never puts forward an ethics in terms of moral principles and codes of behaviour, nevertheless it would be hazardous to affirm that there is no place for the ethical demand in Heidegger's thinking. Even beyond the explicit answers offered in *Letter on Humanism*, the question of Being-with already contains a discourse on ethics, if not explicitly then at least by offering a series of possible developments.

Although Dasein is born and dies in apparent isolation, nevertheless *Being and Time* offers passages – in particular in the discussion of Being-in-the-world and Being-with – in which ideas of openness, sharing, crossing, and circulation of sense play a crucial role. If it is true that Being-with tends to remain polarized between the indifference of the crowd and the destiny of the people, there are enough elements inviting for a third reading, one that takes the Mit as the exposure of singularities to each other. The Da of each singularity responds to the question 'what happens between us'. It offers itself as a reflection on the *between* as the space that makes a 'us' and 'we' possible. When Levinas affirms that the *Da* is already an ethical problem, he seems to acknowledge a crucial development for the concept of Mitsein. The question here would be how Being-with configures the relation of each Dasein when exposed to other singular Dasein*s*. Being-with or being-together impels the rethinking of the opening of Dasein towards a common *Da*, the crossing of many *theres* that does not end in the constitution of a new, higher Dasein (this is in the end what Levinas is preoccupied by).

The measure of the with, if read in this way, should 'evaluate' the distance that singularities constantly cross without giving birth to a higher entity. This defines plurality not as an external or acquired quality of each singularity, but as the very measure of each one of them. Plurality becomes an intrinsic measure calling each time for the engagement of one singularity with all the others, but only each time and not in a heightened or separate dimension. The each time of the crossing happens in the world, also in the midst of the They, for a relative indistinction is needed for a constant opening to be possible. The immeasurable face of the other is respected, for the singular existence is what is at each time at stake: not multiplicity as such, but the multiplicity that is always exposed as singular existence.

This dimension, where the *with* measures the multiplicity opened by each singularity, would also allow for a relation without mediation, exactly what Levinas tries to achieve through a different trajectory. Whilst Levinas' attempt seems to ultimately give in to a Third Term – whose resemblance to an absolutely distant God instigates an ambiguous confusion with neutrality – that appears to act as a mediator in the accomplishment of justice, the measure of the with allows for intersections that respond to nothing else than the originary being-open of a singular existence. The impasse Levinas reaches is well expressed by Leslie Hill: 'if it is the case, as Levinas contends, that the relation with the other is without mediating concept or intermediary of any kind, so it would follow from this that henceforth there is neither God, nor values, nor nature' (Hill 1997: 173).

Levinas' concern though is not only with the crowd. From his writings one can deduce his dissatisfaction towards the essentially solipsistic nature of Dasein. One could say that whilst it is true that Heidegger's system – as Nelson says – rests on *individuation*, this is never fully accomplished. The process is constantly re-opened, resulting in a system of differential relations, rather than promising the constitution of an independent subject.

The fundamental structure of Dasein implies that the work of subjectivity is always 'threatened' by openness. Dasein is in the world as the open. Being-in-the-world means essentially this: that subjectivity is abandoned to its very openness, where my Dasein might never be realised. This struggle for my Dasein is largely played on the level of a sharing out (rather than, for instance, in the modes of self-reflection or discoursing with one's own self). The focus that Heidegger puts on practices (on having to do with) can thus appear not only as the attempt to underline our instrumental appraisal of the world, but as the attempt to describe the world as essentially a system of shared references.

Considering this framework, Nancy's attempt would be to dismantle the concept of the subject starting from Heidegger, in order to construe otherwise the question of relation. This demand seems to be similar in both Nancy and Levinas, but given this common point of departure, a key discrepancy emerges: whilst for Levinas the ethical is infinity as the interruption of finite existing (break in the world, break in the holding on things, break through anonymity thanks to epiphany and proximity), for Nancy ethics is structured as an infinite demand to take finitude into account by challenging the possibility of an ultimate overcoming of finitude.

Where Levinas places the ethical in the altruism coming from infinity, Nancy sees it as the sharing that traverses finitude, 'the question of the between us – which would be in fact the question of the between, according to which there can be a "we"' (Nancy 2008c: 119).

Simon Critchley has moved a Levinasian criticism to Nancy's project for reducing the moments of surprise occasioned by the epiphany of the Other to 'ontic modifications of a fundamental ontological structure' (Critchley 1999: 248). Critchley's analysis, whilst validating the shift in emphasis that Nancy brings to *Being and Time* in order to rescue Being-with from Heidegger's archi-fascism and whilst praising Nancy's attempt to write a non-metaphysical ontology, reproaches the French philosopher for 'neutralizing ethical transcendence' (ibid.: 251). This neutralization reduces Being-with and otherness to relations of juxtaposition and indifference. On the other hand here it has been argued that it is precisely Nancy's focus on the ontological project that allows for a rewriting of the 'with' as singular each-time that guarantees at once separateness and engagement with otherness.

Whilst Levinas starts from an individuality – withdrawal into ipseity (separation) – opening on to others following the call of responsibility, and then achieving justice with the help of God, Nancy begins from the space of the relation, from the 'with' that distances and unites singularities. It is in the space of the 'with', in the endless circulation of sense and the space that this circulation constitutes, that an investigation on singularities becomes possible. Whilst Levinas starts with the one to one and then indicates a Third, a witness, prophet or God to complete the picture, to make the relation a just relation, Nancy starts with the many and the each one, with the space of plurality as essential and proper to singularity. By starting there where Levinas ends, Nancy acquires a position from which he can not simply reinterpret the Heideggerian Mitsein, adjusting its interpretation beyond the crowd and the people, addressing the ethical importance of each *Da*, but also achieves the relation without mediation that Levinas in the end of its philosophical trajectory seems obliged to abandon.

Powers of Existence

Being with the undecidable

The following argument aims on one side to provide a new opening into the analyses carried out so far and on the other to define in greater detail the specific gesture of Jean-Luc Nancy's contribution to philosophy: pushing thinking to the limit-thought of existence.

The analysis will be structured around three moments:

- the notion of Being-with will be analysed once again in light of Levinas' criticism of Heidegger; particular attention will be devoted to the notion of solipsism and its connection with the concept of 'they';
- the attempt by Nancy to undo a general prejudice at work in *Being and Time* – one that tends to highlight the exceptional and the heroic – provides him with the possibility to invest Being-with with a radicalism that Heidegger envisaged but at the same time abandoned. By stressing the *with* as the site of the openness of existence to the work of otherness, Nancy seeks to escape a philosophical performativity that decides over experience by naming it. The result of this is the untying of the with from its destinations and appropriations, and the possibility to open once more philosophy to existence;
- by exposing thinking – always a finite thinking – to existence Nancy emphasises the importance of preserving in philosophy the openness of existence. Existence's undecidability, as its very power, therefore displaces the ontological order. The fact that thinking becomes possible only from the advance of existence with regards to philosophy, understanding, knowledge and interpretation constitutes the very project of Nancy's philosophy. In

his constant debate with Heidegger, Nancy relentlessly evokes powers of existence – singular resistances of existence to the mastering decision of philosophical work, so that philosophy in turn has to continuously loosen its categories and key words in the attempt to decide its course according to what happens between us.

The problem of *Being-with* has been touched upon throughout the current work. It was said that Levinas contests Heidegger for not having been able to disentangle the *with* from both an original solitude and an overarching generalization. The originality of otherness, according to Levinas, is foreclosed by a philosophy that commences with Being and with a 'who' trying to address the question of Being for its own sake. Heidegger bars the possibility of receiving the other in two capacities: on the one hand, Being-with is too general and therefore does not provide any indication about sociality, always sinking the Other in the generality of the crowd; on the other, Levinas insists that the notion of Being-with rests on and refers to a long tradition of solipsism.

Levinas is not satisfied with Heidegger saying *ad nauseam* that 'this being qua Dasein is always already with others and with beings not of Dasein's nature' (Heidegger 1984: 190). According to Levinas it is very clear from the beginning that Heidegger's philosophy is a thesis on solitude. Two motifs already mentioned will be discussed:

- 'they' as the mode of everyday understanding that inevitably embraces and limits the Other and confounds the work of otherness;
- *solipsism* as the original mistake of Heidegger's philosophy, preventing Heidegger from accessing the other.

'They' is the site of the ontical experience of Being-in-the-world as Being-with. Whilst it is true that Heidegger dismisses the 'they' as average understanding that understands everything, it is also true that the 'they' is the very site of disclosedness. Given the structure of Heidegger's analysis, which travels back and forth between the ontical and the ontological to achieve the thinking *of* existence, it should not come as a surprise that 'they' is both the site where everything happens and the place of disengagement. 'They' is always already satisfied, because no one is allowed to say anything that would reach beyond it. However it would be hasty to suggest that the everyday is for Heidegger merely the place of deceit. Heidegger writes that 'the expression "idle talk" is not to be used here in a "disparaging" signification. Terminologically, it signifies a positive phenomenon' (Heidegger 1962: 211).

The conversations taking place in the everyday do not necessarily preclude the experience of existence. Instead what Heidegger implies is that one cannot say anything that would not be immediately recuperated within what the other person (anyone else) is saying. Therefore everything is understood perfectly well. The 'they' is thus not as much condemned as 'everyday', as refused as that moment of the everyday where every day is considered as any other day, where the bursting of existence (a bursting that happens every day, every minute) is therefore suspended in the closure of a past by now deprived of any interest and a future already entirely calculated. The problem – Heidegger says – is that 'understanding and interpretation already lie in what has thus been expressed' (ibid.). The surprise that existence is gets surpassed in the fact that average understanding already knows everything. Existence thus comes to be *comprehended* once and for all: things are qualified once and for all. Authority over existence is established, whilst at the same time existence itself, as a singular decisive event, is passed under silence. It is only because the 'they' is there, however, that one can hear the silencing of existence, that one can understand existence as having been decided upon. It is only because I too am the 'they' that I can encounter myself there and feel uncomfortable. Existence would not be in the world without the 'they', for idle talks and the curiosity that springs from them constitute the very first proof that my world is first of all a shared world. As Heidegger makes clear:

> this everyday way in which things have been interpreted is one into which Dasein has grown in the first instance […] In it, out of it, and against it, all genuine understanding, interpreting, and communicating, all re-discovering and appropriating anew, are performed.
>
> (ibid.: 213)

The attitude just described (an 'I've-seen-it-all' attitude) reveals something about our relation with Others. Heidegger writes that in the everyday

> the Other is proximally 'there' in terms of what 'they' have heard about him, what 'they' say in their talk about him, and what 'they' know about him. Being-with-one-another according to the mode of the 'they' 'is by no means an indifferent side-by-sidedness in which everything has been settled, but rather an intent, ambiguous watching of one another.
>
> (ibid.: 219)

The other is there already in the 'they', its position is that of being surrounded with a curious surveillance. The 'they' therefore offers the sort of indistinction needed for the Other to spring forth. Because the 'they' does not simply negate the other, it tends to reduce both myself and the Other to the same. The 'they' is the negation of singularities in general and their negation in (favour of) the general. It is the everyday before each day. It makes no decision as to what happens between us.

From this one can conclude that the 'they' is necessary to establish at least one façade of an original sociality. The sociality where the other is simply everyone, where everyone is simply an other; another one, upon which to cast a suspicious look. In the 'they' therefore it is not only the Other that disappears, but myself too. As a consequence there disappears also the very possibility of a sociality founded on more than an undistinguished inclusion (perhaps this is the very kind of sociality that a 'multiculturalism' advocating every difference as equal cannot evade).

'They' is precisely the 'same' into which we, the other and myself, are plunged. When Heidegger says that 'this (the They's) Being-with-one-another dissolves one's own Dasein completely into the kind of Being of 'the Others' (ibid.: 164) he is not arguing that Dasein has to overcome the Others so as to retire into a closed interiority, withdrawal par excellence, the ivory tower of consciousness. Quite the opposite: Dasein is included in 'the Others'. The dissolution of Dasein into the Others means that both the other and myself dissolve into a generality into which we both become nobody (*ne ipse unum*). This is also why Heidegger writes that 'existence as together and with one another is founded on the genuine individuation' (Heidegger 1982: 288). Given that Heidegger painstakingly separates his notion of 'self' and 'individuation' from a substantialist approach, one should not read the passage just mentioned from the *Basic Problems of Phenomenology* as indicating that the self should return to itself so as to elude the pressure of other selves. Respectful recognition of the others is respectful only once Dasein has exposed itself to others as a singularity. Dasein's possibility to recognise others happens together with Dasein's recognition of itself as that which is open to existence and not closed within. As Nancy has it: 'any being that one might like to imagine as not distinguished, not dis-posed, would really be indeterminate and unavailable: an absolute vacancy' (Nancy 2000: 96). The problem of Being-with as too general plays out at this level, exactly at the point where the discussion of the 'they' crosses that of solipsism.

Commentators often identify what Heidegger terms *metaphysical egoicity* with solipsism. Heidegger created the term in the 1920s, at a time when his terminology was not fully worked out. With metaphysical egoicity Heidegger describes the possibility for an I–Thou relationship to happen, where the 'Thou' is not simply an ontical replicate of the 'I'. Not an other ego, but a 'you-yourself'.

This very specific kind of existential solipsism is often misunderstood (Levinas is particularly insistent on this) with factual or existential egotism. Dasein's trajectory thus becomes essentially a solitary parade. Dasein would therefore be indifferent to or disinterested in sociality. As François Raffoul remarks though: 'the *solus ipse*, far from signifying the closure of the ego upon itself that occurs with the reduction, in fact opens Dasein to the totality of Beings' (Raffoul 1998: 215). One should be careful not to jump to hurried conclusions, but pay attention instead to the nature of the solipsism Heidegger invokes with the term *metaphysical egoicity*.

A reading of Heideggerian solipsism should not only provide an insight into Being-with, but it could show, perhaps paradoxically, through an exercise of reverse philology, how much what Levinas expresses as 'the other remaining the other' also motivates – up to a point at least – Heidegger's thinking. When Levinas speaks about love he seems to rejoin the necessary movement that cuts across the 'they' and solipsism: 'coincidence is fusion. For me, on the contrary, sociality is excellence, and one should never think sociality as a missed coincidence [...] I think that when the other is "always other", there is the essence of love' (Levinas 2001: 58). One could show that the solipsism Heidegger is describing is in the end not at all different from what Levinas terms 'excellence'.

Heidegger admits that if the determination of Dasein as metaphysically isolated were to mean only that Dasein exists simply to reduce nature and others to its own goals, or that a detachment from the world would allow Dasein to regain some authentic ground, then his philosophical project 'would indeed be madness' (Heidegger 1984: 186).

Heidegger specifies instead that the statement relative to the essence of Dasein as interest into one's own being does not present an ontic ethical egoism. The solipsism he is describing is the instantiation of a singularity; it signals the moment of emergence of a singularity in a fashion opposed to the emergence of a substantial subjectivity. This solipsism makes possible the disclosure of singular/plural existence. It is from this structure that Heidegger proceeds to say that factically Dasein cannot avoid being-with-others, cannot avoid recognising others as singularities. If Dasein were not a singularity, it would not be able to express itself with and through other singularities; quite the opposite, it would have them standing in front of it in a simply empathic relation.

The problem arises when one interprets Dasein as subject, as a substance that stays identical with itself, regardless and through the course of its modulations. One then needs to look back at the entire project of existential analysis, which is aimed at questioning Being so as to reach the most radical concept of singular existence. As Raffoul puts it: 'the question of the meaning of Being "in general" becomes inseparable from the question of the specific mineness of a particular being, the generality of Being harbouring the most radical individuation' (Raffoul 1998: 20). The self in this case becomes a differentiating principle, and Being is a question of 'who' and not of 'what'. To the concept of an egoistic subject Heidegger substitutes that of a singularly decided possibility always open to Being and to others. Always open also means that its relation with itself is an each-time-open. This implies that singular existence can only be understood on the basis of the singular existent's relation to what it decides upon: the world, other beings, other singular existences. Solipsism is therefore still a matter of relation. Whilst subjective theories have posed throughout the history of Western philosophy the self as the moment of closure from which to begin, thus to a large extent presupposing its course, or at least considering it as 'an underlying presence of an entity present-at-hand' (ibid.: 27), Heidegger makes of the singular existent an impossibility: the impossibility of grasping one's own being once and for all. This impossibility produces the constant openness Dasein is, each time open to and for itself. This openness, however, is not configured as a dialectic, which is to say that one is not starting with a self, closed in its consciousness, which subsequently opens to other consciousnesses only to then come back and recognise itself once more. Quite the opposite, with Heidegger one starts with an openness, which can never be reduced; this 'distraction' of Dasein with regard to itself, cannot be reverted back to attention. An absolute subject – abstracted from the world and from others – can at most provide what Heidegger calls a formal indicator, always late with regard to what it tries to indicate: that which does not remain the same.

The problem with the subjectivist tradition – and even Kant according to Heidegger partially falls prey to this criticism[1] – is that it misses out on existence, because it starts with the idea of 'the selfsameness and steadiness of something that is always present-at-hand' (Heidegger 1962: 367). The idea of individuation as the each-time singular event of selfhood instead allows us to grasps the continual and originary exposure of existence to itself.

As Heidegger puts it, the very first gesture of his analysis demands the opening of this anti-subjectivist horizon: 'if the Self belongs to the essential attributes of Dasein, whilst Dasein's "Essence" lies in existence, then "I"-hood and Selfhood must be conceived existentially' (ibid.: 365). As a consequence of this, these concepts demand to be considered from the point of view of an each-time-undecided existence. Dasein has to decide for its own self, which is not given, or better it is that which at any time is only given, but in this given one hears 'delivered over', 'offered' and 'at stake'. The givenness of the self here turns out to have the character of a putting at stake, almost of a gambling. Selfhood is given for articulation, rather than given as that which does not change.

This brings us back to the question of solipsism. Solipsism works along with transcendence. As Heidegger puts it: 'Dasein transcends every being, itself as well as every being of its own sort (Dasein-with) and every being not of Dasein's sort' (Heidegger 1984: 190).[2]

Contrary to what the usual criticism supports, solipsism does not indicate a dismissal of altruism: it is this very idea of the singular and eventual character of existence to commence human community. As Raffoul clarifies further 'Metaphysical Egoicity designates the Being-a-self that is the basis for the I and the Thou, in such a way that the Thou is not understood as an alter ego' (Raffoul 1998: 212). It is only as singular existence that the Other and myself as other avoid being reduced to generality (they). It is only in this way that these singularities can be exposed to one another.

In solipsism one finds the manifestation of a letting others be. At this point for Heidegger sociality is founded on the exposure of singularities to one another, on the surpassing of the notion of a subject always present-at-hand in favor of an openness, whose appropriation is not possible. The singular, as that which at any time stands against itself as much as against others and the world, is that which can never be reduced to anything, that which is constantly committed to existing, to opening, completely, originarily. Only an existent considered as singular (but not as individual) can be this openness, only a singular existent outside participation can live with others in a plurality that 'respects' (this is the term that Levinas says is missing in Heidegger's philosophy) them as singulars. The formula Heidegger offers is that of a relationship between an 'I-myself' and a 'you-yourself'. This means that the singular is not only delivered to others, but it constantly offers itself to others as the singularity that it is. On the other hand, the singular receives others as unique and irreplaceable accesses to the essence of existence, to existence itself. There is therefore no recovery of the authentic value of existence outside the respect for others, the respect for the existence they are. Solitary individuation individuates itself as open, as exposed, always abandoned to this exposure. Solipsism therefore works to prevent the incorporation of Dasein, it aspires to found society outside fusion.

Is this not also what Levinas aims for? Does this not indicate precisely the detachment of the idea of the other from a solitude where the *I* masters itself and therefore masters everything? Is it not precisely this that characterises Levinas' movement in and out of philosophy, the temptation of temptation? When

Levinas formulates the question of otherness in terms of ethical resistance, resistance towards the return to the Same, he is perhaps saying something not too different from Heidegger when the latter argues that the singular finds itself always with-others, but that those others are not same with itself, they are an altogether different exposure of singular existing.

It is perhaps now surprising to read into the fact that on the one hand Levinas accuses Heidegger of promoting with Being-with a fusional ideal and on the other he reproaches *Being and Time* because 'all emotion, all fear is finally emotion for self, fear for self' (Levinas 2006a: 311), solipsism. Perhaps in the interplay between the 'they' as the fusional ideal of common sense and the metaphysical isolation resides a sociality of singular exposures (a contrapuntal sociality to use the terminology employed in the discussion of John Cassavetes).

The gesture of solipsism seems to aim precisely at this: preventing 'the absorption of singularities into a homogeneous Being-together' (Raffoul 1998: 213). At the same time, it also structures singular existence as constantly open to the other, to that which it is not. Solipsism opens to existence as that which must be decided upon but which cannot be appropriated. As Christopher Fynsk presents it: 'when Dasein finds and assumes itself in its constancy, it finds that there is always another with it, speaking to it' (Fynsk 1986: 42). Here lies the Heideggerian concept of otherness, which perhaps (Levinas would probably subscribe to this) precedes also sociality as 'organised otherness', because it anticipates it or better because it insinuates itself both in the singular of 'me' and in the plural of 'us'. Although the concept as such has not been developed, otherness for Heidegger could be said to reside in existence itself as that which we are, but that at the same time stands in front of us, always still to be decided upon. Our own selfhood belongs to the question of otherness. Our existing in the world, the everyday, is a question of otherness, and from otherness – Heidegger seems to say – there is no retreat. As long as existence is in question, as long as it is the question, otherness never ceases to be the point that cuts across everything. Existence and otherness are the same, but they do not rest on the Same. *Otherness is the essence of existence since existence is its own undecided essence.*

Where Jean-Luc Nancy speaks of Being as co-essential to Being-with, one could perhaps translate: existing is the work of otherness, an always inoperative work. The *us* therefore has to rest on this paradox: I am myself the more I am open to the work of otherness, the more I let the perpetual and ephemeral ambiguity of otherness be exposed to me. The more I exist, the more I become incommensurable to myself as 'subject'. In existing (which is the same as experience) the existence that is *mine* exceeds my possibilities of seizing it in comprehension, because it resides elsewhere. At any given time *existence is the elsewhere that I inhabit*. However the otherness that existence works on me is not the approach of an identity that cuts across mine and then returns to itself. Existence affirms itself as the work of otherness without Other, which means that one is not in a position to say who (but also what) the other is. Otherness remains essentially (therefore existentially) ambiguous, itself undecided. The other is not a mediator (as it sometimes appears to be in Levinas' discussion of Justice), because existing is already this combination of given and undecided. The openness of existence, which one could simply call its 'with', is itself extension to the extremity of the other without a manifest, necessary mediation. The otherness in question with regard to existence is the 'not yet' of existence itself, the fact that existence still always needs to be existed and existed anew, at every moment other than itself.

The characterization is at this stage still too general, but perhaps it will turn out that this is also the work philosophy has to attend to, if one pays attention to what Jacques Derrida says in an interview about the 'despair' of beginnings:

> each text belongs to a completely other history [...] It is really as if I had never before written anything, or even known how to write. Each time I begin a new text there is a dismay in the face of the unknown or the inaccessible, an overwhelming feeling of clumsiness, inexperience, powerlessness. What I have already written is instantly annihilated or rather thrown overboard.
>
> (Derrida: 1995: 352)

This last consideration anticipates and delivers the discussion over to the second moment of this analysis: identifying the specific philosophical gesture of Jean-Luc Nancy. The specificity of this gesture, though, cannot be found simply in the re-tracing of an identity, in the identification of a constant signature. What one should look for is not a face-value recognition, the closure brought upon discourse by key words. Nancy's writing sinks key terms, so as to make of them something less and still more than devices of a meaningful presentation. What this writing points to is always an excess of value and the value of excess; the withdrawal of key terms – in favor of existence – is always as important as their birth to presence.

Once more one has to return to the question of Being-with, which somehow constitutes the point of arrival of this work and also the crucial moment when Nancy's reflection both joins and distances itself from Heidegger so that the singularity of his voice becomes more powerful. From now on the analysis will follow on one side the working *on* concepts: Nancy's relation to the constellation of models from *Being and Time*; the extent to which Nancy shapes his own philosophical tone by working his way out of Heidegger, thinking the unthought of *Being and Time*. On the other, it will follow the working *of* concepts, that is to say the way in which Nancy phrases his philosophy and how this brings up the problematic of conceptual presentation as such. In order not to turn philosophical language, even one that stresses interruption, rupture and openness, simply into a justificatory ground, Nancy measures philosophical presentation as such and the *as such* of philosophical presentation. On the one hand philosophy is understood as a reserve of concepts; on the other it is conceived as the struggle of presentation. However these two conceptions never simply rest on opposite ends. The question is therefore the one posed by Lacoue-Labarthe in the following terms:

> whether the dream, the desire that philosophy has entertained since its 'beginning' for a *pure saying* (a speech, a discourse purely transparent to what it should immediately signify: truth, being, the absolute, etc), has not always been compromised by the necessity of going through a text, through a process of writing, and whether for this reason philosophy has not always been obliged to use modes of exposition (dialogue or narrative, for example) that are not exclusively its own and that it is most powerless to control or even reflect upon.
>
> (Lacoue-Labarthe 1993: 1)

What is at stake here is the thin line between on the one hand the purity of philosophical abstraction that always rejoins the heart of concepts available to philosophy and on the other philosophy's complicity with language as a fictional living matter,[3] that which brings philosophy outside of itself and also perhaps closer to existence. Nancy engages with the very question of argumentation as that which leads constantly closer to impasses, so to reveal in the impasse the need for a decisive transgression. It is also always this exhaustion or inability to identify what the right of philosophical discourse is and what is proper to it and to its vocation that Nancy tries to make evident. As he puts it in *Logodaedalus*: 'there is no point in doing philosophy if it isn't to try to accompany this exhaustion of discourse to its limit. Because it is only at the limit that one can try philosophy's luck' (Nancy 2008c: 15).

The in-common of separation

Despite the criticism directed at the notions of solipsism and 'they', it is not there that Heidegger thwarts access to otherness. It is instead in the conceptual constellation leading to destiny that Heidegger produces an irreversible closure. As long as Being-with remains undecided it shows the opening of an access, rather than the closure of otherness.

Nancy exposes this logic in two passages. They appear in the same text, one at the beginning, one at the end, the second perhaps as an answer to the first:

- 'Being-with forms an essential condition for the essence of Dasein. How? This is not easy to uncover because of the limits of the analysis presented by the text. Why this point of resistance and relative obscurity?' (Nancy 2008d: 113);
- 'The limit, the impasse, or the failure, are thus inscribed quite precisely at the place of and owing to the very opening of the text of *Being and Time*' (ibid.: 123).

The insufficiency thus belongs to *Being and Time* itself. Heidegger committed considerable energies to the problem of an irreducible otherness at the heart of the singular's existent in *Being and Time*. Among many others, one could cite these two passages: 'Being-with is in every case a characteristic of one's own Dasein [...] those entities towards which Dasein as Being-with comports itself are themselves Dasein' (Heidegger 1962: 157) and 'the world of Dasein is a with-world' (ibid.: 155).

The idea of the constant work of otherness at the core of singular and eventual disclosures of existence, the thought of existing itself as constant opening to that which stands against it as possible (and unknown, insofar as it has to be assumed); the very conception of something that could work only before and beyond binary constructions (in particular that of subjects and crowds, of singular and plural), that could play the role of un-grounding the latter in the same way that transcendence disengages the subject–object relation, offers extremely rich and compelling material for thinking the question of otherness. Sometimes one has the impression that the co-essentiality and undecidability of Being-with matures almost naturally from the overall structure of the book. Nancy comments that: 'despite this prejudice, there is perhaps no other philosophical text that refers us more forcefully than this one does to the exteriority of the experience it attempts to analyse' (Nancy 1993: 406).

The fact that the question of Being-with remains unresolved perhaps also belongs to the goals of *Being and Time* itself. To put this differently: this notion should remain the very horizon of Heidegger's work and should perhaps therefore be thematized as the gesture that re-opens the volume beyond Heidegger's notorious firmness.

And yet at other times Heidegger retraces the meaning of Being-with towards its very closure. This has to do with the prejudice that Nancy highlights, namely the tendency to grant special relevance to the possibility for the authentically exceptional to appropriate the originary.

Whilst Heidegger insists on Being-with as an existential principle, he seems at the same time to articulate it only as the actualization of a common fate (thus carrying on a gesture similar – as Nancy argues – to certain German Idealism), whose only alternative is an indifferent perpetual activism devoid of any content.

In particular what seems to bring Being-with to a standstill is the fact that Heidegger sublimates it in – and therefore subjects it to – a destination that incarnates the everyday disclosure of existence. This incarnation is the appropriation by a 'powerless superior power' that sacrifices the singular plural play of existence, the fact that at each time what is at stake is a singular decision towards existence as the plural otherness that cannot be appropriated but that nevertheless one must make one's own. The *with* suddenly transforms into an essence that has always already appropriated and expropriated existence, the latter being relegated to a vanishing point 'already guided in advance': fate [*Schicksals*] as the possibility that Dasein 'has inherited and yet has chosen' and its crossing with destiny [*Geshick*]. As Fritsche says, the past 'demands of us that we subjugate ourselves to it and defend or re-realise it' (Fritsche 1999: 36). It is in the past that one ought to seek the actualization of the authentic, whilst the inhauntetic constantly projects itself in the future: 'with the inconstancy of the they-self Dasein makes present its "today". In awaiting the next new thing, it has already forgotten the old one' (Heidegger 1962: 443).

Heidegger proposes a structure where the processes of mastering and appropriation are always left open, never properly resolved, but tied together in the form of separation. Possibilities are never fully grasped or exhausted, what Dasein understands is never completely understood. This is the case for Dasein's own individuation – mineness is an each time, Being one's own is a recurring threshold – but also for its relation to others – the voice of the friend cannot be identified in a specific 'who', fascination and guilt disappropriate without then being recaptured in and by understanding and theory, Being-with does not offer the rule of a unity but makes possible a relation across distance. In the end not even resoluteness – factual existence firmly determined in remaining in the open of possibilities, 'letting itself be encountered' (ibid.: 374) – or decision – where the fact of existence is exposed in all its *immemorial passivity* – does provide a closure to Dasein's stretching between birth and death. The moment of mastery remains always conceived as a deferral.

On the other hand though Heidegger seems to reconfigure an almost opposite constellation around the terms *connectedness*, *fate* and *destiny*, according to which authenticity is realised: 'Dasein's fateful destiny in and with its "generation" goes to make up the full authentic historizing of Dasein' (ibid.: 436). The problem is less that Being-with is not developed enough. Instead the focus should be on the fact that in its development it comes to master itself; its existential character is exceeded and it becomes – in spite of itself – a calculated category, understood now simply according to 'fate', 'the ground for destiny, by which we understand Dasein's historizing as Being-with Others' (ibid.: 438). In this section of *Being and Time* resoluteness becomes the grasping of one's fate. The everyday has to be bypassed and experiences have to be connected into a destined future, an already decided destination. The tension between the ahead-of-itself and the having-been is resolved in a common destiny that gathers them together and brings their work to a halt. Future as the moving back towards the fact of already existing, of always already being in the face of existence, now becomes realised only in the possibility given by a destined community that sidesteps singularities. In this connectedness the concept of participation, against which Heidegger had struggled whilst discussing the notion of the 'they', reappears: a connected community identifies its hero surmounting the undeter- mined *who* of the voice of the friend. Guilt is expiated as response to the call of destiny. Responsibility becomes responsibility not towards all our destinies, but towards the destiny of *All*, a gathering together in the sublimation of singular fates. The only trait that distinguishes the togetherness of destiny from the confused homogeneity of the 'they' is that whilst in the latter difference was blocked off by a curious dis-interest, here difference is foreclosed by a creative catastrophe, where the singular rather quickly turns and locks itself in the order of a plural *unicum* (one could also name this – with Nancy – an *immanentism*[4]).

The everyday, which in the first part of the analysis gave the impression of being the moment, the 'at stake' of a decision for existence, is now delimited as the floating 'coming to pass'. Encountering the everyday means only reabsorbing it into a wider, better rooted, purpose.[5] The dispersal of the 'between' stretching from birth to death must be made into unity. What comes to pass has become fate. Every characterization of each day as the moment of a deferred mastering of one's own possibility proves to simply be a momentary step towards the constitution of a horizon channeled by destiny. The between Dasein is – the fact that 'existentially birth is not and never is something past and death is just as far from having the kind of Being of something still outstanding' (ibid.: 374) – finds an ultimate, but then also infinite, end.

Heidegger says that Dasein is a stretching along. If the value of this is to be preserved, then it should not result in a destiny whose only freedom is that of giving up. In this way Dasein is destined at every moment to a precise moment, which becomes exactly the moment of an ultimate presence. In Heidegger's words, in fact, a 'moment of vision' is a principle that exceeds every now. Destiny comes here to represent the 'right now' of existence, where existence concludes its deciding upon possibilities. In destiny everything has been made actual.

According to this configuration, the world is not only the dispersion of *each times*, the eventual spacing and relatedness of singular existences, but the plane where a destiny is played out. The future becomes that which is acted out by being sent, its directionality is decided once and for all. The structural connectedness that ends up revealing – in a moment of vision – the flowing of fates into a destiny demands that existence closes its work towards the future: the now of existence has finally occurred. At this point it is only by way of destiny that the community of humanity can subsist.[6] The 'connectedness of life' makes of discrete 'current nows' a final 'Now', where an ultimate 'revolution' becomes possible: Dasein turns towards itself and recognises its always having been in view of the destiny in which it now participates. This means also that existence is no longer open to the decision of what still lies outside itself; it is no longer that which constitutes itself only by being approached (possibilities). The work of existence as resolutely maintaining itself in the deferral of appropriation, where what is grasped is also re-sent to a further grasping, finds in destiny its right time, where no delay is allowed. Singular existence becomes selfsame and still completely oblivious of itself (solitary) in the plural unicum, the only one that can legitimately express plurality.

The call of fate is a final and last call, where 'the future is all used up', where every *who* calling from the unknown has been individuated and every *we* or *us* has ceased to happen as a sending/receiving but is already and infinitely named in the radical individuation of destiny. Silence derives not from listening, but from the infinite – and final – submission of existence to a *single decision*, which has, it goes without saying, nothing to do with a *singular decision*.

In this constellation the very possibility of a repetition both of decision and of resolution, therefore the possibility for the constant work of existence as unfinished opening to otherness, is foreclosed. The finitude of existence, and therefore also its eventual character (the each time), seems to get sucked up in an infinite permanence where existential possibilities are disclosed only as monuments.

The only possibility remaining is that of 'giving up', freedom becomes the freedom to 'give up in accordance with the demands of some possible Situation' (ibid.: 443). The throwness of existence is finally 'accepted', and 'incorporated' in what appears to be an 'ultimate moment of vision'.

Being-with at this stage has lost its bond with the promises and the powers of existence. Rather, it seems that the notion simply collaborates in sending forward the connection of dispersed experiences in the together, in unity and destiny. Being-with becomes the ground through which Dasein 'pulls itself together out of its dispersal and thinks up for itself a unity in which that "together" is embraced' (ibid.: 442).

Heidegger therefore seems to close off and efface the very radicality of his own propositions. If it is true that he displaces any appeal to a sociality that derives simply from the identity of a subject, he seems at the same time to counterbalance this with a gesture in the opposite direction, that of presupposing the solution of the problem of relation in an incarnated community, the destiny of the *Volk*.

It is at this point that Nancy's reading of Heidegger becomes an appropriation from a distance. Right after the formulation of Being-with as coessential with Dasein, Nancy's reading becomes something more, a decision.

Why with Being-with and not with some other Heideggerian notion? Nancy decides on Being-with because its co-essentiality is both the most explicit attempt at articulating the question of an existence in the world beyond individual subjectivity and also the point at which Heidegger seems to fall outside of himself, outside perhaps of existence as he had defined it. For Nancy it is crucial to expose this co-essentiality: Dasein and Being-with happen each time at the same time. Otherness happens before the self, but not in the connotation Levinas ascribes to it, rather in the sense that exposure to the plurality of existence happens before and cuts across every possibility of firm identification.

The other comes only once and never leaves, which also means that it never comes back.

This is possible though only if the *with* is thought as being the measure of an incommensurability. By stressing the notion of destiny, by putting the accent on the choice of the hero and in general by privileging epic suggestions over the ordinary, Heidegger imposes on existence a measure. To counterbalance this Nancy talks instead of 'measures of the incommensurable' (Nancy 2000: 81), that can take place only within a finite thinking, that is within a thinking which renounces itself – justice towards itself – in order to be just to existence. This is a thinking that loses its properness and assumes itself to be signaling and exposing powers of existence. This could also be said in the following, more concise way: thinking exposes itself as the thought of singularities, *attempting to think the other without abandoning the other of thinking*. One will have to repeat this many more times in many ways (repetition is in the nature of what is being said; finitude requires a *pollakos legomenon*, the spoken-in-many-ways [Nancy 1993: 36]), but to use Nancy's words: 'existence the truth of which consists in leaving its sense always beyond or short of any apprehension' (Nancy 2001a: 21).

If read in this way then the *with* should be thought of as that which measures the nothing and everything between us. *With* is the measure of what happens between us – eight billion bodies – even when nothing happens, in the figure of indifference or of mystic dis-interest,[7] or when – and this is perhaps its crudest modality – the nothing happens,[8] but also and still when everything happens (even for Heidegger the gift of love confronts and works in the openness of the *with*).

One could rephrase these remarks by saying that the *with* is the open into which 'we' maintains itself and sense keeps circulating, from us to us: 'to us: to the upsurge of our existences, together, as the surging up of sense' (Nancy 2002: 78). The *with* as the open thus is the place from which and to which we address, as already addressed, existence: work of an open otherness, immeasurable measure between us.

All this amounts to saying that the *with* itself is nothing, but only because it is what is always 'a question of'. The impossibility of turning the *with* into a political strategy or into an absolute moral principle proves its necessity and its necessarily open character. Its articulation is always both a naked fact and an impossible question, but no mediation can resolve the two into a synthesis, the *with* always comes with and imposes both sides. What the with measures is a logic of separation, which makes 'we' co-essential with 'I', but only there where in their turn neither I nor we can simply be subjects of a self-presentation or of a presentation of the self. As Nancy writes, the *with* remains 'imperceptibly and insuperably exscribed' (Nancy 1993: 320). The presentation of the *with* therefore escapes the right measure of presentation, after having escaped demonstration.

The with is the open itself: it manifests itself only there where one touches in us, between us both our inextricable evidence (the fact, for example, of being hopelessly involved in queues and crowds) and the insufficiency of our programs (the *with* produces cracks both in the theme of recognition and in that of seduction, in the social and libidinal order). This is not a deficiency, or at least not only a deficit. Quite the opposite: it presents itself as an affirmation (and an ultimately ethical one). The various forms and manifold figures that attempt to present the *with* once and for all fall always short of its openness and at the same time perform an excess of appropriation: never plural enough, but also too firm in designating the identity of the plural. The *with* thus remains separated from them, it withdraws and still keeps pushing forward (the fact that in the face of wars one can always still glimpse some kind of moribund piety or 'humanity' – a generous gesture towards the prisoner – does not spring from the essentially good nature of humanity but responds to the nakedness of the *with*, it comes, so to speak, from its evidence).

With celebrates also every relation from me to me, the each time of mineness. As Nancy writes,

> 'Each time' is the singular-plural structure of the disposition. Therefore, 'each time mine' signifies primarily 'each time his or hers', that is, 'each time with': 'mineness is itself only a possibility that occurs in the concurrent reality of being-each-time-with'.
>
> (Nancy 2000: 97)

'Mine' is nowhere else than in the openness of the 'with'. Love as well catches a glimpse of itself here. If it is true – as Heidegger wants to show – that love is a task and an ultimately nude task (there is no knowledge available and even so one has to fight for and through it) than it is there that one can express most vividly the logic of the *with*, its being nothing. The *with* announces the breaking up of every relation with *us*, whilst constantly setting up all possibilities for relation, so to produce a logic according to which *relation with the 'with' is the* with *out of relations*.

Powers of existence

The *with* then can only be occasioned to name a phenomenon of the retracing of common sense: with makes possible such retracing by withdrawing at the moment of appropriation, by escaping a properness that would reduce it to the opposite of itself, that is to say to a principle of identical presence. Sense in this way shows that *with* is the logic of every existence that cannot simply afford to say: 'I and the other' but that necessarily has to put up with the fact that the inside of every *I* would still be *with*, because it would still have the structure of an each time mine. The *Je* in the Heideggerian *Jemeingkeit* must be re-existed each time.

If sense is therefore exposed as *with*, there is then no common sense, but only the questioning, the putting back into question of this commonality. In a way sense is common only when sense is dead (death itself is the most communal of common senses). A reflection on sense thus means sense's explosion, the bending and re-bending of sense.

Existence therefore is not the particularization of a universal essence or the degrading of principles, but rather the fact that 'at the point where we would expect "something", a substance or a procedure, a principle or an end, a signi-fication, there is nothing but the manner, the turn of the other access' (Nancy 2000: 14).

Exposing principles (the Heideggerian existentials) to the each time of the manners and the turns of existence constitutes the ethical problem at the heart of existence, but also the anticipation of every ethical program, an 'archi-ethos' as Nancy calls it.

With a tone that recalls the Heidegger of *Letter on Humanism* one could argue that an ontology can be written only as an ethics and that every ethics is also an ontology, or better that ontology not only is ethical but that it must be so as long as a questioning of existence is necessarily also a way not to betray this existence by closing its horizon (whether in the name of the I, the Other, or the National Community).

Heidegger writes: 'only if the inquiry is itself seized upon in an existential manner as a possibility of the Being of *each existing Dasein*, does it become at all possible to disclose the existentiality of existence and to undertake an adequately founded ontological problematic' (Heidegger 1962: 34). Nancy makes of this Heideggerian thesis the chance to revert Being into the responsibility towards each parcel of sense, thus making of principles a dispersal, perpetual exposure to the otherness of undecided existing.

It is here that one discovers something like *powers of existence: existence as the force of the each time eludes a thinking of its beginning as it eludes that of its closure.*

The expression *powers of existence* does not mean affirming an ontical priority over the ontological – a paradigm of the banal as it were – nor on the contrary does it aim at establishing the anteriority of the ontological rearguard over the facts of the everyday. Rather, powers of existence indicate the utter exposure of both these registers to the otherness of undecided existing.

Powers of existence would thus operate in planting the responsibility of mundane existence always as first concern, concern and pre-occupation against a principle or value which teleologically imposes itself on existence (such as the People) or that dissolves existence and its decisions (such as the Crowd).

Powers of existence define philosophy as a *responsible decision made in view of the impossible on always factual and urgent possibilities.*

The intention here is to find under the articulation of powers of existence the very gesture of Jean-Luc Nancy's philosophy. This articulation seems to constitute both the opening and the displacement of ends operated in Nancy's often fragmentary writing (fragmentation itself is perhaps the very enactment of those powers, their mode).

In discussing sense, the body, freedom, community, art, the order of ontology, the rule of philosophical presentation, Nancy constantly evokes powers of existence: moments that keep true to the claim of existence. The latter demands an opening, an always inaugural decision against the absence of any horizon (unless this is the circulation of sense). Existence demands that this decision be inextinguishable (in front of community, meaning, but also ethics and politics, and every recognition that runs in and out of those, infinitely piercing them and fixing them to a ground).

Existence demands to be essentially open to the other, to the otherness over which it casts its eventual decision. As Nancy writes 'existence presupposes itself and calls itself infinitely as meaning – as the entirety of meaning, absolutely. But, at the same time, in existing, existence denies that it has meaning as a property [...] Existence is the appropriation of the inappropriable' (Nancy 1997a: 80).

Powers of existence indicate moreover a decision always belonging only to 'some factical Dasein at a particular time' (Heidegger 1962: 345). It is this decision that responds by keeping existence un-answered – *in the answering* – but constantly in view; in view in the given (that is the only thing we have) as that which cannot at any time be received as simply given.

Freedom and community, world and sense, body and otherness: these concepts have to be existed, that is they have to be crossed over, sliced open by existence, by the singular touch of existence.

Existence is already the very exposure to the other as deciding for possibility. This ambiguity – decision is only always a decision towards more openness – should not as someone suggests determine the end of philosophical work;[9] quite the opposite, it delivers philosophy over to existence, over perhaps to a lateness around which philosophy does not recollect itself, but keeps opening to otherness.

The very idea of a power of existence imposes therefore on philosophy an act ex-scription of experience. Philosophy will neither try to recuperate within its own system the exteriority of experience (this teaching, the letting be of experience, is Heidegger's, even if it is precisely what Levinas contests him), nor to cap experience with a factical ideal that would pose an asymptotic principle or a 'better way'. Philosophy rather attempts to expose the singularity of the each time as the founding of existence, to return thinking to the play of specificity, rather than restricting it to the passage of abstract formulations.

In this way, experience remains both the very site of a philosophical resolution and that which thinking can only grasp without deciding for it once and for all. Philosophy survives only if it ventures beyond (and against) conservation instincts. This seems to confirm the formulation proposed by Adorno when he writes: 'the very wish to be right, down to its subtlest form of logical reflection, is an expression of that spirit of self-preservation which philosophy is precisely concerned to break down' (Adorno 1996: 70).

By philosophical resolution we mean here that philosophy measures itself against the questions opened within experience – philosophy is not something foreign to experience, therefore it does not have to recuperate it – as the act (or praxis) that brings the questioning of experience back to the point of undecidability: this is experience's ex-scription. For this same reason experience always remains in advance of philosophy and maintains open an intrinsic difference through which philosophy cannot (and should not) pass intact (this is also the gesture that Levinas advocates for his own thinking).

It is not a question about the foundations or the logic of existence, but a question about the *resonance* of the singular event of existence, at once able to transform the sense of the world and incommensurable to any other stroke.

The question of the 'who' is perpetually the question of existence because it is always a matter of coming up to what happens at the level of the singular sparkle of existence, thus neither what it is before it happens, nor how it repeats itself.

The kind of philosophical reflection that powers of existence need is one that proceeds not by recollecting in the inside, but by bouncing back from existence. What Heidegger refers to as *Widerschein* should here be invoked to name the work of philosophy itself, 'not shut ourselves off from the phenomena by a framework of concepts' (Heidegger 1982: 160). What one should now read in reflection is the fact that philosophy does not withdraw from experience and from the fact that experience is existence (not that experience makes existence). Philosophy does not retire into its own foundation, into the very site of its self-preservation; rather, it finds itself – it finds its own saying as well as its very 'philosophy' – in the midst of existence and only there. It does not have to turn backwards towards itself. It reaches itself and at the same time attempts not to remain identical with itself 'in those things that daily surround it' (ibid.: 159). Reflection as the understanding of powers of existence, reflection as the gesture of Nancy's philosophy, is the giving of itself to the inception of existence. This would be a peremptory, unconditional affirmation of philosophy (its passion, so to speak): that of never abandoning existence, everything that is as that which always still has to be existed, what Heidegger calls a 'going-along-*with* the givens' (ibid.: 161). Philosophy, given to existence, receives its action from it.

Such constellation also respects what Heidegger calls the philosopher's loyalty, 'the loyalty the philosophizing individual has to himself' (Heidegger 1984: 17) that becomes in the end the only verification of good philosophy. Being loyal to oneself means also having entered the hard thought, the limit-thought of existence as that which does not have foundations or essence: having decided to decide. It means precisely to have resolved some kind of freedom to existence, to the possibilities of existence, to have already entered 'the remaining uncertainty and gaping discord' (ibid.: 18).

Nancy seems on the whole to respond to two claims advanced by Heidegger:

- that philosophy does not in its working produce a world-view and also fights against this tendency almost natural to philosophizing itself;
- more importantly that philosophy has to start (and possibly end) right at existence, at current existence, at 'mine', 'yours', 'hers', 'theirs', understood outside properties and only in their existing. As Heidegger writes: 'philosophy remains latent in every human existence and need not be first added to it from somewhere else' (ibid.: 18).

Reflection is not the act of coming back to itself (therefore of affirming the substantiality of the given), but rather of exploding (circulating) in the midst of experience. Every singular each time of existence is a reflection. Philosophy neither casts it on existence, nor names it; it puts it in a space where its necessity is open to a regime of interconnections.

Given the definition Nancy offers of existence as 'being-determined according to indetermination' (Nancy 1993: 104), one could develop the argument that, whilst existence is given, it is given to be existed; therefore not simply given and not simply received. It gives itself as an offering whose reception is undecidable. That the essence is existence therefore always means having to affirm existence (and not simply something about it, as Levinas also reproaches philosophy for doing). 'All thought frees the existing of existence because thought proceeds from it' (Nancy 1993: 18): this is the command that falls upon thinking when thinking aims to be more than a gathering of information, the substitution of one particular rhetoric with a new one or the regaining of a self-assurance as the right of philosophy to exist always as what it is.

The emergence of incommensurable measures with regard to the body, sense, the world, the opening of an incommensurable space or of a measure of incommensurability do not respond to an awareness as to the end of philosophical action. At the opposite they answer a different call: the affirmation of existence. One should therefore see a program here – *moments of incommensurability* could be another title for it – perhaps the entire program of Nancy's philosophy. It belongs to the nature of thinking to open a field of possibilities rather than to close upon them with an ultimate decision. Nancy is quite clear about this: 'thought has no decision of practical, ethical, or political action to dictate. If it claims to do so, it forgets the very essence of the decision, and it forgets the essence of its own thinking decision' (ibid.: 118).

And yet what can be deduced from this is not the great refusal of thinking. Thinking does not decline action nor does it remain 'indifferent' or 'disengaged'. Thinking cannot be indifferent towards action, there is not such a thing as 'disengaged thinking', thinking oblivious of difference. The exposure of moments of incommensurability responds to a gesture of affirmation, rather than to a withdrawal: to expose an immeasurable measure as the practice of thinking.

If this prevents philosophy from enacting the prescription of general rules, at the same time it keeps philosophy as the very affirmation of existence and of existence alone as its own essence.

Coda

Love: A broken heart and the exposed being

The Heideggerian thinking of the *with* as a moment of sublimation, where the stripped juxtaposition of our existences grows into destiny, seems then to indicate Being-with as the capping of individual experiences. It represents thus the very closure of powers of existence.

On several occasions when confronted with the Heideggerian development of Being-with Nancy seems to elude the impasse produced by Heidegger's heroes and destinies by turning to love.[10] It is in fact in the few remarks on the possibility of love that Heidegger – without ever systematizing his thinking in this direction – seems to put the notion of Being-with back into question.

One should be extremely cautious in trying to formulate a Heideggerian thinking of love simply by reconstructing the sincere, but nonetheless sketchy, remarks one finds in the *Letters to Hannah Arendt*.[11] These letters contain intriguing formulations, but also some noticeable contradictions (Heidegger speaks of love mainly as the affirmation of the Other, but sometimes he refers to it as an ideal unity). Although the letters date from the period during which Heidegger was completing *Being and Time*, one cannot be too sure as to how far the equation between the man in love and the philosopher of *Being and Time* can be meaningfully carried out. The aim here, therefore, is to problematize Nancy's turn towards 'Heideggerian love', whilst always keeping in mind both Being-with and the thinking of existence at large. Without a doubt the letters do contain significant considerations. In a surprisingly blithe fashion Heidegger insists mainly on three points:

- to pose love 'as such' contradicts the very expression of love;
- in love the otherness of the other bursts forth without ever being reabsorbed (according to St Augustine's *volo ut sis*);
- love is the most explicit undertaking of existence; the moment where taking existence upon oneself remains beyond and in excess of every possible knowledge, theory or programme.

In the letter from 9 July 1925, Heidegger writes: 'love as such does not exist'. Love is always only 'my' or 'your' or 'our' love, it can be determined solely on the basis of the singular stroke of the ones who share it. No singular expression of love can be adjusted to fit into the horizon of a thinking about love in general or of absolute love. As such, outside its singular eventuality, its singular measure of Being-with, love does not take place.

Also, Heidegger proceeds to say that 'only such faith – which as faith in the other is love – can really accept the "other" completely' (Arendt/Heidegger 2004: 20). The other appears here as the *gift of love*: 'you – just as you are and will remain – that's how I love you'. The possibility to understand the other, as the positive affirmation of an unknown, is the way love sustains itself always beyond mimesis and integration: 'only then love is strong for the future'. Only then is love future itself.

This delivers the argument to a third declaration: 'to be in one's love: to be forced into one's innermost existence' (ibid.: 21). Love emerges here as the moment of existence that cannot be assimilated: 'for anything else there are methods, aids, limits, and understanding'.[12] Love is then the fiercest power of existence, it keeps itself open, 'always beyond or short of any apprehension'. Faith for *co*-existence. To confirm this Heidegger adds: 'being allowed to wait for the beloved – that is what is most wonderful – for it is in that waiting that the beloved is present' (ibid.: 18).

The minute space Heidegger makes for love allows one to glimpse for Being-with a different trajectory from the thematizations available in *Being and Time*. It is perhaps not surprising that the possibility of Being-with to offer a logic of separation is maintained right at the point where Heidegger is at the most distant from philosophical presentation proper (and the tone at times seems almost to resonate with Levinas): 'here (in love) being close is a matter of being at the greatest distance from the other [...] the other's presence suddenly breaks into our life – no soul can come to terms with that' (ibid.: 4–5).

This impossibility of love – 'we want to thank the beloved, but find nothing that suffices' (ibid.) – perhaps indicates something more. Not being able to think the *with* without transforming it into an essence (fate, generation, community, sacrifice) or dispersing it in the apparent apathy of existence as routine (they, indifference, idle-talk, scribbling) – thinking it as what remains in-common in separation, what signals a non continuous contact, the play that always puts at stake both actualized occasions and indefinable possibilities – is 'a paradox common to all philosophy' and not only a Heideggerian deficit. Philosophy seems to fall short of our being-together as that which is stretched across a distance (and always an other distance, a newly born one) rather than united in a point.

In *Shattered Love* Nancy attempts to articulate the concept of love beyond metaphysical and dialectical significations aimed at completion. In Nancy's view love interrupts the law of a subject that always returns identical to itself. Love triggers a transcendence that works as the 'disimplication of an immanence' (Nancy 2003: 249). Love breaks into the reflective work of the subject.

To the scheme that wants love as absolute representation running on the fulfillment of the subject (reflecting subject–love–fulfillment), Nancy opposes the logic of the heart (broken heart–love–promise) where love is a singular movement that expresses itself as the arrival of a promise (this arrival, though, does not imply that the promise is kept and therefore concluded). If one understands love according to the first articulation, one hears in it the work of possession. Possession is not of the object possessed – it is not, as it were, simply the grasping of the object – but it shows the subject realising itself as property. Understood as the law of the broken heart, love instead constitutes the exposed being, that which 'is not completed by the dialectical process, it incompletes itself to the outside, it is presented offered to something that is not itself' (ibid.: 252). Here the affirmation and negation proper to dialectic are not eliminated, but posed to the outside of a 'you'. What the heart exposes is finitude, the impossibility of appropriation through love, impossibility of finding one's own property 'either in itself or in a dialectical sublimation of the self' (ibid.: 262).

Therefore the experience of love is experience of the outside: experience of a subject that cannot maintain itself simply on its self-presence, but has to pro-pose itself to itself in terms of discontinuity. Love rests on this outside that is not the outside of me balanced by the outside of the other. It is not enough to say that the other's identity has traversed me, because it is not the work of another identity that exposes me. The other as well comes always as other, already disjoined, never itself. What the other approaches when he approaches me is not an integrity called 'me', but a movement towards otherness. As Nancy puts it: '[love's] coming is only a departure for the other, its departure only the coming of the other' (ibid.).

This structure, Nancy says, is nothing else than the ontological determination of Dasein. Love is the law of a subjectivity that starts in singular sharing, not in the mastery of the 'I' or in its sublimation through the other (in this case one would have to assume again the other as closed immanence). If it is true that this trajectory owes its formulation to Heidegger, it is also true that in *Being and Time* Heidegger remains silent about the possibilities of love. According to Nancy, Fürsorge 'is still thought starting from an "I" or from an "identity" that goes toward the other' (ibid.: 269) (but even for Levinas love remains nothing more than the moment of a process: love expresses the face, but is then surpassed by the absolute distance and novelty of filiation, the child. Love remains ambiguous, it 'does not transcend unequivocally' [Levinas 2005: 266]. To love is also to return to oneself. It is only in going beyond its terms – and so in the child and in fecundity – that love can manifest 'a unity that is not opposed to multiplicity, but, in the precise sense of the term, engenders it' [ibid.: 273]).

The space and the logic described by Nancy can be found in Heidegger's thinking only if one pays attention to the letters to Hannah Arendt. There one can glimpse Being-with thematized as faith in the possibility of the other, in otherness itself as the decision for existence. In this series of love letters something is opened that does not find space in *Being and Time*: a singular sharing names the absolute singularity of being, 'that which remains "self" when nothing comes back to the "self"' (Nancy 2003: 262).

Beginning to think

Jean-Luc Nancy's philosophical project resides largely in a reading of the unthought in Heidegger's work. To read the unthought means responding not only to the call coming from Heidegger, to Heidegger's legacy as it were, but to that which in Heidegger's thinking resists thinking, resists presentation: existence, an opening into Heidegger's thought, at the very outset of Heideggerian presentation. As Nancy writes:

> the existential analytic of *Being and Time* is the project from which all subsequent thinking follows, whether this is Heidegger's own thinking or our various ways of thinking against or beyond Heidegger himself [...] It does not signify that this analytic is definitive, only that it is responsible for registering the seismic tremor of a more decisive rupture in the constitution or consideration of meaning.
>
> (Nancy 2000: 93)

Thinking the unthought thus means something other than thinking according to this rule: 'letting every thinker's thought come to us as something in each case unique, never to be repeated, inexhaustible' (Heidegger 1968: 76). It means thinking with Heidegger, according to a logic of separation, where the distances – whether minimal or absolute – in the Heideggerian praxis of thinking make up resistances. Thinking the unthought in Heidegger's work means thinking that which resists him. The unthought in this sense would be that which is not presentable under the strategies of *Being and Time* and the action of thinking. Resistance of philosophy to itself. That which is un-thought in Heidegger is the beginning of his own thinking. *The unthought becomes that which cannot be enclosed by thinking, the threshold of its beginning, that which by exhausting thinking from the start makes thinking take its course. Existence and its powers of exposure to the undecidable-having-to-be-decided.*

By thinking the unthought in Heidegger's writing, Nancy thinks the unthought itself anew: affirmation of existence beyond philosophical presentation and, at the same time, urgency following which we begin philosophy.

To pay attention to powers of existence, to follow their course, thus means unleashing the *with-ness* from within the subject that philosophizes and from within the subject of philosophy. Unachievability here should not simply indicate the failure to complete a program, an identity infinitely deferred: it should structure the program itself, the power of thinking-with, silently happening and immediately exposed between us.

Notes

Chapter 1

1 Derrida reminds us of the problem of foundation between the two: 'Is or is not Vorahndenheit founded on Zuhandenheit?' (Derrida 2008: 44).

2 For an analysis of the relation between Heidegger and Merleau-Ponty's thought see Aho 2009.

3 Judith Butler proposes 'a return to the notion of matter, not as site or surface, but as a process of materialization that stabilizes over time to produced the effect of boundary, fixity, and surface we call matter' (Butler 1993: 9).

4 I have here avoided making use of the word aestheticization for at least two reasons, a positive and a negative one. By speaking of an aesthetic body, we run the risk of falling into an irreversible tautology, for the body is already aesthetic, the fact of feeling being proper to the body, or better yet it is bodies alone that can access and create an aesthetics, the space of senses. Any body is aesthetic in itself, since the very beginning, because it is the very force expressing and expressed by the verb αἰσθάνομαι. On the other hand the word beauty bears here a particular connotation, relevant to the discourse we hope to stimulate. Beauty, from the late Latin *bellum* – a milder version of *bonus* – means first of all comfortable and suitable, indicating then that which follows a certain code or standard of conduct.

5 A second and most intriguing line of enquiry could then be developed from Nancy's apparently casual remark that 'an existence is an individual essence' (Nancy 2010: 60).

6 Thomas Aquinas for instance writes in the *Summa Theologica*: '*viventes scilicet in corpore mortali, quod est quasi quidam carcer animae*'.

7 The demonstration to EII, P2 is not given, but, Spinoza writes, it has the same character as that of P1. I am here reconstructing the demonstration following P1.

8 One would need here a detour on the question of making love for it is in making love that the problem of the here and there manifests itself in all its vividness, for the more I try to find ways in and around one's innermost being, both in its physical and psychological connotations, the more that person remains there and keeps occupying a space which I cannot fully access. One could say that this gap both sustains and denies the relation.

9 In a similar way Nancy writes that 'the coming to the world is also the coming of the world' (Nancy 1997b: 159).

10 'The individual thus composed will, moreover, retain its nature whether it moves or be at rest, or whether it move in this or that direction, provided that each part retain its own motion and communicate it as before to the rest' (Spinoza 1949: 94).

11 To mention the question of the wound inevitably means interrogating the surroundings of the wound itself. If there is a wound there should be a totality, originally intact and then slit open. To attempt a first answer: there is no totality, for the wound itself, as it is, opened, a displacement, is the place of the coming to presence. The only way one can conceive of this kind of wound, of Being as wound, is if one takes the wound itself as the totality, but the totality always already broken in. The wound as totality is a wound without a surrounding body, but body itself, a body of a particular nature, always open.

Chapter 2

1 The French original uses the word *diction*, which the word *determination* does not do justice to. *Diction* refers both to the choice of words and to the way words are pronounced, how we confront sound unities.

2 Nancy has spoken of 'transimmanence' in (Nancy 2007b: 55); however, in *Adoration* he writes: 'I have at times spoken of "transimmanence": the semantic combination is clear, but the thought remains labourious, deprived of intuitive form for linguistic sentiment' (Nancy 2010: 31).

3 Heidegger interrogates this issue in *Basic Problems of Phenomenology* by writing: 'If the world is not something extant but belongs to the Dasein's being, if the world is in the Dasein's way of being, then it is something subjective [...] But the principal problem [...] is, after all, to determine exactly what and how the subject is' (Heidegger 1982: 167).

4 There is a ground in nature' – 'This ground ought to be in some real being or cause' – 'That being is the ultimate ground of things and is usually designated by the one word GOD.'

5 Among the many interpretations not contemplated here because of lack of space and time, it is worth recalling here two main directions that will remain out of the frame, although it would be worth considering them elsewhere. One has to do with Heidegger's statement that *the world is always spiritual* in *Introduction to Metaphysics* (Heidegger 2000: 47) and the analysis Derrida devotes to this in *Of Spirit* (Derrida 1989: 47) and the other with Wittgenstein claim that *the sense of the world must lie outside the world.*

6 Of *Todtnauberg* Philippe Lacoue-Labarthe writes that it is 'barely a poem, a singular nominal phrase' (Lacoue-Labarthe 1999: 33). We know that Celan

visited Heidegger in his mountain Hütte in the summer 1967, following Heidegger's interview in *Der Spiegel*. Celan came to Heidegger to hear one single word, but received silence: 'just a single word: a word about pain. From there, perhaps, all might still be possible. Not "life", which is always possible [...] but existence, poetry, speech. Language. That is, relation to others' (ibid.: 38).

7 It is interesting to note how Nicholas of Cusa's concept of *docta ignorantia* – referring to the limited understanding we can produce of the working of the universe – acquires new validity in the physics that follows the Copenhagen Interpretation at the beginning of the twentieth century. Heisenberg draws interesting parallels between philosophy and the principles of quantum theory in his informative *Physics and Philosophy* (Heisenberg 2000).

8 That the world plays could also mean that it produces a sound, but this sound is the product of its revolution, of the two ends of this same world extending one toward the other and touching each other. One has here lost the *harmonia celestis*, the music of the stars – we can't hear it anymore, but what we can lend an ear to is the music of the revolution of the world on itself (revolution = return to the point from where a movement has started).

9 In *Dis-Enclosure* Nancy writes: 'After all modern signifies a world always awaiting its truth of, and as, world, a world whose proper sense is not given, is not available, is, rather, in project or in promise' (Nancy 2008b: 34–5).

10 *The World*, prod. Hengameh Panahi, Takio Yoshida and Chow Keung, dir. Jia Zhangke, 105 mins., Celluloid Dreams, 2004.

11 See in particular the pages devoted to Rossellini and Bresson in (Revault d'Allonnes 1994).

12 In *The World Viewed*, written few years before the publication of Deleuze's books on cinema, Stanley Cavell speaks of cinema as making manifest the impossibility of distinguishing reality and fantasy, for the former is already immersed in the latter (Cavell 2001). Whilst Cavell's reading of cinema responds to a different agenda, a comparison between the works of the two philosophers may nonetheless prove very productive.

Chapter 3

1 Heidegger himself warns about the peril of such a venture: 'What a thinker has thought can be mastered only if we refer every thing in his thought that is still unthought back to its originary truth. Of course, the thoughtful dialogue with the thinker does not become any more comfortable that way, on the contrary it turns into a disputation of rising acrimony' (Heidegger 1968: 54).

2   The original French text says: 'Nous n'allons fonder la relation avec l'étant respecté
    dans son être sur l'être au monde, sour le souci et le faire du Dasein heideggerien.
    Le faire suppose déjà la relation avec le trascendant' (Levinas 1990: 111).
3   Levinas writes: 'every object offers itself to enjoyment, a universal category of the
    empirical – even if I lay hold of an object-implement, if I handle it as a Zeug. The
    handling and utilization of tools, the recourse to all the instrumental gear of a
    life, whether to fabricate other tools or to render things accessible, concludes in
    enjoyment' (Levinas 2005: 133)
4   The distinction between categories and existentials has already been explored in
    the section entitled 'Desire in the world' of this work.
5   Walter Biemel in talking of 'others' puts it like this: 'Je peux les découvrir comme
    co-existants parce que je suis moi-même *être-avec*, c'est-à-dire ouvert aux autres en
    partageant avec eux mon ouverture sur les étants' (Biemel 1987 : 93).
6   It is worth here reading the entire passage, whose lyrical quality matches its
    analytic density: '"Would we accept being alone?" – "Alone, but not each one
    for his own sake; alone in order to be together." – "Are we together? We aren't
    completely, are we? We're only together if we could be separated"' (Blanchot 1999a:
    19).
7   On a different level, it would be interesting to discuss Nancy's analysis of
    the *Divine Wink*: 'Man is in connivance with God. Connivance is mute; it is
    content with the Wink, and, in it, it exceeds sense, the look, and, finally, the god
    himself. That is the divine trait or gesture: God is exceeded in his own passage.
    In fact he comes there and leaves from there; he is the passing of it' (Nancy
    2008b: 119).

Chapter 4

1   This question should in fact be read in particular in light of Heidegger's
    re-appropriation of Kant in *Being and Time, The Phenomenological Interpretation
    of the Critique of Pure Reason* and *The Basic problems of Phenomenology*. For the
    time being this sentence could suffice to render the tone of the discussion: 'But
    how does it come about that whilst the "I think" gives Kant a genuine phenomenal
    starting-point, he cannot exploit it ontologically, and has to fall back on the subject
    [...] and does not Kant himself keep on stressing that the "I" remains related to its
    representations, and would be nothing without them?' (Heidegger 1962: 367).
2   Given the premises, it should not come as a surprise that in the following
    paragraph Heidegger recalls Kierkegaard's choosing oneself as 'absolute choice' or
    as 'primordial choice'. Kierkegaard is a thinker with whom Levinas shows to have a
    profound affinity.

3 Deploying a similar tone Giorgio Agamben writes of the prolongation of language beyond itself: 'where language stops is not where the unsayable occurs, but rather where the matter of words begins' (Agamben 1995: 37).

4 Nancy defines it as such: 'a community presupposed as having to be one of human beings presupposes that it effect, or that it must effect, as such and integrally, its own essence, which is itself the accomplishment of the essence of humanness' (Nancy 1991: 3). This question owes a lot to the reading of Heidegger's 'national-esthétisme' (Lacoue-Labarthe 1990) and opens up to the assessment of a possible politics of Being-with. The first gesture would be to follow Nancy's refusal of the community and therefore concentrate on displacing the political from the heart of the community, whilst still pursuing the in-common, the dismantling of the community as substance in favor of the sharing of sense. If there is a destiny – and perhaps there has to be – it is one that remains without destination. It would run parallel to the Derridean interest in what 'ne se dépêche pas' (Derrida 1987). What makes our collectivity is an affirmation that resonates as a response to the demands of existence. If the political has so far presupposed the collectivity it addresses, the logic of the with (which is never a simple logic, rather a finite opening) imposes on the political the bond of the singular. This open space from which a unitary tension arises but in which it is not resolved is what one could call a properly political space, or the place of the politically proper.

A second gesture is then required, so that our 'faith in existence' does not become itself a substantial ground. The rights of man, our rights, otherwise called the rights of life, are not always necessarily progressive; we cannot simply refer to them or simply open a well-rounded debate that would once more validate their nature. One needs an affirmation of a different kind. Everything we have instituted already asks us questions, it does so from the very moment of its institution, because it rests and is decided between the naked arrogance of the fact of existing with (existing in the middle of existence) and the impossibility of enclosing this existence in the givenness of 'what is'. In talking about the possibility of the 'left' Nancy says that the 'leftist' exigency arises 'neither out of a foundation (or archi-subjectiveity) nor out of a legitimacy (or archi-citizenship)' (Nancy 1997b: 113) but, rather, without foundation and without right, incommensurable, unassignable.

However what is interminable is not simply the end, but the beginning, the fact again that existence is its own essence. The unachievable becomes the program and not simply a property of the program. What is interminable therefore is not a normative end (aim and closure at the same time) but the instigation of the program.

The ethos of such a politics would be the same of thinking itself: politics would perhaps start thinking the meaning of *action*, rather than simply calculating the consequences of its actions.

5 It could be particularly interesting here to read Blanchot at the moment where he
   writes: 'The Everyday: what is most difficult to discover' (Blanchot 1993: 238)

6 One should compare this passage from *Being and Time*: 'Resoluteness implies
   handing oneself down by anticipation to the "there" of the moment of vision; and
   this handing down we call "fate". This is also the ground for destiny, by which we
   understand Dasein's historizing in Being-with Others' with the one just quoted
   from *The Metaphysical Foundations of Logic* (Heidegger 1984: 190).

7 For a discussion on dis-interest see Gaston 2005.

8 Lacoue-Labarthe writes: 'we are told that when Holderlin went "mad" he
   constantly repeated, "Nothing is happening to me, nothing is happening to me"
   (Lacoue-Labarthe 1999: 21).

9 Paul Ricoeur for example insists on 'the need to maintain a certain equivocalness
   of the status of the Other' and concludes that 'with this aporia of the Other
   philosophical discourse comes to an end' (Ricoeur 1995: 355).

10 Confirmation of the revealing character of Heideggerian love comes from Giorgio
   Agamben, who attempts a similar path: 'Love, as passion of facticity, may be what
   makes it possible to cast light on the concept of the Ereignis' (Agamben 2002: 202).

11 Hannah Arendt's work on St. Augustine and its relation with Heidegger's thought
   would deserve a separate treatment, which cannot be afforded here. The proposal
   is to run a parallel analysis of Heidegger's care and St. Augustine's idea of love as
   craving as treated in (Arendt 1996).

12 In this same letter one should take into consideration also the final passages
   where 'thank you' is repeated three times, until the final 'thank you for your love'.
   Here perhaps one could attempt a triangulation on thinking as gratitude to the
   impossibility of love.

Bibliography

Agamben, G. (1993), *The Coming Community*. Trans. M. Hardt. Minneapolis: University of Minnesota Press.

—(1995), *Idea of Prose*. Trans. M. Sullivan and M. Whitsitt. New York: SUNY Press.

—(2002), *Potentialities: Collected Essays in Philosophy*. Trans. D. Heller-Roazen. Stanford, CA: Stanford University Press.

Aho, K. (2009), *Heidegger's Neglect of the Body*. New York: SUNY Press.

Alweiss, L. (2003), *The World Unclaimed: A Challenge to Heidegger's Critique of Husserl*. Athens, OH: Ohio University Press.

Arendt, H. (1996), *Love and St. Augustine*. Trans. J. Vecchiarelli Scott and J. Chelius Stark. Chicago: University of Chicago Press.

Armstrong, P. (2009), *Reticulations: Jean-Luc Nancy and the Networks of the Political*. Minneapolis: University of Minnesota Press.

Biemel, W. (1987), *Le concept de Monde chez Heidegger*. Paris: Librairie Philosophique J.Vrin.

Blanchot, M. (1986), 'Our clandestine companion' in R. Coen (ed.), *Face to Face with Levinas*. Trans. D. B. Allison. New York: SUNY Press.

—(1988), *The Unavowable Community*. Trans. P. Joris. New York: Station Hill.

—(1992), *The Step not Beyond*. Trans. L. Nelson. New York: SUNY Press.

—(1993), *The Infinite Conversation*. Trans. S. Hanson. Minneapolis: University of Minnesota Press.

—(1995), *The Writing of the Disaster*. Trans. A. Smock. London and Lincoln, NE: University of Nebraska Press.

—(1999a), *Awaiting Oblivion*. Trans. J. Gregg. London and Lincoln, NE: University of Nebraska Press.

—(1999b), 'The one who was standing apart from me' in G. Quasha (ed.), *The Station Hill Blanchot Reader: Fiction and Literary Essays*. Trans. Davis, L. New York: Station Hill.

—(1999c), 'Two versions of the imaginary' in G. Quasha (ed.), *The Station Hill Blanchot Reader: Fiction and Literary Essays*. Trans. L. Davis. New York: Station Hill.

—(1999d), 'When the time comes' in G. Quasha (ed.), *The Station Hill Blanchot Reader: Fiction and Literary Essays*. Trans. L. Davis. New York: Station Hill.

—(2003), 'Le discours philosophique' in C. Bident and P. Vilar (eds), *Maurice Blanchot: Récits critiques*. Tours: Éditions Farrago.

Bloechl, J. (ed.) (2000), *The Face of the Other and the Trace of God: Essays on the Philosophy of Emmanuel Levinas*. New York: Fordham University Press.

Bonitzer, P. (1985), *Decadrage : Peinture et Cinema*. Paris: L'Editions de l'Etoile.

Bruno, G. (2003), *Cause, Principle and Unity*. Trans. R. de Lucca. Cambridge: Cambridge University Press.

Buber, M. (2007), *I and Thou*. Trans. W. Kaufmann. London: Continuum.

Butler, J. (1993), *Bodies that Matter*. London: Routledge.

Carney. R. (1985), *American Dreaming: The Films of John Cassavetes and the American Experience*. Berkley, CA and London: University of California Press.

—(2001), *Cassavetes on Cassavetes*. London: Faber & Faber.

Cavell, S. (2001), *The World Viewed*. Cambridge, MA: Harvard University Press.

Critchley, S. (1996), 'Il y a' in C. Bailey Gill (ed.), *Maurice Blanchot. The Demand of Writing*. London: Routledge.

—(1999), *Ethics, Politics, Subjectivity: Essays on Derrida, Levinas and Contemporary French Thought*. London: Verso.

Deleuze, G. (1988), *Spinoza: Practical Philosophy*. Trans. R. Hurley. San Francisco: City Lights Books.

—(1992), *Expressionism in Philosophy: Spinoza*. Trans. M. Joughin. New York: Zone Books.

—(2004), *Cinema 1: The Movement-Image*. Trans. H. Tomlinson and B. Habberjam. London: Continuum.

—(2005), *Cinema 2: The Time-Image*. Trans. H. Tomlinson And R. Galeta. London: Continuum.

Derrida, J. (1982), *Margins of Philosophy*. Trans. A. Bass. London: Harvester Press.

—(1987), *De l'esprit*. Heidegger et *la question* Paris: Galilée .

—(1989), *Of Spirit: Heidegger and the Question*. Trans. G. Bennington and R. Bowlby. Chicago: University of Chicago Press.

—(1998), *Monolingualism of the Other or The Prosthesis of Origin*. Trans. P. Mensah. Stanford, CA: Stanford University Press.

—(1995a), *On the Name*. Trans. T. Dutoit. Stanford, CA: Stanford University Press.

—(1995b), *Points: Interviews, 1974–1994*. Elisabeth Weber (ed.), trans. P. Kamuf. Stanford, CA: Stanford University Press.

—(1997), *Politics of Friendship*. Trans. Collins, G. London: Verso, 1997.

—(1999), *Adieu to Emmanuel Levinas*. Trans. P. A. Brault. Stanford, CA: Stanford University Press.

—(2002), *Writing and Difference*. Trans. A. Bass. London: Routledge, 2002.

—(2005), *On Touching – Jean-Luc Nancy*. Trans. C. Irizarry. Stanford, CA: Stanford University Press.

—(2006), *Geneses, Genealogies, Genres, and Genius: The Secrets of the Archive*. Trans. B. Brahic. New York: Columbia University Press, 2006.

—(2008), *Psyche: Inventions of the Other, Volume II*. Trans. J. Leavey and E. Rottenbergh. Stanford, CA: Stanford University Press.

Dreyfuss, H. (1990), *Being-in-the-World: A Commentary on Heidegger's Being and Time, Division I*. Cambridge, MA: MIT Press.

Fritsche, J. (1999), *Historical Destiny and National Socialism in Heidegger's Being and Time*. Berkeley, CA: University of California Press.

Fynsk, C. (1986), *Heidegger: Thought and Historicity*. Ithaca, NY: Cornell University Press, 1986.

Gaston, S. (2005), *Derrida and Disinterest*. London: Continuum.

Gordon, P. E. (2008), 'Fidelity as heresy' in S. Fleischacker (ed.), *Heidegger's Jewish Followers: Essays on Hannah Arendt, Leo Strauss, Hans Jonas, and Emmanuel Levinas*. Pittsburgh: Duquesne University Press.

Harman, G. (2002), *Tool-Being: Heidegger and the Metaphysics of Objects*. Chicago: Open Court.

Heidegger, M. (1962), *Being and Time*. Trans. J. Macquarrie and E. Robinson. New York: Harper & Row.

—(1968), *What is Called Thinking?* Trans. G. Gray. London and New York: Harper & Row.

—(1978), *Basic Writings*. Trans. D. Farrell Krell. London: Routledge.

—(1982), *The Basic Problems of Phenomenology*. Trans. A. Hofstadter. Bloomington, IN: Indiana University Press.

—(1984), *The Metaphysical Foundations of Logic*. Trans. M. Heim. Bloomington, IN: Indiana University Press.

—(1996), *The Principle of Reason*. Trans. R. Lilly. Bloomington, IN: Indiana University Press.

—(1998), 'On the essence of ground' in W. McNeil (ed.), *Pathmarks*. Trans. W. McNeil. Cambridge: University of Cambridge.

—(2000), *Introduction to Metaphysics*. Trans. G. Fried and R. Polt. New Haven, CT: Yale University Press.

—(2001), *Zollikon Seminars*. Trans. F. Mayr and R. Askay. Evanston, IL: Northwestern University Press.

—(2002), *Identity and Difference*. Trans. J. Stambaugh. Chicago: University of Chicago Press.

—(2003), *The End of Philosophy*. Trans. J. Stambaugh. Chicago: University of Chicago Press.

Heidegger, M. and Arendt, H. (2004), *Letters 1925–1975*. Trans. A. Shields, Ursula Ludz (ed.). Orlando: Hartcourt.

Heisenberg, W. (2000), *Physics and Philosophy*. London: Penguin.

Henry, M. (1975), *Philosophy and Phenomenology of the Body*. Trans. G. Etzkorn. The Hague: Martinus Nijhoff Press.

—(2000), *Incarnation: Une Philosophie de la Chair*. Paris: Seuil.

Hill, L. (1997), *Blanchot: Extreme Contemporary*. London: Routledge.

Hutchens, B. (2005), *Jean-Luc Nancy and the Future of Philosophy*. Montreal: McGill-Queen's Press.

James, I. (2006), *The Fragmentary Demand: An Introduction to the Philosophy of Jean-Luc Nancy*. Stanford, CA: Stanford University Press.

Kafka, F. (1974), *The Diaries of Franz Kafka*. Trans. J. Kresh, M. Brod (ed.). London: Penguin.

King, M. (2001), *A Guide to Heidegger's Being and Time*. New York: SUNY Press.

Kouvaros, G. (2004), *Where Does it Happen? John Cassavetes and Cinema at the Breaking Point*. Minneapolis: University of Minnesota Press.

Koyré, A. (1957), *From the Closed World to the Infinite Universe*. Baltimore: Johns Hopkins University Press.

Lacoue-Labarthe, P. (1990), *Heidegger, Art and Politics: The Fiction of the Political*. Trans. C. Turner. London: Blackwell.

—(1993), *The Subject of Philosophy*. Trans. H. J. Silverman. Minneapolis: University of Minnesota Press.

—(1999), *Poetry as Experience*. Trans. A. Tarnowski. Stanford, CA: Stanford University Press.

Leibniz, G. W. (1975), *Philosophical Papers and Letters*. Trans. L. Loemker. London: Springer.

—(1977), *Monadology and Other Philosophical Essays*. Trans. P. Schrecker and A. M. Schrecker. Indianapolis: Bobbs-Merril.

—Levin, D. M. (1999), 'The ontological dimension of embodiment' in D. Wellton (ed.), *The Body*. London: Blackwell.

Levinas, E. (1986), 'The trace of the other' in M. Taylor (ed.), *Deconstruction in Context*. Trans. A. Lingis. Chicago: University of Chicago Press.

—(1987a), *Collected Philosophical Papers*. Trans. A. Lingis. Dordrecht: Martin Nijhoff Publishers.

—(1987b), *Time and the Other*. Trans. R. Cohen. Pittsburgh: Duquesne University Press.

—(1994), *Nine Talmudic Readings*. Trans. A. Aronowicz. Bloomington, IN and Indianapolis, IN: Indiana University Press.

—(1995), *The Theory of Intuition in Husserl's Phenomenology*. Trans. A. Orianne. Evanston, IL: Northwestern University Press.

—(1997a), *Difficult Freedom: Essays on Judaism*. Trans. S. Hand. Baltimore: Johns Hopkins University Press.

—(1997b), *Outside the Subject*. Trans. M. Smith. Stanford, CA: Stanford University Press.

—(1998), *Of God Who Comes to Mind*. Trans. B. Bergo. Stanford, CA: Stanford University Press.

—(2001), *Is It Righteous to Be? Interviews with Emmanuel Levinas*. J. Robbins (ed.). Stanford, CA: Stanford University Press, 2001.

—(2003a), *Existence and Existents*. Trans A. Lingis, A. Pittsburgh: Duquesne University Press.

—(2003b), *On Escape*. Trans. B. Bergo. Stanford, CA: Stanford University Press.

—(2005), *Totality and Infinity: An Essay on Exteriority*. Trans. A. Lingis. Pittsburgh: Duquesne University Press.

—(2006a), *Entre nous : Thinking-of-the-other*. Trans. M. Smith and B. Harshav. London: Continuum.

—(2006b), *Otherwise than Being or Beyond Essence*. Trans. A. Lingis. Pittsburgh:
Duquesne University Press.

Lewis, M. (2005), *Heidegger and the Place of Ethics: Being-with in the Crossing Of
Heidegger's Thought*. London: Continuum.

Llewelyn, J. (1995), *Emmanuel Levinas: The Genealogy of Ethics*. London: Routledge.

Manning, R. (1993), *Interpreting Otherwise than Heidegger: Emanuel Levinas's Ethics as
First Philosophy*. Pittsburgh: Duquesne University Press.

Marion, J. L. (2000), 'The Voice without Name: Homage to Levinas' in J. Bloechl (ed.),
*The Face of the Other and the Trace of God: Essays on the Philosophy of Emmanuel
Levinas*. Trans. J. Bloechl. New York: Fordham University Press.

Merleau-Ponty, M. (1968), *The Visible and the Invisible*. Trans. A. Lingis. Evanston, IL:
Northwestern University Press.

—(1988), *In Praise of Philosophy and Other Essays*. Trans. J Wild, J. M. Edie and
J. O'Neill. Evanston: Northwestern University Press.

Mulhall, S. (1996), *Routledge Philosophy Guidebook to Heidegger and Being and Time*.
London: Routledge.

Musil, R. (1995), *The Man Without Qualities*. Trans. S. Wilkins. New York: Alfred Knopf.

Nancy, J. L. (1979), *Ego Sum*. Paris: Flammarion.

—(1990), 'Sharing voices'. Trans. G. L. Ormiston. In G. L. Ormiston and A. D. Schrift
(eds), *Transforming the Hermeneutic Context: From Nietzsche to Nancy*. New York:
SUNY Press.

—(1991), *Inoperative Community*. Trans. P. Connor, L. Garbus, M. Holland and S.
Sawhney. Minneapolis: University of Minnesota Press.

—(1993a), *The Birth to Presence*. Trans. B. Holmes et al. Stanford, CA: Stanford
University Press.

—(1993b), *The Experience of Freedom*. Trans. B. McDonald. Stanford, CA: Stanford
University Press.

—(1996), *The Muses*. Trans. P. Kamuf. Stanford, CA: Stanford University Press.

—(1997a), *The Gravity of Thought*. Trans. F. Raffoul G. and Recco. New York:
Humanity Books.

—(1997b), *The Sense of the World*. Trans. J. Librett. Minneapolis: University of
Minnesota Press.

—(2000), *Being Singular Plural*. Trans. R. Richardson and A. O'Byrne. Stanford, CA:
Stanford University Press.

—(2001a), *La Pensée Derobée*. Paris: éditions Galilée.

—(2001b), *L' 'il y a' du rapport sexuel*. Paris: éditions Galilée.

—(2001c), *The Evidence of Film*. Trans. C. Irizarry and V. Conley. Brussels: Yves
Gevaert Éditeur.

—(2001d), *The Speculative Remark. (One of Hegel's Bons Mots)*. Trans. C. Suprenant.
Stanford, CA: Stanford University Press.

—(2002), *Hegel: The Restlessness of the Negativ*. Trans. J. Smith and S. Miller.
Minneapolis: University of Minnesota Press.

—(2003), *A Finite Thinking*. S. Sparks (ed.). Stanford, CA: Stanford University Press.

—(2005), *The Ground of the Image*. Trans. J. Fort. New York: Fordham University Press.

—(2007a), *Listening*. Trans. C. Mandell. New York: Fordham University Press.

—(2007b), *The Creation of the World or Globalization*. Trans. F. Raffoul and D. Pettigrew. New York: SUNY Press.

—(2008a), *Corpus*. Trans. R. Rand. New York: Fordham University Press.

—(2008b), *Dis-Enclosure: The Deconstruction of Christianity*. Trans. B. Bergo, G. Malenfant and M. Smith. New York: Fordham University Press.

—(2008c), *Logodaedalus: The Discourse of the Syncope*. Trans. S. Anton. Stanford, CA: Stanford University Press.

—(2008d), 'The Being-with of Being-there' in F. Raffoul and E. S. Nelson (eds), *Rethinking Facticity*. Trans. F. Raffoul and D. Pettigrew. New York: SUNY Press.

—(2010), *L'Adoration: Déconstruction du christianisme*, 2. Paris: éditions Galilée.

Nelson, E. S. (2008), 'Heidegger and the ethics of facticity' in F. Raffoul and E. S. Nelson (eds), *Rethinking Facticity*. New York: SUNY Press.

Norris, C. (1991), *Spinoza and the Origins of Modern Critical Theory*. London: Blackwell.

Pierre, S. and Comolli, J. L. (1986), 'The Two Faces of Faces' in J. Hillier (ed.), *Cahiers du Cinema: The 1960s. New Wave, New Cinema, Reevaluating Hollywood*. Trans. W. Williams. Cambridge, MA: Harvard University Press.

Plato (1998), *Cratylus*. Trans. C. D. C. Reeve. Indianapolis: Hackett Publishing Company.

Raffoul, F. (1999), *Heidegger and the Subject*. Trans. D. Pettigrew and G. Recco. New York: Humanities Press.

Revault d'Allonnes, F. (1994), *Pour le cinéma "moderne": Du lien de l'art au monde*. Liege: Yellow Now.

Saramago, J. (1993), *The Gospel According to Jesus Christ*. Trans. G. Pontiero. London: Harper Collins.

Sheppard, D., Sparks, S. and Colin, T. (eds) (1997), *On Jean-Luc Nancy: The Sense of Philosophy*. London: Routledge.

Singer, I. B. (1973), *The Spinoza of Market Street*. Trans. E. Gottlieb. London: Jonathan Cape.

Spinoza, B. (1949), *Ethics*. Trans. J. Gutmann. New York: Hafner Press.

—(1969), *Letters to Friend and Foe*. Trans. D. Runes. New York: Philosophical Library.

Thomas, E. (2004), *Emmanuel Levinas: Ethics, Justice and the Human Beyond Being*. London: Routledge.

Walser, R. (2009), *The Tanners*. Trans. S. Bernofsky. New York: New Directions.

Watkin, C. (2009), *Phenomenology or Deconstruction: The Question of Ontology in Maurice Merleau-Ponty, Paul Ricoeur and Jean-Luc Nancy*. Edinburgh: Edinburgh University Press.

Wolfson, H. (1967), *The Philosophy of Spinoza: Unfolding the Latent Processes of his Reasoning*. Cambridge, MA: Harvard University Press.

Filmography

A Child is Waiting, prod. Stanley Kramer, dir. John Cassavetes, 102 mins., United Artists, 1963.

Faces, prod. John Cassavetes and Maurice McEndree, dir. John Cassavetes, 130 mins., Faces International Films, 1968.

Gloria, prod. Sam Shaw, dir. John Cassavetes, 123 mins., Columbia Pictures, 1980.

Husbands, prod. Al Ruban and Sam Shaw, dir. John Cassavetes, 138 mins., Columbia Pictures, 1970.

Love Streams, prod. Menahem Golan and Yoram Globusm, dir. John Cassavetes, Cannon Films, 1986.

Minnie and Moskowitz, prod. Al Ruban, dir. John Cassavetes, 115 mins., Universal, 1971.

Opening Night, prod. Al Ruban, dir. John Cassavetes, 144 mins., Faces Distribution Corporation, 1977.

Shadows, prod. Maurice McEndree and Nikos Papatakis, dir. John Cassavetes, 87 mins., Faces International Films, Inc, 1958.

Too Late Blues, prod. and dir. John Cassavetes, 103 min., Paramount, 1961.

A Woman Under the Influence, prod. Sam Shaw, dir. John Cassavetes, Faces Distribution Corporation, 155 mins., 1975.

Index

Lightning Source UK Ltd.
Milton Keynes UK
UKOW06f1038180315

248076UK00001B/74/P